VOLUME II

CHURCH AND STATE

LUIGI STURZO

With an Introduction by

A. Robert Caponigri

UNIVERSITY OF NOTRE DAME PRESS • 1962

PART II

THE CHURCH AND THE MODERN STATE

(continued)

CHAPTER IX

THE PROBLEM OF RELIGIOUS TOLERATION

§ 33.—Several times in the two preceding chapters we touched upon the problem of religious toleration, as the course of events of Reformation and Counter-Reformation threw into relief the need for truce and peace. But, in the period we considered as extending from the beginning of Luther's revolt to the Peace of Westphalia (1517–1648), all attempts at toleration had no other result than to consolidate the principle of State religion (*cuius regio illius et religio*), and the religious, civil, and political inferiority of the dissenting minority.

At the same time, the idea of religious toleration, in the sense of an equal right of worship for all Christian persuasions, with no disability, either civil or political, attaching to religious faith, little by little gained ground among certain sects and men of culture, and penetrated the closed circles of courts and churches. We are not speaking of a merely political pragmatism, which has existed since the world began, usually under the aspects of choice of the lesser evil, or the practical interest of monarchy, country or church. We are speaking of a theory which, as such, had to find its place in a system of thought and its foundations in an ethical and social conception.

Readers will remember what we said of the theory of the two moralities, thrown into new light during the period of the Renaissance as an aspect of the theory of the two truths. It was logical that such a period should reach that typical toleration, when people of culture, the humanists, were fully free to speak and write as they did, under the aegis of popes and kings, with hardly any religious or moral limits to impede their philosophical research or artistic expression. Such tolerance reached the point of licence and undermined both religion and civil society, since it deprived truth and morality of their true value, reducing the first to an adaptation of the mind and the second to social utility.

It was natural that spirits thirsting for a truth to which an inner morality could correspond should react in the direction of reform. But the Lutheran reform, unable to resolve the antinomy born of the severance of social from inward morality, stripped the individual of his free will and made of social morality a legal and outward conformity. The logical solution, unforeseen though it was, was a State religion and intolerance towards dissenters; these might be left, as compensation, an individual freedom of enquiry and interpretation of the Bible, which did not resolve itself into ethical freedom—that is, an inner, autonomous complex, with no counterpart in political and social life. There are two truths and two moralities in Lutheranism also, which, instead of leading to the licence of the Italian Renaissance, led to the persecutions and wars of religion.

Among anti-Catholic critics, Lutheranism is generally given the credit for introducing into civil society the principle of religious freedom, which bore fruit in toleration; the tardy development of toleration they would explain as due not to the principles of the Reformation but to adverse historical circumstances before which the chief reformers had to give way. This reasoning (which certain superficial Catholic apologists also tend to accept, from an opposite standpoint), is invalid both historically and sociologically. The free enquiry proclaimed by Luther and spread by the Reformation was not, and could not be, an element isolated from the theological and political syntheses of the various Protestant theories. We cannot attribute to it an autonomous and thus a negative value. Free inquiry would have no meaning if, in the Lutheran conception, it were detached from Justification by Faith, the servile will, and the concentration in the Sovereign of all external powers, even where ecclesiastical matters were concerned; which implies politico-religious intolerance. Nor in Calvin's system of thought can free inquiry be separated from the theory of predestination or from the rigid religious-political structure of his communities. Luther and Calvin were therefore logical when they maintained the right of banishing or burning heretics, sectarians, and all those who by denying one of the dogmas resulting from the common interpretation of the Bible, denied at the same time the new Christian society and the basis of social power.

The historical process leading to religious toleration has other theoretical and historical roots than Protestantism. The case of Michael Servetus, burned alive in Geneva in 1553, through the intolerance of Calvin and the Calvinists, was the outstanding occasion for an explicit theory of toleration to be formulated by the so-called Italian 'Academicians' who had taken refuge in Geneva. They were humanists, who sought in the Reformation a higher spirituality and a rational purification, as hard for them to find in Geneva as anywhere else, in spite of the neophyte fervour of the Calvinistic communities of the time. They were opposed to the intolerance that this neophyte spirit carried to extreme lengths. Among the many who had gathered together in Geneva were Lelio Sozzino, or Socinius, and Bernardino Ochino of Siena, Castellione of Savoy, Gribaldo Mofa of Chieri, Blandrata of Saluzzo, Curione of Moncalieri, and Gentile of Cosenza, who, with several others, formed not so much a sect as an *élite* of free spirits, termed in contempt 'Academicians'. Religious as they were, wishing to be religious, they were rationalists before their time. They brought into the Reformation the critical spirit of Humanism.

To Lelius Socinius was attributed the pamphlet, published under the pseudonym of 'Martinus Bellius' a few months after the burning of Servetus, and entitled: '*De haereticis an sint persequendi et omnino quomodo sit cum eis agendum doctorum vivorum tum veterum tum recentiorum sententiae liber hoc tam turbolento tempore pernecessarius.*'[1]

Critical scholarship has led to the opinion that the book was mainly composed by Castellione in collaboration with Curione and perhaps with other Italian refugees from Bâle, where the spirit of Erasmus of Rotterdam still breathed. Castellione had already come into conflict with Calvin when, in 1551, he had published a Latin version of the Bible with, in the preface, a fierce invective against the use of torture and the stake. '*Quis non putet Christum aliquem esse Molochum aut eius generis aliquem deum si sibi vivos homines immolari comburique velit?*'[2] Théodore de Bèze replied immediately in defence of the Calvinists

[1]Of heretics, whether they should be persecuted, and in general how they should be treated, this book, very necessary in so turbulent a time.

[2]'Who would not esteem Christ a Moloch or some such god if He wished live men to be sacrificed to Him and burned'?

with '*De haereticis a civili magistratu puniendis libellus adversus Martini Belli farraginem et novorum academicorum Sectam*'[1] (1554). Castellione, for his part, renewed his attack with his well-known '*Dialogus inter Calvinum et Vaticanum*', which also for a long time was attributed to Socinius. The latter was the central figure of the Italian *élite*, and imprinted on the rest his powerful personality and his ideas.

Persecuted as heretics, some succumbed, others were reduced to silence. Ochino and Blandrata took refuge in Poland, where anti-trinitarianism began to develop, spreading as far as Lithuania and Transylvania; here it took the name of Unitarianism. Faustus Socinius, Lelius's nephew, summoned from Florence, joined with Blandrata to form its most important and active centre. The principles of their doctrine, called after its two true founders, uncle and nephew, by the name of Socinianism, were established in the Rakau Catechism, published in 1605, shortly after the death of Lelius.

Religious toleration in Socinian thought assumes a different aspect from that which it had in the Renaissance under the influence of the two truths. The Socinians sought to unify supernatural with natural truth, reducing the supernatural to a rational system. Some modern scholars have defined Socinianism as a 'supernatural rationalism', others as a 'rational supernaturalism'. The Socinians rejected the Old Testament, and in the New retained as matter for religious belief all that is accessible to human reason. All that transcends it, mysteries, prophecies, miracles, was set aside and left to free opinion. They thus hoped to find a unity of Christian thought in the points on which all the churches were agreed and to which reason assented by its own virtue. Since everything else was beyond the compass of reason and would not form an object of faith, no ecclesiastical or temporal authority could have the right to make belief in it compulsory. The theory of toleration thus received a fairly logical basis, through which motives of dogmatic dispute in the politico-social field would be avoided, and in which the State could count on a wide conformity. We say 'a fairly logical basis', not because such discrimination as to the value of the truths of the Gospel was logically or critically exact,

[1]Pamphlet on the punishment of heretics by the Civil magistracy against the nonsense of Martinus Bellius and the new Sect of *Academicians*.

but because, that principle once granted, however mistaken it might be, the consequence derived from it followed logically.

Protestants and Catholics opposed Socinianism as the worst of heresies, not only because of its denial of the Trinity, but because, while presenting itself as a religious sect and practising Christian worship, it led directly to rationalism and to a deism no longer Christian and supernatural. Therefore the Socinian theory of toleration, thus formulated, could find neither theoretical nor practical support. The Socinians were attacked and driven away almost everywhere, but in spite of this they survived in Poland and Transylvania, and penetrated into Germany, Holland, England, France and America. Their thought had an influence on the intellectual *élites* over a long period. With their evangelical rationalism and the theory of political toleration they combined a whole assortment of humanitarian notions. They denied the right of capital punishment, private vengeance, the legitimacy of personal self-defence, and the right of war. The more extreme went so far as to deny the secular authority altogether, influenced in this by the Anabaptists, with whom they were in almost constant contact. All this gave the Socinians something of the character of an anti-social sect, cast up from the depths of the medieval soul, coloured by the rationalism of the Renaissance and the mysticism of the Reformation.

It was in Holland that the Socinian theory of toleration was first and characteristically put to the test within the structure of the Calvinist State-Church. The Low Countries had been a prey to the struggles and wars between Reformers and Catholics, they had suffered the repression of the anti-Spanish revolt, they had been involved in the wars between England, Spain, and France. It was thought that the religious problem had been settled by the Pacification of Ghent (1576); it came up again at the Peace of Religion of Antwerp (1578). The Protestants soon after formed the Union of Uretcht (1579), and the Catholics retaliated the same year by forming the Union of Arras, in alliance with Alessandro Farnese and Spain. This was typical of what was happening all over Europe. Protestants refused freedom of worship to Catholics, Catholics to Protestants. Hence civil wars and general wars, revolts and conspiracies, truces and peace-pacts, edicts of toleration issued only to be violated or revoked.

A first movement of thought towards toleration grew up in Holland among the various Reformed currents, but excluding the Catholics or Papists, who, a month after the formation of the Union of Utrecht, had been deprived of such concessions as they had been granted. The sense in which the dogma of predestination was understood was a motive of dissent and division. Gaspar Coolhaers maintained, with the Socinians, the universal brotherhood of Christians. Theodore Coornhert had shortly before confuted the assertion of Joest Lips, that heretics must be persecuted with fire and sword; his book was published in 1593, a few years after his death, with the title *Defensio processus de non occidendis haereticis*. Others were of the same opinion, either by method or by system, and since the universities and congregations of the faithful in Holland were in a state of upheaval over questions rising from the dogma of predestination, the problem of toleration of dissenters was bound up with the latter.

At the University of Leyden the two parties called themselves by the names of their leaders, Arminians or Gomarists. On the death of Arminius (1609), the guidance of his party fell to Episcopio and Uytenbogaert, who published what was known as the Remonstrance, summing up in five articles the points on which they dissented from the Calvinists. The reply, the Counter Remonstrance, followed immediately, and thenceforth the two parties were also known as Remonstrants and Counter-Remonstrants. The upheaval that followed was so violent that the States published their decree of toleration, with a prohibition of any discussion of it in public. But Maurice of Orange, who had gone over to the Counter-Remonstrants, promoted the condemnation of their adversaries (1618). Oldenbarneveld was put to death, Hugo Grotius and his wife escaped from perpetual imprisonment, Episcopius and Uytenbogaert took refuge in Brabant, and others in Germany. On the death of Maurice, the Remonstrants were allowed back and were granted rights of worship and teaching on the same footing as the rest (1630–34).

It must not be thought that from the political standpoint the toleration granted to the Remonstrants or Arminians of Holland, who returned from exile in 1630, differed in spirit or motives from the toleration granted the Huguenots by the Edict of Nantes, in 1598, or from other similar edicts frequently renewed in Europe, according to the outcome of agitations or wars, or changes in princes or ministers. There was, however, a difference which insensibly crept into the world of culture and into the formation of the mind of the XVII century, under the influence of Dutch thought, then predominant throughout Europe. The difference was that such toleration grew up (1) *between kindred confessions*, (2) *within similar political conceptions*, (3) *on a rationalistic basis*.

Socinianism, which brought the leaven of toleration into Europe, could itself never receive it, for from the religious standpoint it was reputed a negation of Christianity and from the political, an anti-social theory. While providing the rationalistic basis of toleration, it could provide neither the confessional nor the political basis. On the other hand, Catholicism in Protestant countries, and Lutheran or Calvinistic Protestantism in Catholic countries, could never obtain true toleration because, while there might be agreement on a given political conception, both parties ruled out the rationalistic plane, and on the confessional plane they had no sort of affinity. It was for this reason that Catholics and Protestants fixed upon the system of a State religion, and on a mutual intolerance mitigated by *modus vivendi*.

In the case of the Arminians, we find above all a confessional affinity. Though dissenting from Calvinistic orthodoxy, they were imbued with it both as spirit and as system. Therefore differences of interpretation led them towards a moderate rationalism on which to base toleration and in the unity of a State of federal tendencies they found the necessary practical elasticity. Though they differed from the Socinians, they too sought to restrict the body of Christian doctrine to the points common to the other Reformed confessions, to eliminate rigid interpretations, to resolve dogma into morals, and to deprive churches, synods, congregations of all effective authority, which they would hand over entire to the secular power.

This rationalistic tendency was seething in the midst of violent theological battles, and corresponded to the positive temperament of the Dutch. The Natural Law School found in Holland its precedents and its first ripe expression. Huig van Groot (Hugo Grotius), who like the Socinians declared against the death penalty, and who had suffered prison and exile, in 1625 published in Paris his *De jure belli et pacis*, which marks a date in history. In 1646 he published at the Hague *De imperio summarum potestatum circa sacra*.

In the first work, Grotius developed the thesis of a *consociatio* as the origin of society, distinguishing between *consociatio in populum*, the society of the State, and *consociatio ex populis*, international society. Since the *consociatio* is made up of parts, either taken individually or as particular groups (*consociatio privata*), he declares that the original agreement to constitute a society attributes to the majority the power to act as a whole only in matters concerning the members as a whole—*ut universi*—and this cannot be said of religious matters. In his second work, Grotius distinguishes between a 'directive' régime and a 'constitutive' one; the first carries no obligation, the second does so. This may be constitutive *ex vi imperi*, or *ex consensu* ; the first has an imperative character binding all subjects, the second has no imperative character, but that of a *universitas legitima*. For Grotius, all true authority in both civil and ecclesiastical matters resides in the State, of which the *summa potestas* springs from Natural Right. Any other right recognised to autonomous bodies or to the Church is held to be delegated by the sovereign, since by its very nature the Church is merely a directive régime deriving from the *consociatio privata*.

The theory that all the particular communities, including autonomous regions, free cities, universities with their immunities, had no authority of their own but received it from the sovereign, was already widespread. Suarez had accepted and defended it. But Catholics put the Church beyond the compass of particular communities, in virtue of its supernatural and universal character. The Arminian current, and Grotius, who was imbued with its spirit, considered the churches as so many particular communities, religious 'colleges' freely formed by the faithful, co-existing within a State and subject to the sovereign authority. There was no objection in Protestant circles to investing the sovereign with ecclesiastical jurisdiction, so long as he was not the head of a determined official church, but the guardian of the rights of the State, of ethics, of order, of religion, of the hierarchy, of economic justice; it was for the ecclesiastical colleges to co-operate to ensure that such rights were respected, and to respect them themselves; the clergy had no powers, but solely an office of persuasion, direction and moral and religious training. In all this Grotius anticipated the formation and development of Protestant 'collegialism' and Catholic 'jurisdictionalism', both founded on the conception of the Natural Right of the State as distinct from, and independent of any ecclesiastical right of supernatural origin.

§ 34.—When the Arminian current penetrated into England—through which the Socinian theories, brought by the Italian, Jacopo Aconcio, had been creeping for half a century—it received the name of Latitudinarianism. The persecutions of Catholics, which had followed each other with ever fresh ferocity, from the time of Henry VIII onwards, had produced among these no philosophical or mystical movement in favour of toleration. The Anglicans considered them as Papists, subject to a foreign power enemy to England, so that, forced on the defensive, they did not wish to seem less English than the rest or less faithful to the Crown. The question of the Oath of Allegiance divided them for a long time, into those who resisted, backed by the papal condemnations, and the others who wanted to find a compromise or who ended by taking the oath. A large part of Catholic efforts was directed to winning over kings and courtiers, so that Catholicism might be restored or at least given parity with the State Religion. But these hopes were nearly always ill founded, for in the political game between the Stuarts and their Parliaments, the two opposing churches, Episcopalian and Presbyterian, had more influence, and there was no room for a third church, enemy to both.

Thus in England, as in Holland, no theoretical basis existed for toleration of Catholics, who in these countries were the persecuted, excluded from civil life. The Act of Indulgence of Charles I in their favour was followed by harsher persecution. Milton, the champion of freedom of opinion and of the press, fierce fighter against the censorship, and favourable to religious toleration as he was, excluded Catholics, whom he wished to see treated as idolaters, allowed neither public worship as scandalous, nor private worship as an insult to God.

Cromwell during his Protectorate was harsh towards Catholics, not only for the sake of political conquest, as in Ireland, but from religious zeal. During this period the struggle was for the supremacy of the State Church. The Stuarts stood for the Episcopal Church, and under Charles I the Civil War broke out through his attempt to enforce Episcopalianism in Scotland. Under Cromwell, on the contrary, Episcopalianism was suppressed and the Independents and Presbyterian Puritanism triumphed. The Stuart Restoration meant a return to Episcopalianism, to the Act of Uniformity and to anti-Puritan persecution. If the Catholics, for a short time, were then tolerated, this was not so much because of the Catholic Queen, as because they supported the absolutist theories of the Monarchy. But Parliament was watchful, and reacted with the Test Act of 1673, obliging all State officers to prove that they were Anglicans; thus James, Duke of York, lost the command of the fleet. James's Declaration of Indulgence of 1687 roused the country against him, and when he had his infant son baptised with Catholic rites, William of Orange, grandson of Charles I, with his wife Mary, daughter of James II, were summoned to take the Crown. The Act of Settlement of 1701 finally excluded the succession of a Catholic to the throne.

Within the religious struggle between the Churches, the struggle for political supremacy was taking place, and the two were so intertwined that for a long time they could not be envisaged apart. James I had an unlimited conception of the Divine Right of Kings; the royal hereditary succession was to him a constant realisation of the divine will. The King was as the trustee of this divine will, and was responsible to God alone, not to men. Parliament had been given to the people by a sovereign concession which could always be revoked, and it had no rights over the Crown.

To maintain this thesis in practice, James had need of a force that could be opposed to Parliament, and this force was the Episcopal Church. Parliament, for its part, claiming as it did that it represented the people in an autonomous and legal manner, that Ministers must enjoy its good graces and answer to it for their actions, that it had the right to limit the powers of the King, had no other mode of asserting itself than by leaning on the opposite forces, principally on Presbyterianism and on the other anti-Episcopal currents.

The support of opposing churches either to Monarchy or Parliament carried with it the favour of the secular power to one church and intolerance towards the other. The vanquished fled either to France or Holland, or to the transatlantic colonies which were already developing. The famous Pilgrim Fathers of the *Mayflower* in 1620 opened the way for those impelled at once by attachment to their religious faith, by quest of a livelihood and by desire for adventure. The alternating political vicissitudes of the eighty years of the stormy Stuart period, and the resulting successive religious persecutions suffered by all the Churches and sects existing in England, Scotland and Ireland, provided the impetus and motives for the development of ecclesiastical latitudinarianism and of the political speculation that culminated in Hobbes and Locke. The latitudinarian theory percolated into a wide portion of the intellectual *élite* under two aspects: on the one hand continual persecutions brought a sense of the need for religious appeasement, and the most suitable means for mitigating the conflicts over ritual and theology seemed the reduction of Christianity to the points common to the various antagonistic confessions, while on the other the defence of freedom and parliamentary privileges led men to seek the basis of political society and of a certain religious toleration in the idea of Natural Law.

An early latitudinarianism was the fruit not of theories but of sentiments and of a certain religious pessimism, which Francis Quarles (1592–1644) expressed in his verses. John Dury (1596–1680) is the first to give systematic form to latitudinarian principles. (He was in touch with the famous Calixtus, who was working for the unification of the churches.) His *Summary Discourse concerning the work of Peace Ecclesiasticall* appeared in 1639.

Side by side with the latitudinarianism of Arminian origin, there developed the Erastian current (called after the German Erastus, who had denied the Church the right of excommunicating and of withholding of the Sacraments); this maintained the complete supremacy of the State in religious matters, so that a subjection by conviction should lead to an external pacification in uniformity. Sir Francis Bacon (1561–1626) was not sensible of religious problems; his philosophy was at bottom not so much rationalistic as utilitarian. Thus his appeal for religious moderation sounds a note of detachment rather than of effectual intervention. His attempt to construct a tolerant Anglican church led him to deny the Church any religious authority, which passed to a conformist and tolerant State. It was Erastianism, as conceived in England. But the two terms were contradictory; a State-cum-Church as such could not be tolerant.

On this point ideas were in ferment and the choicest spirits carried away by passion. Milton in his *Areopagitica* (1644) defended freedom of the Press against the censorship which had been restored by the Presbyterians, then triumphant. This specific problem revealed the other and deeper one of religious toleration, which the Independents championed against the strict discipline of both Episcopalians and Presbyterians. Milton's position was a political one, concerned with the English parliamentary system, which implied freedom of opinion and of the Press; it was also politico-religious, since, considering the question of hierarchy and worship to be secondary to that of inner spiritual revelation, he envisaged the co-existence of the various religious opinions and sects, the Catholic excepted, as part of a free political régime. Cromwell sought to bring about something of the kind with the 'Protectorate Establishment', by which he created not a State Church but an institution for 'preaching and teaching', without hierarchy, rites or Sacraments. It was natural that this should lead to ecclesiastical persecution (apart from the persecution of Catholics) and to intolerance.

Thomas Hobbes sets aside the religious or ecclesiastical preoccupations that were still strong in the latitudinarian Independent and Parliamentary currents, taking his stand on the conception of Natural Law, which he substituted for the Divine Right of Kings. Thus he secularised absolute power but maintained its character of entire and unlimited sovereignty. He was the first who, with the modern conception of society, sought to overcome the dualism of People and Sovereign, which still existed (as it does in Grotius) through the survival of the medieval idea of corporation. For Hobbes there is no true contract between the people and a head either chosen or imposed by circumstances, for the people without a head is an amorphous mob with no organic cohesion. Only when it has a head is there society; in that moment the multitude ceases to be a multitude and becomes an organism. This transition, by force of nature, leads to a concentration of powers in the head, powers plenary and illimitable; it is therefore a completed and irrevocable act. Any retrogression, any limitation of powers, would mean the resolution of society into an incoherent and disorderly multitude; the social organism would cease to exist. By transferring their freedom to the head, individuals remained deprived of it, but in becoming members of a society by a kind of natural determinism they acquired a faculty of action that liberty alone did not assure to them.

Hobbes had thus an intuition of the essence of the modern State, but he suppressed all dynamism that might result from the duality 'people and head'; this duality he would abolish by resolving it into a formal monism of power. There was no room in such a conception for any individual religious liberty, nor for any toleration of dissenting denominations. By a series of tortuous interpretations of pre-Christian religions and of Christianity itself, he cuts away the foundations of an individual obedience to the law of God in conflict with the law of the State, for, since the establishment of Christianity in the world, the sole interpreter of divine and natural law is the sovereign, who has therefore the right to decide to what persuasion his subjects must belong. This conception did not seem strange in the mental climate of the age, when the Peace of Westphalia had confirmed this faculty to the princes of Germany by the *jus reformandi* and when in England war was waged for the supremacy of the official church. Hobbes' *Leviathan* was published in 1651, after the Civil War and under the Protectorate; it was written in Paris at the beginning of the reign of Louis XIV, during the *Fronde*.

When he returned to London, after the Restoration, Hobbes engaged in prolonged philosophical and political controversies, especially on liberty. His determinism irritated the religious currents and his absolutism the parliamentary ones. The ferment of ideas and passions at that period was remarkable. It was the time when George Fox started to spread Quakerism, founding the Society of Friends, insisting on the personal aspect of religious experience and maintaining the possibility of complete victory over sin. The spread of Quakerism was swift in certain zones intolerant of ecclesiastical formalism and political conformity; therefore it was fiercely opposed by both Episcopalians and Presbyterians. Cromwell's Parliament treated the Quakers with extreme harshness. Persecution continued under the Stuarts, and many emigrated to the Colonies. They saw in individual liberty a means of forming strong social nuclei, and thus permeating society with their religious spirit through the efficacious action of groups. Through freedom, as political method, truth finds its own way in the midst of errors; through freedom conceived as spiritual union with God, the way is opened for the duty of conscience. Thus for the Quakers toleration was not a sign of religious indifference, but a possibility of proselytism. They, however, far more than the Arminians and Latitudinarians, had emptied Christianity of dogmas, sacraments and rights, reducing it to a mystical moralism. From Socinianism they had taken its opposition to war, to the death penalty, to torture, and, in general, to absolutism of power.

In 1666 John Locke published his *Essay Concerning Toleration*, in which he anticipated certain of the leading ideas he would treat in his maturity, after his experience of political life, his exile, and his acquaintance with the various centres of culture in France and Holland. Educated in Puritanism, he had felt its narrowness and intolerance; the Independents disgusted him by their arrogance; in contact at Oxford with the Anglican Platonists, he disliked their formalism and was repelled by their spirit of domination. Socinians, Latitudinarians, Arminians in Holland, Cartesians and Rationalists in France, exercised an influence on his mind, dedicated as he was to scientific research and philosophical speculation, and involved in political vicissitudes as a follower of Lord Ashley, later Earl of Shaftesbury. The question of toleration came again to the fore in all the Protestant centres of Europe during the acute period of Huguenot persecution in France, which culminated in the Revocation of the Edict of Nantes in 1685 and in the dispersion of the Huguenots to England, Holland, Germany, Sweden and elsewhere.

Immediately afterwards, affairs in England came to a climax. The flight and deposition of James II, the result of his 'Papistry' and of his absolutism, gave the triumph to Parliament. The latter, in giving the crown to William and Mary (1688) wished to proclaim its rights in a solemn document; it is from this moment that the State begins to move towards democracy.

But the problem of religious toleration still remained unsolved. William took the initiative. With the Arminian ideas he had brought with him from Holland, he wished to establish Protestantism as the State religion, reducing it to a minimum of beliefs compulsory for all, while allowing the several communities freedom in interpretation and rites. It was a compromise between the theory of a State Church and free collegialism. But the proposal was thrown out in the Commons, both by the Episcopalians, who did not wish to give up their hierarchy and ritual, and by the Independents, Baptists and Quakers, who would not consent to even a minimum of hierarchy and ritual. Finding it impossible to discover a religious formula acceptable to all, William introduced civil toleration by the Act of Toleration of May 24, 1689, by which Protestant dissenters were exempted from the penalties and disabilities established by former laws, when practice of the official religion was obligatory. By this Act, they were allowed the public practice of their form of religion; Presbyterians, Independents, Baptists and Quakers benefited by it, while Unitarians or Socinians and 'Papists' were excepted. Against these, political and religious prejudices were strong. In regard to the Catholics, no further reason was required than their dependence on the Pope, considered as a foreign Sovereign and Head of a Church that claimed authority over kings. There were at that time lively repercussions, in every court of Europe, of the Gallican dispute between Rome and Paris.

It was in the year of the Act of Toleration that Locke published his famous *Epistola de Tolerantia*, followed by other letters, printed a year later (1690), when he also published his Two Treatises on Government. Locke too is a jusnaturalist, but differs from Grotius and Hobbes in stressing the individualist tendency that would dominate the thought of the next century. For him, the community is merely a co-partnership of individuals, who remain as such even once they have united in a society. The social contract does not deprive them of their personal rights, but introduces an order and regulation, to be fully determined by the majority; the majority law, too, must be established by contract. Locke bases the problem of religious toleration on a naturalistic conception. Starting from the idea (which is perfectly correct) that the State has not and cannot have authority over souls, he denied it the right to oblige its subjects to profess a given form of religion or to constrain them by penal laws. As against the system of a State religion, on the other hand, for him the Church is merely a voluntary society formed by the faithful who accept a given creed and submit to a discipline of their own; if they do not want to belong to it, they have but to leave it; if the Church authority finds a member of the faithful to be incorrigible, it can expel him if it so wills. In such a system, the co-existence of the Churches (which Locke bases on mutual respect and the spirit of charity), must be tolerated by the State, which cannot but allow their public worship.

To this system of religious freedom Locke foresaw four exceptions —first, those who professed subversive theories against the State and the well-being of society; secondly, those intolerant sects that maintained that their members were not obliged to keep faith with heretics and boasted that they could depose an excommunicated king; thirdly, those who went over to the foreigner as head of their religion, and were therefore ready to fight against their own sovereign; fourthly, atheists, for atheism is contrary to the consistency of society. The second and third exceptions were aimed at Catholics, as they then appeared even to enlightened Protestants. The difference between Milton and Locke, where Catholics were concerned, was that Milton considered them from the religious standpoint as idolaters, Locke from the social-political standpoint as intolerant, disloyal and dangerous to the State, since they were subject to a foreign sovereign.

The half-century or less that separates Milton from Locke had brought the affirmation of a Natural Law common to all men, and forming the basis of society; the secular conception of the State, as freed from religious features and functions, is on its way. Whereas the Socinians and Arminians sought a basis for religious toleration in a rationalistic reduction of the Christian creed, the jusnaturalists sought it in the free co-existence of all religious confessions, without the direct intervention of the State. The universal Christian Church through the Reformation had been reduced (except for Catholics) to territorial churches; toleration brought the further stage of collegial churches. Historically, Universal Church, territorial churches, collegial churches, clash and interpenetrate and develop according to the conditions of the various countries. The persecutions and measures of toleration which alternated in Great Britain, drove the persecuted and the refractory to the American colonies, where they sought independence and religious liberty, together with those others who sought wealth and adventure. Thus, in the XVII century, here and there in the English colonies we find interesting and characteristic experiments in religious toleration, together with extreme intolerance.

George Calvert, Lord Baltimore, received from Charles I in 1632 the grant of the territory of Maryland, under the condition that he and his successors would never exercise the rights conferred on them in such a manner as to bring prejudice to the '*Sacrosanctae Dei verae christianae religioni*'. He and other pioneers, mostly Catholics, opened the colony to all those who accepted the Christian religion, inviting from other colonies both the Puritans persecuted by the Episcopalians and the Episcopalians persecuted by the Puritans. In order that no-one should find practical obstacles in the way of profession of his particular faith, Lord Baltimore and the assembly of colonists decreed that cases connected with marriages or wills should fall within the competence of the civil magistracy. This régime of toleration was revoked a first time when the majority of the Assembly became Puritan. Encouraged by the triumph of Puritanism in the mother country, they rebelled against Lord Baltimore and for the Act of Toleration of 1649 substituted the Act Concerning Religion of 1654, by which they denied all liberty to 'Papists and Prelatists', that is, to Catholics and Episcopalians. With the Stuart Restoration, Lord Baltimore regained his rights, and, with an Assembly that was in part Catholic, restored the régime of 1649. All this lasted only till the accession of William of Orange. The English Act of Toleration of 1689 was extended to the American colonies, and even in Maryland Catholics lost all rights.

Another English colony in America into which toleration was introduced at a time of harsh persecution was Providence, founded by Roger Williams, a man of Arminian tendencies. He, after suffering various persecutions in the English colonies, from 1631 to 1636, decided to found a new colony with a democratic government which would not interfere in religious matters, allowing all full freedom of conscience. After Providence, he founded other colonies, assisted by the dissenters of various persuasions. At the same time Samuel Gorton was founding new centres open to all.

The most famous of such colonies was that founded by William Penn and called after him Pennsylvania, where the Quakers, so harshly persecuted in the other colonies, could have complete freedom and offer it to many others, including Catholics, towards whom Penn had always shown sympathy. But—the residue of prejudices and struggles—in Pennsylvania Catholics were denied access to public office, unless they declared in writing that they did not believe in Transubstantiation and that the cult of the Virgin was a superstition.

The movement towards toleration, which had grown up in the English colonies on American soil, was facilitated by the fact that the colonists could migrate from one State to another, found new cities and new independent centres, and themselves fix the forms of their civil and religious life. But the prevailing spirit in English America was one of intolerance and confessional rigidity; the colonies received the backwash of religious-political movements in the mother country. When Episcopalians or Presbyterians were persecuted in England, they were persecuted in the colonies, with the sole difference that here dissenters had not to seek a refuge on foreign soil, but could go from one colony to another. By the Act of Toleration of William of Orange all Protestants and dissenters received equal rights in America, except, as we have seen, Unitarians or Socinians and Catholics. Thus the XVII century closed in Great Britain and her colonies, with '*toleration among kindred confessions within similar political conceptions on a rationalistic basis*'.

§ 35.—In Germany, jusnaturalism found its first real exponent in Johannes Althusius, who in 1603 published his *Politica metodice digesta*. He was not a Lutheran but a Calvinist, and as such combined the popular conception of the State with a close connection between State and Church. His political system, however, led him to secularise the State, making it the expression no longer of Divine Right but of Natural Right. Unlike his great Latin contemporaries, Bodin and Suarez, who attributed to the State alone the character of an authoritarian society, from which all other bodies derived their rights as concessions, Althusius maintained the originality of each social form (family, guild, city or municipality and province), and made of the State a federation of municipalities and provinces. According to him, every social entity springs from the contractual will of individuals, either as single persons or as already constituted groups. The sovereignty of the State is compatible with the autonomous existence of the other groups, for the State is an *universalis publica consociatio* with a *potestas publica universalis*. But at every stage of association, the social contract, by developing a specific life in common, creates the correlative power necessary to its complete existence. This power would be initially a *potestas privata*, as in the family or corporative association (*Genossenschaft*), but when a group succeeds in asserting itself as a territorial whole, it then becomes a *potestas publica*, where its specific functions are concerned, till the stage is reached of universal political society in the State. The State therefore is of a federal type, neither absolutist nor absorbing everything into itself or, as we should say to-day, totalitarian.

Althusius sought to reconcile the medieval corporative conception with that of modern jusnaturalism; he represented a phase of transition.

With Pufendorf we reach the maturity of German political thought of the XVII century; his influence was considerable and assumed a special character in regard to religious toleration. Between Althusius and Pufendorf there lay the Thirty Years' War, the Peace of Westphalia, the growth of Dutch Arminianism, Cromwell, Hobbes, the Quakers, and the Stuart Restoration in England. When he wrote his *De habitu religionis christianae ad vitam civilem*, the Revocation of the Edict of Nantes had had an immense repercussion throughout Germany. Pufendorf bases his theory of toleration on a kind of natural religion. No one should be forced to adopt a given religion. Those who would not accept a minimum of natural religion should be expelled from civil society, or else tolerated on condition they behaved decently and refrained from propagating any subversive ideas. He went further than Locke on the path of toleration, since he did not exclude Catholics from the free profession of their religion, and accorded to atheists a possibility of escaping pursuit. This breadth of view sprang from the purely naturalistic conception of society, as culminating, either federally, as maintained by Althusius, or monistically, as maintained by Hobbes, in the State. The idea of a universal Church independent of the State and under certain aspects superior to it, was alien to the jusnaturalist system, even if its writers recognised the supernatural character of the Christian revelation and held the Bible as an inspired book. Although formally they dealt with the relations between State and Church as between two entities, and considered the various Christian denominations as corporate bodies, free associations, *systemata subordinata*, and the like, in substance they dealt with the relations between individuals and society, and with this approach there could be no relations other than those of a natural order, fundamentally individualistic. The Church no longer integrated the State as in the Middle Ages. It was not absorbed by the State, as in Lutheranism. It did not form with the State a single spiritual complexus, as in Calvinism. But it fell within the orbit of the State as simply an activity of individuals, who could freely meet together to that end, so long as they did not conflict with the ends, activity and responsibility of the public power. This does not mean that the jusnaturalists ignored the importance of religion and the office of the Church, but only that the theory they upheld led logically to the secularisation of the State and to social individualism in the religious field.

We must realise that jusnaturalism had its greatest and most characteristic development in Protestant countries, through Protestant thinkers. The State in these countries had between the XVI and XVII centuries assumed the form of State-cum-Church. The Head of the State was the Head of the Church. The State had its own religion. In Germany and the neighbouring countries the Peace of Westphalia had definitely consolidated the principles of the Peace of Augsburg of 1555, with all the adjustments, whether on the change of religion of a sovereign, or the question of usurped or confiscated properties, or ecclesiastical communities, or nonconformist minorities, that had been introduced in the course of the experience of nearly a century.

In the Empire three confessions were allowed, the Catholic, the Lutheran, the Reformed: '*sed praeter religiones supra nominatas nulla alia in sacro Imperio Romano recipiatur vel toleretur.*'[1] Thus the *Instrument of the Peace of Osnabrück*. These three confessions enjoyed legally exact

[1] 'But besides the religions above-mentioned, no other shall be received or tolerated in the Holy Roman Empire.'

and mutual equality—*exacta mutuaque aequalitas.* In actual fact, every sovereign or prince of the Empire, Austria excepted, enjoyed the *jus reformandi*, through which he could opt for one of the three confessions, and, by the *jus reprobandi*, expel from his State those who did not wish to follow him. On the other hand, the dissenting minorities could ask hospitality from another prince, and he could accept them in virtue of the *jus recipiendi*. This implied among the dissenting populations the *beneficium emigrandi* from one State to another. The system was based on two fundamental conceptions: (*a*) the territoriality of the religious community; (*b*) the Protestant type of State-cum-Church. Even the Catholic countries of the Empire, though depending on Rome in religion, formed State-cum-Church units. The jusnaturalist conception undermined these foundations, since it made of the State the universal and sovereign natural society on its own territory, with no bonds or limitations from any given church, and it reduced the Church to as many free collegial communities as there were forms of religion.

To this jusnaturalist conception Pufendorf gave a juridical structure centred in the idea of the *persona moralis*. He distinguishes between the *persona moralis simplex*, the individual under a given aspect or legal quality (such as the *paterfamilias*, the *civis*, the *minister*), from the *persona moralis composita*, that is, the social forms, from the family to the State, and including the Church. When the will of one unites with the will of others, in due manner and for characteristic ends, then the composite *persona moralis* is formed. Pufendorf sees every group of persons under the aspect of moral-juridical relationships, which acquire a clearly defined consistency from the moment they have a head invested with authority. Whether society be conceived of as co-participation or as community or as representation, it will have an ethico-legal value in so far as it succeeds in becoming a *persona moralis*, that is, a characteristic mode of being of the actual persons who have joined together. The *persona moralis* is in itself finalistic, and in its finality autonomous.

Although Pufendorf's theory of society soon fell out of fashion before the advance of the theory of individualistic representation, it nevertheless fulfilled a useful function in the evolution of law and the consolidation of the new political conception, which was tending towards the release of the State from the influence of the official Church. The close union between the two, in Germany and elsewhere, had become a stranglehold. The type of State that was then developing in Prussia had undoubtedly an influence on Pufendorf's thought. Prussia was beginning to set the example of a State which through its financial and military organisation had liberated itself from the nobles and from the Church. The monarchs of the XVII century sought to subject nobles, clergy and middle classes to their dominion. But, since the States had neither an independent and stable finance, nor a large and well-organised army, they had to have recourse to nobles, clergy and parliaments in order to keep the royal treasury in a sound condition and to maintain and renew their armies and fleets. Hence, in return, continual concessions to the clergy for the supremacy of their church, to the parliaments and nobility for their privileges and their display. In Prussia, from the time of Frederick-William I, the Hohenzollerns conceived of a military State, based on the bourgeois people, free from clergy, nobility and assemblies; a State, strong in itself, which thus became the sole and effective territorial authority. The idea of achieving a State complete in itself, with no need to lean for support on clergy or nobility, unhampered by parliaments, and which at the same time would be the expression of each individual resolved into the authority of the head, was bound to allure the German theorists, who sought to overcome the religious-political dualism by unification of the State and religious freedom.

Speculative research was complemented by positive research; religious toleration was studied in the interpretation of German law. Among the Protestants there came into being a current which interpreted the treaties of Westphalia in a liberal sense; the three authorised confessions were considered from the standpoint of public worship, never as domestic or private religion. Since religion was an intimate personal concern, freedom of conscience could be denied to no one; not only the prince had the right to choose his own religion, but each of his subjects. Such was the theory of J. H. Boehmer; his pupil C. H. Fuehrman developed the same thesis in his study on the *Civil effects of religious toleration in the letter and in the spirit of the Peace of Westphalia.*

Through the influence of the Natural Law School in Germany the idea of toleration for dissenters outside the three authorised confessions gained ground steadily. The system of territorial churches persisted, but with a perceptible tendency towards the collegial system. In practice, the aversion between Catholics and Protestants remained, even in the following century, through the position of irreducibility each maintained towards the other, in spite of practical compromises dictated by political exigencies and by the tangled dynastic interests which the wars of the time brought to the fore and rendered urgent, and which were favoured by unexpected successions. The multiplicity of the German States made it easy for dissenters from one State to be received in another; the opportunity of developing industries and trades and of procuring specialised workers made the princes ready to avail themselves of the *jus recipiendi*. Wars, dynastic successions and practical interests provided frequent motives for applying to religious confessions the toleration preached by the jusnaturalist theories, which developed in spite of the opposition of the clergy and of the Westphalian traditionalists.

The Baltic countries, Denmark, Sweden and Norway, which had become Lutheran more through political interest than through religious crisis, after the first period of struggles and truces, became the most enclosed and intolerant States of Europe, and maintained the rigidity of their system till the XIX century. The few concessions made to the Huguenot refugees were due to the reaction provoked by the revocation of the Edict of Nantes; others, to Catholics, were of a diplomatic character, the result of pressure from the courts of Paris or Vienna, or else in order to obtain from other States specialised workers for new industries. No current of thought penetrated the Baltic countries till the period of the Encyclopaedia. There was no effectual mitigation of the system of a single State religion, the Lutheran, which unified Church and State.

In Switzerland, the problem of toleration was raised from the first period of the Reformation. From then till 1712, in German-speaking Switzerland there were four periods of war, followed by four peace pacts. The principle at stake was that of *intercantonal parity* between Protestant and Catholic lands, which led to *cantonal parity* between religious majorities and minorities. The wars were caused by mutual intolerance and ended with the most meticulous prescriptions to equate the rights of the victorious party with concessions to the vanquished. The system of territorial churches and the *jus reformandi* of the Protestant majorities were the outcome of the peace of 1529; parity was won only with the peace of 1712.

In French-speaking Switzerland, though there were no wars between the cantons—only wars with the princes of Savoy, against an attempt to restore Catholicism—yet religious intolerance lasted without mitigation. The influence of Alfonso Turrettini, a Genevan of Italian origin (1671–1737), who preached universal appeasement and mutual toleration, had small effect on the development of Swiss thought. In Switzerland, the conception of the canton, as city and State, combined with the strictest religious observance and the safeguarding of the independence of the country, formed a strong and inelastic nexus. Local wars assumed the character of a defence of families, villages, communities, local traditions and interests. All this strengthened the ties between civil and religious life, between magistrates and ministers. The jusnaturalist currents could find no supporters behind the Swiss mountains. Aspirations to freedom of conscience in order to pass from one to the other of the two recognised confessions or to profess another form of religion, found no motives in men who for two centuries had fought with arms and with their votes (in the cantonal administrations), to defend their own religions, to which each family was bound by traditions of loyalty and heroic memories.

Owing to the rigidity we have noted in the Baltic countries and in Switzerland, and also to the various vicissitudes of the German Empire, through wars, struggles, persecutions and intolerance, the Protestant churches were riddled with sects and undermined by philosophical and juridical speculation. The tendency towards toleration came most to the fore where the need was greatest, that is, where the absolutism of the monarchy and the intransigence of the clergy were strongest. It gained credit through the support of the Universities; it spread with the books, pamphlets, reviews and papers, published chiefly in Holland (the undisputed centre of culture in the XVII century), which poured into every country in Europe, in spite of the watchfulness of the customs officers and the rigour of the criminal and religious laws.

§ 36.—In Catholic countries, or those where the majority and the monarchy were Catholic, there was no real basis for a movement of ideas and feelings towards toleration, neither moralistic, naturalistic, nor mystical. The Socinian current remained crystallised in Transylvania and a few scattered centres, in small local sects, the most notable that of the Polish Brothers, or among isolated scholars. In spite of this, the Socinian spirit circulated in various guises, but it was less a question of true Socinianism than of a residue of the humanistic currents of the Renaissance, which had filtered through the discipline of the Counter-Reformation. Stoicism had an attraction in the intellectual and moral fields. Montaigne was its most famous and loftiest exponent. The Libertines, (when they were not simply *bon vivants*), were not concerned with religious dogmas, and whittled down individual morality to the point of licence. In philosophy they were moderate Epicureans, like Gassendi, or else sceptics of the type of Saint-Evrémont's *honnête homme*.

The man who had an immense influence not only in France but in many other parts of Europe, and on Catholic culture itself, was Descartes. His rationalism, it is true, brought him into conflict with traditionalists, scholastics and mystics, but his attitude of questioning everything, starting from systematic doubt and resting on the certainty of his own thought, was for many a liberation from the authoritarian systems of culture and a vindication of the power of reason. To reconstruct everything in the geometric spirit, to eliminate the obscure movements of reality in obedience to the '*idées simples et claires*' was a means of reuniting the world of metaphysical certainty to the physical world of mathematics. Galileo in Italy with his scientific criticism was attacking the a-priorism and dogmatism of the scholastics of his time, as applied to the physical and astronomical sciences; Descartes in France was building modern philosophical rationalism on criticism of thought.

The first application of rationalism to criticism, in history, scholarship and religion, showed at once the need for a limit, the lack of which made Bayle himself feel the imminence of a general scepticism. Rationalistic criticism furnished the basis of history in its two-fold aspect of ascertainment of fact and systematic exposition. It is true that the first encounter between rationalism and historical criticism gave a dizzy sense of destructive pyrrhonism, but immediately after came Leibniz,

Mabillon, Muratori, Vico. The same thing happened in the other fields to which rationalistic methods and criticism were applied, including the Bible and morals. But, whereas biblical criticism remained confined to a circle of erudite scholars, and met with immediate obstacles from the traditionalists and the Church itself—among Catholics, the boldest, Richard Simon, was several times condemned, and had to assume a dozen pseudonyms in order to gain a hearing—moralistic criticism, under the name of casuistry, became one of the most passionately pursued problems of the XVII century, and remained, in the general culture of Europe, a problem never entirely solved.

It would be here out of place to give the history of casuistry, or of the struggles between Jansenists and Jesuits, culminating in the intervention of Pascal, who, with his *Lettres Provinciales*, transferred the quarrel from Paris to the whole cultured world of his time and of succeeding centuries. Here it is of interest to note that the movement improperly known as casuistry had a character of its own, which related it on the one hand to the rationalistic and critical currents and on the other to the two extremes, the Stoics and the Libertines. This may seem a hazardous view, but only by a thorough study of the widespread and general tendency after the Reformation and Counter-Reformation to escape from political constriction and religious intolerance, towards a rationalism which would, it was believed, bring appeasement both inwardly, in the mind and will, and outwardly, in society, can we understand the import of the phenomena we are now considering.

In the Catholic countries—where, in the XVII century, the activities of dissenting churches and diverse sects could find no suitable field, and where, therefore, the problem of toleration did not present itself in the same manner, nor so urgently as in Protestant countries—the individualist and particularist spirit developed on the margins of Church and State, and also within them, under a marginal aspect. Escape was not sought in release from a conformity imposed by the two-fold bond of religious and social tradition, but in rational and critical culture, in the moral attitude of Stoics or Libertines, in Jansenist or Quietist mysticism. In France, and, under other aspects, in all Catholic countries, there was a further need—that of evading the Gallican stranglehold of the Court and the Sorbonne, and a traditional rigorism in the clergy who seemed themselves Jansenists before their time. In the struggle against both, the Jesuits were in the forefront, and threw themselves into the fight.

We have seen how they had defended popular power against monarchic absolutism, and how they had therefore been driven out of France as subversive and tyrnnaicidal; how, on their return, they had defended the papal power under Bellarmin's formula of indirect power, and how they had been obliged to repudiate their own teaching and to subscribe to the most trenchant assertions of Gallicanism. At the same time, other struggles had arisen, which nourished disputes and animosities between the parties concerned—Molinism, Casuistry, Anti-Jansenism. These struggles would continue under other aspects in the next century. In all this, the Jesuits were not animated, as they seemed to Pascal, by an anti-Christian will of world dominion, but sought to utilise, by their own, and sometimes disputable, methods, a rationalist reorientation, of which the need was then felt by many. But, even though they maintained such reorientation within the bounds of Catholic orthodoxy, there were inevitable deviations now towards Pelagianism, now towards Laxism.

The theory of free will, as defended by the Jesuits, derived both from the decisions of the Council of Trent and from the voluntarist asceticism of St. Ignatius Loyola. In seeking to give a theologically rational explanation (not indeed as an explanation of the mystery of grace), Molina and his followers met with violent opposition from the Thomists and Augustinians in Spain and in all the centres of university culture, from Louvain to Paris, Vienna and Rome. This was at the close of the XVI century and the opening of the XVII. Rome was flooded with complaints, books, pamphlets, controversies, declarations, inquiries of the Spanish Inquisition and messages from the Courts—Philip III of Spain and the Empress Maria of Austria were for the Jesuits. Clement VIII in 1598 formed a special congregation, the *De Auxiliis*, to examine the theological dispute between Molinists and Thomists. But after nine years of work, it was suspended by Paul V, who forbade either party to qualify the adverse opinion as censurable. The Jesuits, who had been accused of semi-Pelagianism, cried Victory! They could henceforth defend Molina's theory without risk of censure.

Hence, festivals in their colleges, festivals in their churches, inscriptions that read: '*Molina Victor!*' At Villagarcia in Spain even a bull-fight was organised in celebration. Such manifestations, which might be judged as springing from an exaggerated *esprit de corps* and from theological and university jealousies, had at the same time a remarkable repercussion among the public, both lay and clerical, who for nearly a century had listened to the most acrimonious discussions on Grace and Free Will in the schools and pulpits, for and against Luther, Calvin and Baïus.

The higher free will was exalted, the higher the exaltation of human reason, from which it springs. The revision of moral theology on a casuistic basis was merely the effort to bring to light its link with reason. Thomist scholasticism had already taken an important step in this direction when it had philosophically developed Christian ethics in accordance with the Ethics of Aristotle, not by reducing the gifts of grace to natural virtues, but by basing the supernatural structure of ethics on the natural, bringing out its rationality. Casuistry went still further. On the one hand it sought to seize the psychological laws of the human act, not in general but in the concrete, to ascertain its intrinsic value and responsibility; on the other it studied the rational means, both inward and outward, of overcoming practical doubt on the morality of actions. In doing so, the casuists sought to avoid any subjectivism, natural or supernatural, such as was derived mainly from the Protestant theories, from intuitionist conceptions and from the mysticising forms of Illuminism, Quietism, Visionism, in short from everything in morals that could not be appraised by reason; but they avoided also individualism of personal judgment as liable to be affected by passion or ignorance. Hence the double office of reason and authority. For both it was necessary to give a scientific character to the human method of probability, as commonly used, even unconsciously, in practical life, in doubtful cases, whether moral, legal or technical. From Bartolomé de Medina onwards this was called *Probabilism*, and was contrasted with the system urged by the zealots in favour of obligation, which was therefore known as *Tutiorism*. The polemic (it was an age of polemics) became general and did not lack asperity. Any opinion maintained by an authoritative moralist or by several moralists was termed probable; the intrinsic reasons of the probability were seen by many in terms of the extrinsic value of the authority.

Deviation was already advanced. Acute, subtle, bold, hyper-logical casuists took to using reasoning so as to justify many violations of the moral law and to mitigate its bonds; to such a pitch that the Libertines themselves, who believed in morality for others, cried scandal. The rigorist current among the clergy opposed the Probabilists in the name of tradition. Rome intervened, and in 1603 placed on the Index the *Aphorismi confessariorum* of Father Sa and the *Summa theologiae moralis* of Father Henriquez; the *Summula casuum conscientiae* by Father Condignat followed, and in 1640 it was the turn of the famous Father Bauny. Finally, after the Pascal controversy (and it was Pascal's achievement), Alexander VII in 1665 solemnly condemned 'Laxism', the excess and also the caricature of casuistic Probabilism.

Pascal confused Laxism with Casuistry; he condemned both the intrinsic probabilism based on reason and the extrinsic probabilism based on the authority of the moralists; he attenuated the rights of reason and of free will, emphasising in the Jansenist manner that of grace. But his condemnation of casuistry has remained till the present day without appeal for the world of general culture (though not for that of the specialists), for in reality he struck not at the substance of casuistry but at the exaggerations of the rationalistic and legalistic methods of the time. These whittled down the value of the voice of conscience, giving an escape from its inward judgment to the external authority of the theologians; they paid insufficient attention to the duty of holding fast to the moral law, and abounded in quests for means of evading obligation or attenuating it. Thus the descent towards Laxism was only a matter of degree.

Pascal failed to understand that all this was on the one hand a reaction against an oppressive conformism, political, religious and social; against a rigid traditionalism which in morals took no account of the economic, cultural and professional developments of the time, or the needs they created. He thus confused a permanent and eminently human problem, that of the morality of actions in the concrete of each particular case, with the positions adopted by casuistry as he had seen it—in the Jansenist controversy, in Laxist application, and disintegrating into formalism. Rationalism and criticism released those of small religious belief or small religious observance from the bonds of dogmatic faith, producing the so-called Libertines. Intellectual and moral libertinism had an influence on the rich and cultured class which travelled over the world and kept itself, by its scepticism, untouched by profound passions. Casuistry, where it degenerated into Laxism and legal formalism, allowed certain sections of the upper and middle classes to take their ease in external religious observance and worldliness of spirit. All these evaded the problems raised by religious conflicts, whether within their own consciences or in the outer sphere of society and politics: the individual and the collective spheres came to form two separate worlds.

These were the motives through which the religious persecutions and political intolerance against Jansenists, Huguenots and Quietists in France aroused no disquiet, no opposition, no protest among the intellectuals, philosophers and responsible men, but rather agreement and approval. Not a single proposal was made to limit the powers of the Monarchy, or to grant some practical concessions to dissenters, in the name of a principle of humanity and Christian sense. As long as the governments of the two great Cardinals, Richelieu and Mazarin, lasted, the toleration to which the French Monarchy had pledged itself by the Edict of Nantes was more or less observed. Since both Cardinals sought to transfer the centre of European politics from Spain to France, and to render France a strong and compact State, they made it their business to put an end to factions, to humble the aristocracy, to tame the clergy and Parlements, and to magnify the absolute power of the King. They had therefore no interest in exciting the Protestants of North and South by religious persecutions. But the exaltation of the absolute power, the teaching of Gallican doctrines already associated with the Divine Right of Kings, and rendered binding upon all and put into practical effect, carried further-reaching consequences than the political and moral unification of the State.

In England monarchs by Divine Right, like the Stuarts, were at odds with their Parliaments; Charles I ended on the scaffold, and James II lost his throne. In France, Louis XIV was at odds with the Pope, and very nearly reached the point of schism. But the Stuarts were caught between the jaws of two churches; by favouring one, they divided the country and were defeated. Louis XIV had the clergy behind him, nearly all the clergy, even the Jesuits, who were forced yet again to subscribe to the Gallican doctrines. With such support he could fight at once against Rome on the one hand and the Huguenots, Jansenists and even the unimportant Quietists on the other. The intolerance of Louis XIV was based on his motto, which summed up the theory of Divine Right: '*Un roi, une loi, une foi!*' The support of the Gallican clergy, moreover, gave it the clearest and most decisive theological formulation that had been known since the time of the Council of Constance.

Friction with the Roman Curia was not wanting in any Catholic court of the age. Jurisdictionalism was practised everywhere. Political complications and theological disputes provided continual motives for diplomatic quarrels. Louis XIV was personally in conflict with Alexander VII; Cardinal Mazarin's struggle against the worthless Cardinal de Retz, who was supported by Rome from canonical motives and by the Jansenists for practical reasons, made history. The mission of the Duc de Créqui to Rome (an arrogant, inflated fellow, who with his insistence on etiquette and precedence hoped to convey to the Romans the greatness of his King) complicated relations to such a point that Louis occupied the Comté de Venaissin and threatened the papal States with armed invasion. After much tergiversation, Alexander gave way and the Treaty of Pisa followed, in 1664. This dispute so excited Louis and his court, that he seized upon one of the many debates in the Sorbonne on the papal power and Gallican liberties, to procure a resounding means of humiliating the Pope and making the official theory final. The Faculty of Theology (in 1663) was invited to define its doctrine; it did so in six articles in negative form, thus avoiding pronouncing upon the limits and positive value of the propositions set forth, but the theory of the Divine Right of Kings received full consecration, as also that of the superiority of Council to Pope, and the other, that the Pope had no power to depose Bishops. The Parlement of Paris registered the Six Articles, the King approved them, and ordained that they should be registered at all courts and that their teaching in all the faculties and schools of the kingdom should be compulsory.

The most resounding and gravest dispute between Louis XIV and the Papacy was that over the 'regalia,' which lasted twenty years, from 1673 till 1693. Louis claimed the right to exact the revenues of the vacant bishoprics throughout France, as regalia, whereas in reality he had the right to do so only in certain bishoprics not yet 'exempted'. Summoned by the King to give explicit recognition of his rights, no Bishop dared resist; only two from the South appealed to the Pope, who decided in their favour. The dispute, a question of pure Canon Law, was widened, bringing into question, as usual, the powers of the Pope. Louis, wishing to strike a decisive blow, in 1681 convoked the delegates of all the clergy of France, to decide the dispute over the regalia in his favour. The clergy at the same time sent Innocent XI a letter of justification, and besought him to avert a new conflict. But the conflict was what the King wanted. He demanded from the assembled clergy a formal declaration on the Gallican theory, so as to put an end to the claims of popes who might threaten to excommunicate and depose him. In Bossuet he had at once a courtier, a zealous bishop, and an enlightened theologian, whose authority was undisputed. Bossuet drew up the famous Four Propositions—corresponding, in a positive form, to the six approved by the Faculty of Theology of the Sorbonne in 1663—and submitted them to the Assembly. The first declares that kings are not subject in temporal matters to any ecclesiastical power, and that the Pope cannot depose them either directly or indirectly, and has no power to absolve their subjects from their oath of allegiance. The second, while recognising to the Pope full spiritual power, recalls the decrees of the fourth and fifth sections of the Council of Constance on the superiority of the Council. The third maintains the right to assert, in respect of the Pope, the canons and traditional privileges of local churches. The fourth declares that though the Pope plays the principal part in matters of faith, his judgment is still not final without the consent of the Church.

Louis XIV hastened to approve the Four Propositions and to impose them on all France. Innocent XI protested, and refused to give canonical investiture to priests promoted to bishoprics, if they had taken part in the assembly of 1682, so that in a few years over thirty-five bishoprics lacked their incumbents. Alexander VIII continued the resistance and declared the Four Propositions null and void. The French bishops, fearing a schism, in 1693 signed a retractation of the Four Propositions, and Louis wrote to Innocent XII that in consequence he would rescind the order for their enforcement. But the Pope yielded over the question of regalia, recognising them to the French monarchy. It seemed as if peace had been reached, but Louis engaged Bossuet to finish his '*Défence de la Déclaration*', which he had begun to write, but did not dare to publish. In actual fact, the Four Propositions remained as the authorised expression of the Gallican theory and spread over Europe; in spite of papal condemnations they were maintained and taught by various national clergies.

It is in the mental climate of Paris between 1663 and 1693, in the union between clergy and monarchy and the influence of the Jesuits on the Court, in the growing friction with Rome and the inflated conception of the Divine Right of Kings and their role as guardians of the faith and of the Church, that we find the explanation of the persecution of the Huguenots, of the revocation of the Edict of Nantes, of the rigours against Jansenists and Quietists, of the King's continual interference in Church matters, even in convents of nuns and country parishes. His Catholic zeal was mingled with a punctilio to do more and better than the Pope (in which he copied Philip II of Spain), while feminine influence played an equal part in exciting his zeal which ended by becoming, after his fashion, sincere.

The method of the 'Dragonnades' to force the Huguenots into conversion was one of the worst that has ever been devised by a tyrannical king and bigoted councillors. The dragoons were sent into Huguenot homes, to install themselves as in time of war, tormenting women and old men and children with the most brutal and most refined methods, threatening them even with death. In a short time these singular missionaries produced thirty thousand conversions. But the Protestants were too many, nor were protests and attempts at resistance wanting. The final decision was the revocation of the Edict of Nantes, the suppression of all toleration, the exile of over three hundred thousand Frenchmen, the apparent conversion of many others, while a large number of families fled into the forests and mountains. The Protestant countries, forgetting their own persecutions against Catholics, were filled with indignation at Louis' action, in stamping under foot the edict which Henry IV had declared perpetual and irrevocable. They received the refugees, and gave them means to defend themselves and to rouse Europe against the great injustice committed by the new Antichrist. Rome was annoyed by the revocation, judging it inopportune, but in France all approved the action of the *Grand Monarque*—Fénélon, La Bruyére and La Fontaine, Racine, the Jansenist leaders Nicole and Arnauld. Bossuet wrote that it was the greatest enterprise of the second Constantine. The old Chancellor, Michel Le Tellier, on countersigning the decree, declared himself happy to end his career by the grandest act of his life. Madame de Sévigné wrote: '*C'est la plus grande et la plus belle chose qui ait jamais été imaginée.*' Even Fontenelle was favourable, and with him the rationalists and libertines. Saint-Evrémont had written: *Je ne trouve rien de plus injuste que de persécuter un homme sur sa créance, mais je ne vois rien de plus fou que de s'attirer la persécution.*'

If among all the philosophers and politicians, rationalists and libertines and dissident clergy, we do not find one who could see the persecutions of Louis XIV in their true light, the chief reason is the universal acceptance of the political theory of the Divine Right of Kings, even by the Jansenists and by the Huguenots. Montesquieu and Rousseau were not yet born. The only men to formulate political theories whose names carried weight were Bossuet and Fénélon. Bossuet was the theologian of the Divine Right, of the absolutism of kings, to the exclusion of any human control, popular, civil or ecclesiastical. Fénélon sought timidly to introduce a consideration of the interests of the people into the conception of absolute sovereignty. But neither could envisage religious toleration as anything but a mere matter of political opportunism, of which the sole judge was the King. The intolerance of the Catholics was met by a like intolerance in those they persecuted. The Huguenots fought in defence of truth, of Christianity, of the only true Church of God, which was their own; the clash between two truths, held as such by either side, brought them disaster, but it was within the logic of their religious system.

The Jansenist leaders, who openly applauded the revocation of the Edict of Nantes, inasmuch as they considered themselves Catholics, indeed, more Catholic than the rest, had already experienced persecution, and were to experience it again in a more comprehensive and effectual form. No sooner had the Pope condemned the Five Propositions of Jansenius, than Louis XIV convoked the clergy in the Louvre (1660), to inform them that Jansenism must be suppressed. Pascal's *Lettres Provinciales* were burnt by the public executioner, a good number of Jansenists were put in prison, and the great Arnauld went into exile. In the course of a second persecution, Louis XIV went so far as to cause the nuns of Port Royal to be driven out by troops, who violated the tombs of the dead and destroyed the monastery so that no trace of it remained. The persecution of Huguenots and Jansenists would be renewed under other forms in the following century.

Similar phases of truce and toleration, struggle and persecution, are to be found in other Catholic countries where there were dissenting factions, as in Poland, Hungary, Transylvania, and even in the small State of Piedmont, where the Waldensians were victims of the notorious 'Piedmontese Easter' (the massacres of 1665), which was followed by the Peace of Pinerolo the same year. But in 1686, toleration was revoked, in imitation of Louis XIV. The flight of the Waldensians into Switzerland followed, then their reconquest of the valleys in spite of the resistance of French and Piedmontese—the 'Glorious Return' of 1689. There were five more years of struggles and disputes before peace was made in 1694 between the Waldensians and Victor Amadeus II, when the latter had broken with Louis XIV. In Italy there were no other Protestant communities, save in Venice, where toleration assumed a commercial and economic character and persecution a political character. In Spain there were no Protestant sections, and the Inquisition saw to any who showed signs of suspect ideas in regard to religion and the monarchy. Towards the end of the XVII century there was only a faint echo in Catholic countries of the jusnaturalist theories that had ripened in Holland, England and Germany, while Catholic theologians and philosophers had already abandoned the theories of the popular origin of governing power, as maintained by Bellarmin, Suarez and Mariana.

§ 37.—After the Peace of Westphalia, a movement had taken shape in Germany towards a possible understanding between Catholics and

Protestants, which interested a certain number of ecclesiastics, intellectuals and university professors, diplomats and princes; there was for a short while the idea of remaking a new Christendom. Christopher de Rojas, in 1661, was one of the first to urge the study of such a project. The Emperor in 1675 decided to collect in Vienna the declarations of Protestant theologians as a basis for discussion. The famous George Calixtus (1586–1656) had already maintained the thesis of accepting the dogmas common to the various churches as syncretic elements of faith and practical union. This idea, which was at first received with hostility, came to appeal to the minds of many, and plans were formulated by both Catholics and Protestants. Rome waited on events, giving encouragement with reservations; the attempt might come to nothing, like other attempts before and after the Council of Trent.

Among the most authoritative and unwearying champions of the union of the churches was Leibniz. In 1676 he had entered the service of John Frederick, Duke of Hanover, who in 1651 had been converted to Catholicism and laboured much in the various courts to this end. Leibniz wrote his *Systemata theologorum* (1683), in which he seems to have sought less the exposition of his own ideas than that of the state of the questions debated among Catholics, Protestants and Reformers. However we may judge this work, Leibniz had for a long time been pursuing a plan of convergence among the Christian churches, in order to reach a politico-religious structure of Europe as a new Christendom. An element in this plan was the conquest of Egypt, which he had urged upon Louis XIV, in order to strike a blow at the Turks and distract their forces, then pressing on Vienna and Budapest. He hoped for the conversion of China to Christianity through the Jesuits. He foresaw and encouraged the development of Christian Western civilisation in Russia (it was the time of Peter the Great), as an intermediary between Europe and Asia. He conceived and dreamed of a unified Germany, a united Europe.

It was needful to root out the causes of disunion, among them religious intolerance, the absence of powerful centres of culture, and the struggles and wars between Christian States. Therefore Leibniz, like other men of his time, thought it would be possible to reach a religious understanding on a minimum of dogma common to the various churches, with a comprehensive spirit of toleration and charity towards conflicting opinions. For Leibniz, the Catholic Church was not the universal church, and though he held that the Pope should be the common head of all Christians, and considered as valid the theological concept of tradition (denied by Protestants), he did not agree with either the Jesuits or Bossuet on the infallibility of the Church. Nor could Bossuet accept Leibniz' idea that a heretic was not a man who denied a dogma, but only one who persisted obstinately in his opinion. Leibniz started from a sound premise, which Bossuet rejected, that recognition of the goodness of God contained implicitly recognition of the Redeemer, and that this therefore was enough for a pagan, who had conceived a love of God and sorrow for his sins, to find salvation. From this premise, he drew a wider consequence, that the basis of the Church was not faith in a broad dogmatic complex, but simply faith in God and charity. Leibniz' discussion with Bossuet was a prolonged one, but it could have no success. For Bossuet, the reunion of Europe in a new Christendom could be effected only through the return of Protestantism to Catholicism. The method of discussion and persuasion was the method the Church preferred; the political method of constraint might be useful; Catholic monarchs in the hands of God were the ministers of His glory and His vengeance. Bossuet, for his part, was ready to fulfil the task of persuasion that fell to him as bishop and writer, by means of discussions and historical and dogmatic demonstration. To this he gave much of his labour, from his youth up, till he was a sick, old man. From this standpoint he did not refuse to respond to the insistency of Leibniz, though hoping nothing from his plan, unless, perhaps, the conversion of his great correspondent.

When his hopes for an understanding between Catholics and Protestants came to nothing, Leibniz confined his plan to a reunion of the Protestant and Reformed churches. But even this attempt was doomed to failure. No form of religious syncretism could provide a basis, either for Christian minds—for which faith cannot be simplified into elementary data, without leading to more complex developments and wider and deeper applications to individual and social life—or to those who were moving further and further away from religious thought, towards secularising conceptions, like the jusnaturalists and the rationalists, who consciously or unconsciously were seeking the basis of a unified human society in natural religion. Religion syncretism was merely a transitory and interpretative phase of the passage from a Christian conception of society to that of Natural Law; it is the accidental aspect of all religious latitudinarianism on the point of losing its theological physiognomy.

Leibniz did not found his ideas purely on a syncretic latitudinarianism, nor on a naturalistic and rationalistic theory, but on a philosophy inspired by Christianity. Only by bearing in mind his philosophy can we understand the significance of his efforts and his dream of a new Christendom. He was anti-Cartesian and anti-Spinozan by reaction and by conviction. Descartes reduced nature to a mechanism in the realisation of all possible forms; like the Nominalists, he made all physical and moral laws depend on an arbitrary Divine Will, thus denying the intrinsic rationality of the real. Spinoza made of reality a single Absolute, geometrically deterministic. For Leibniz, Descartes led to atheism, Spinoza to pantheism; both falsified the nature of created reality and denied it all finalism. In spite of this, in both there were two fundamental truths which could provide the basis for a new philosophy—in Descartes, the *idea of contingency*, brought out by the concept of the dependence of all things on the Divine Will, (as against Spinoza's necessity); in Spinoza the *idea of order*, as dependence on a geometrical, (or better, rational) necessity. Leibniz thus arrived at his idea of the '*principle of the best*': the present world is the best of possible worlds.

This realistic optimism in Leibniz animates all his theoretical systems and all his practical activity. His complete and active monad, quivering with inner life, ordered to itself and at the same time harmonised in the complex of other monads, is the concrete revelation of the contingent and finalistic optimism of his philosophy. The organism of monads seeks its end, just as does each separate monad; a pre-established harmony unites them, and all respond to their ends and to the more complex ends of the whole, which manifests the power and glory of God. Finalism is apparent in the movement of all being towards God—in inorganic matter through strength and motion; in organic matter through life; in man through moral act. Reason unites man to God and to the other created spirits; through reason we see the complex harmony of creation, the laws that show forth the divine wisdom, the historical continuity by which everything conspires to an end, which cannot be other than the City of God and the reign of love.

This optimistic vision was in contrast to the disunion of the Christian churches, the mutual intolerance, religious and political, the dissensions between Christian princes, the menace of the Crescent in Europe (it was the period of the siege of Vienna and the victory of John Sobieski). Hence the necessity for a plan corresponding to the spirit of such a philosophy. Philosophical finalism becomes historical finalism; events intertwine with things in a continuous interconnection, tending towards a better future by the law of continuity and progress, towards the realisation of the providential plans. Leibniz, the philosopher of history, in his conception of Providence, joins hands with Bossuet the apologist, the author of the *Discours sur l'Histoire Universelle*.

He was a happy man, for his optimistic ideal never failed him, in all the conflicts of his life, the collapse of his dreams, his abandonment by men. Though Leibniz was not a mystic, he must have been allured by the great visions of the mystics, thus to transcend all the pessimism of life in a higher conception of a divine end. Unfortunately, his finalistic optimism found no response in the world of philosophic thought of the time, imbued as this was with naturalistic rationalism and Spinozan pantheism, nor in the religious world, where Lutheranism denied free will, Calvinism established an iron, predestined determinism, and Jansenism, already widespread among Catholics, froze all effusion of grace.

There was another optimism during this period, that of the French classical culture of the XVII century, based on a conception of order, authority, tradition, on the stability of reason, the poise of morals, the harmony of art. Such a world, tending as it did to be fixed and static, could not appreciate either social dynamism or spiritual unrest. Pascal stands outside the world of Corneille and Descartes, just as Boileau, Bossuet and Malebranche stand outside the world of Pascal, whose intuitions attained a clarity in profundity. Racine and Moliére sought to break through the static world, but, lacking an optimistic philosophy, failed to reach the vision of a higher dynamism. Another world which was moved by optimistic motives was that of the Jesuits, in the widest sense of the word, including not only the Jesuits themselves but their followers, admirers, patrons and pupils. Here were free will, probabilist morals, finalistic intention, utilisation of all human possibilities, means and inventions, art and science included, for the conquest of the Kingdom of God. But this world carried the counterweight of an exterior formalism, of hazardous undertakings, of worldliness of means, of a predominance of fancy over feeling, reason over intuition, and was continually agitated by acrimonious controversies and by the almost constant opposition of a large portion of the clergy and of official culture as represented by the Sorbonne.

Classical optimism and Jesuitic optimism, which found in the France of the second half of the XVII century a centre from which to radiate through all Europe, were shattered against Jansenist pessimism, which gained the ascendancy, creating a deep gulf between the social and mundane reality and the spiritual intimacy of conscience. One man alone, Pascal, was able to overcome this dualism on a higher plane on which philosophy and mysticism formed a synthesis, yet the *Pensées* remained unfinished notes of an Augustinian vision of the world. After Pascal, only Fénélon sought a synthesis between the inner and outer. He saw the classical world of order and authority crumbling; he sought to give more room to the imagination and the heart; he felt the crisis that was approaching, but he was not of a stature to provide a philosophy for modern thought, nor a sure mysticism for the spiritual man as St. Francis de Sales had done in his day.

The XVII century opened with the religious pessimism of the Jansenists, which, in spite of condemnations from Rome, the Sorbonne and the French clergy, already invaded the Catholic camp. To this was added a growing unrest and a dissatisfaction with logical rationalism, juridical naturalism, moral laxism, religious formalism. On the other hand, the national clergies, especially the bishops, were so closely bound up with the monarchic power, and thus constituted so integral a part of the dominant oligarchies, as to create an immense gulf between them and the mass of the faithful, of whose spiritual and material conditions many were wholly ignorant.

The mediation between the political power and the people was left to the active religious orders, especially those that had been founded for educational purposes, like the Christian Brothers of St. Jean-Baptiste La Salle, and the many charitable institutions created and inspired by the work of St. Vincent de Paul and his imitators. The mystical currents showed vigorous life through the whole of the XVII century; it is sufficient to mention St. Francis de Sales, St. Maria Maddalena dei Pazzi of Florence, St. Jeanne de Chantal, St. Jean Eudes, St. Joseph of Cupertino, St. Marie Marguerite Alacocque, Blessed Claude de la Colombière, Cardinal de Bérulle, and l'Abbé Rancé, the reformer of the Trappists. The Catholic mystical influence penetrated to many sections of the people, who needed something to restore them from the oppression of Jansenism, and found comfort in the cult of the Sacred Heart of Jesus, which was then spreading. But such apostolic and mystical currents remained on the margins of organised society and could no longer, as in the Middle Ages, permeate general culture, philosophy, law, economics, politics. The prevailing motives escaped the inward rhythm of Christian life; philosophical and critical rationalism, political and legal jusnaturalism, formalistic or syncretizing religiosity, laid hold on Europe. The various Catholic forces which, in the different countries, might have opposed a valid resistance, were paralysed by the jurisdictionalist struggle between State and Church, which prevailed in the XVIII century till the eve of the Revolution.

CHAPTER X

JANSENISM, JURISDICTIONALISM, THE ENLIGHTENMENT

§ 38.—No sooner was Louis XIV dead (in 1713) than his corpse was abandoned by his huge host of courtiers. Only his confessor, Père Le Tellier, and the Captain of the Guard followed the bier to St. Denis, and the mob insulted it like that of a common scoundrel. As Louis XV was still a minor the Duke of Orléans was appointed Regent; he hastened to make the Parlement of Paris annul the will limiting his powers in favour of the Duke of Maine, the bastard son of the *Grand Monarque* by Madame de Montespan. This the Parlement did the more readily in that it was visibly regaining a power reduced and mortified by Louis XIV. At the same time the Regent, an irreligious and unscrupulous individual, in order to mark a change in ecclesiastical policy hitherto dominated by the Jesuits, set the Cardinal de Noailles at the head of the *Conseil de Conscience*, which was a kind of ecclesiastical ministry, very powerful and influential. The Cardinal had favoured the Jansenists and was looked upon askance by the Jesuits.

Louis XIV had left the anti-Jansenist struggle at an acute phase, which had originated in 1703 over the celebrated 'Case of Conscience'. Canon Périer, the son of Pascal's sister, set before the Theological Faculty of the Sorbonne, in writing, a case of conscience in order to get from it an authoritative reply. In discussing the most subtle cases these learned doctors were in their elements. The time had passed when discussion turned on whether the Five Propositions were or were not in the *Augustinus* of Jansenius; Rome had replied that not only did it condemn the propositions but condemned them in the sense Jansenius gave them. The Jansenists would not accept defeat; Canon Périer put the case of whether it was possible to give absolution to a priest who, accepting the condemnation of the five propositions and signing the formulary without reservations or mental restrictions, remained uncertain whether the propositions were really to be found in Jansenius and, on this subtle point, observed a submission not of conviction but only of respect and silence. To-day at a distance of two centuries it is incomprehensible how such a question could have assumed public importance; then it was otherwise. Forty doctors of the Sorbonne signed a decision in favour of absolving a priest thus troubled in conscience. The matter was dealt with between Périer and the theologians as if they were a kind of Sacred Penitentiary Congregation, but, through an indiscretion, which was certainly not involuntary, the decision was known and circulated. Bossuet flared into indignation and sent the Cardinal de Noailles a polemical tract entitled: *Réflexions sur le cas de conscience*.

The matter was denounced to the Pope, who at once sent two Briefs disapproving the decision of the Sorbonne, the one to the Archbishop of Paris, the other to the King, ordering that the signatories should receive exemplary punishment, for which he called upon the assistance of the secular arm. All the doctors involved, except Petitpied, Professor of Scripture, withdrew their signatures. The bishops, to whom the brief was communicated by the King, hastened to publish it, accompanied by special charges, but the magistrates, many of whom were Jansenists or the friends of Jansenists, raised the question that papal briefs, before they could take effect, had to be supplied with royal letters patent, registered by the Parlement. Louis XIV recognised his mistake: such was the Gallican and publicistic rule. The bishops' publications were null, the Briefs without legal effects. But he at once saw to it that the Jansenists should be robbed of their satisfaction, asking the Pope to issue a solemn Bull which would put an end (or so he thought) to the dispute. Clement XI in 1705 issued his *Vineam Domini Sabaoth*, and the King himself, in sending the Bull to the bishops, wrote that 'it was on his instances that Jansenism had been freshly condemned by the Pope', and that, according to the Gallican use, 'he addressed to the assembly a copy of this Constitution: he exhorted the deputies to deliberate at once on the acceptance of the Constitution, so as to send out as soon as possible the letters patent necessary for its execution.'

Both the King and the Clergy Assembly in accepting the Bull were careful to reaffirm the Gallican doctrine and praxis, but there were bishops, with the Cardinal de Noailles at their head, who slipped in Jansenist reservations; thus the efficacy of the Bull, once believed decisive, was so reduced that far from appeasing past controversies it kindled a new one. It is not to be thought that the whole of France was roused to enquire up to what point grace or free will had prevalent or concomitant efficacy. If a thesis, whether theological or philosophical or scientific, is to arouse the passionate interest of a large and complex public, it must end by touching sensitive fibres in a wide zone of opinion and by becoming a psychological impulse. Jansenism had in its favour mystical elements which agreed with the medieval spiritual tradition, and its ethical rigorism was widespread among the country clergy, the provincial bourgeoisie, certain religious orders like the Augustinians and Dominicans, and the intellectual middle classes. Such looked with horror upon Laxism, which was confounded with casuistry; they were ill-disposed towards the Jesuits, as these presented themselves to the popular imagination—confessors of kings, nobles, courtiers and worldly ladies, educators of the wealthy classes, their colleges and churches thronged by the aristocracy; among them too were certain fathers dedicated to the profane sciences, writers and polemists of note. In the Clergy Assembly of 1700 Bossuet, who had drawn up and caused to be condemned five further propositions tainted with Jansenism, took care, to balance the position, to obtain the condemnation of no less than a hundred and twenty-three propositions taken from the 'relaxed casuists'. Behind the latter were the Jesuits, who were carrying on the anti-Jansenist struggle to the last ditch, attacking not only their theological theses on grace but also the Gallican premises which served them to frustrate condemnations from Rome and to render vain the efforts of the French bishops and of the court to reduce them to discipline.

The most uncomfortable position was that of the French bishops. In majority they were against the Jansenists and with the Pope over the dogmatic question, but they were against the Jesuits and dissented from the Roman Curia over Gallicanism. For their anti-Jansenist campaign they needed not only the backing of the Court but also that of the Sorbonne, the Parlements and the law-courts; but while the Court was against the Jansenists, the others were in favour of them. The bishops' action was thus paralysed. The intertwining of sentiments, interests and political passions with theological questions and with ecclesiastical positions helps to explain how, up to the middle of the XVIII century, in a period of intellectualistic and naturalistic culture, France was so deeply stirred by the Jansenist struggle. At bottom there was also the unconscious and instinctive resentment of the lower clergy, living in economic hardship, against the upper clergy, wealthy and protected by the court; of the bourgeoisie, which had to work for a living, against the aristocracy that exploited the lands it had forsaken and the royal exchequer at the expense of which it often lived; of the working classes of the countryside, of the artisan and workman in the incipient industries, who, brought more into contact with the bourgeoisie, mistrusted the debt-laden nobles living remote from the provinces. It is not possible to draw a clear distinction between Jansenist and anti-Jansenist sections of society; there is no economic determinism or religious idealism that can regulate in fixed form movements mainly psychological and instinctive. Feelings are always fluctuant, and therefore public opinion is fluctuant, unless exceptional events polarise it towards a definite goal.

One of such phases was that of the rebellion against the Bull *Unigenitus* by which Clement XI in 1713 had condemned a hundred-and-one propositions of the Oratorian Quesnel, then leader of the Jansenists. The bishops had accepted the new Bull and the Parlement had reluctantly registered it, when the Sorbonne came into open opposition. The magistracy condemned to the flames the episcopal charges in its favour. The ferment was such throughout France that the bishops themselves had to ask for enlightenment from the Pope and four of them, with the support of the Sorbonne and of many priests and friars, appealed 'to the future Council'; while conferences were set on foot between Jansenists and orthodox with a view to an understanding. In the meantime Louis XIV had died, and the Regent—bored and irritated by all this clerical hubbub which he could not dominate, and at the same time unwishful to irritate the Pope who in 1718 had condemned the appellants—decided on the one hand not to publish the papal condemnation and, on the other, ordered that no one henceforth should speak either for the Bull *Unigenitus* or against it. As was to be expected, given the general excitement, no one obeyed him. Clement XI was succeeded, in 1721, by Innocent XIII. The regent had wanted a Cardinal's hat for his minister, l'Abbé Dubois, whose moral conduct left much to be desired. The Jesuits favoured his nomination, counting on him to ensure the favour of the court in the fight against Jansenism and to neutralise the influence of Cardinal de Noailles. The future Pope gave the requisite undertaking, thus assuring the support of France; Dubois became Cardinal and in 1723 was elected President of the Clergy Assembly. The bishops hoped that he would obtain them the support of the Court in their fight against the Parlement; by now their position was such that everything depended on the King. To such subjection had they been reduced by Louis XIV, and thus they continued under the regency. No sooner was Louis XV of age, than they wrote to him: '*Sa Majesté est très humblement suppliée de vouloir faire attention aux affronts qu'a reçu le Clergé de France en ces dernières années, par une foule d'arrêts qui sont autant d'entreprises sur les droits les plus sacrés de l'Episcopat, et qui ne tendent à rien qu'à saper par le fondement toute l'autorité de l'Eglise.*' And the bishops continued their lament as follows: '*On s'en est pris personnellement aux évèques; on a fait saisir leur temporel, on les a menacés des plus grandes peines; leurs mandements sur des points de doctrine ont été déclarés abusifs ou supprimés; des particuliers de l'un et de l'autre sexe ont été autorisés à se soulever contre les mandements de leurs évèques, unis au Saint-Siège . . . Des pretres, des curés même, se font un titre de ces arrêts pour mépriser les censures dont ils avaient été liés par leurs supérieurs et ont continué impunément, sans s'en faire absoudre, l'exercice des fonctions les plus saintes . . . plusieurs arrêts ont été rendus sur le réquisitoire des procureurs et avocats généraux qui combattent par des propositions téméraires, fausses et erronées, la doctrine que les éveques enseignent à leur peuple*'.[1]

[1]'His Majesty is very humbly prayed to turn his attention to the affronts suffered by the Clergy of France in recent years, through a host of awards that are so many encroachments on the most sacred rights of the Episcopate, and which seek nothing but to sap the foundations of the whole authority of the Church. . . . The bishops have been personally called in question; their temporalities have been seized, they

In short, these poor court bishops, having lost all effectual authority over their priests and people, asked the King for a tribunal independent of the Parlement, to which to carry disputes arising out of appeals *ab abusu* or for other reasons, against episcopal orders in execution of the papal Bulls. How pettifogging was the mentality of these Gallican bishops! A question of spiritual conviction, of religious discipline, and in large measure a psychological sickness, in their eyes was a question for the legal competence of a royal tribunal which would examine appeals against their acts. Their apostolic powers in the face of a rebellious clergy were reduced to denouncing to the King the intervention of the Parlements, which supported the Jansenist party. They did not see to the bottom of the problem, which involved the old Gallican organism, they did not understand the genuine spiritual distress of so many of the faithful. On the one hand they egged on the papal authority, on the other they called upon the royal authority, when in reality they lacked any true pastoral authority, not in the legal or formalistic sense, but in that of paternal and apostolic ministry.

Their action was, indeed, tainted with Gallicanism and remained impotent. It was a moral impossibility for them to make their episcopal authority carry weight. In execution of the Bulls *Vineam Domini Sabaoth* and *Unigenitus* they inculcated not only submission but intellectual assent to the papal condemnation, *de jure* and *de facto*, but they themselves when the Pope had condemned the four Gallican propositions of 1682 went on acting in the spirit and letter of these propositions—in spite of the fact that in 1693 many of them had signed the retractation and declared they submitted to the Pope. This submission, indeed, had been external and formal, with greater intellectual and practical reservations than those of the Jansenists referred to in

have been threatened by the gravest penalties; their charges on doctrinal points have been declared abusive or suppressed; individuals of either sex have been authorised to rebel against the charges of their bishops in union with the Holy See. . . . Priests, even parish priests, consider that these awards give them the right to despise the censure by which they had been bound by their superiors, and continue with impunity, without absolution, the exercise of the most sacred functions. . . . Many awards have been made on the accusations of the Attorneys General and Advocates General who by rash, false and erroneous propositions fight the doctrine that the bishops teach to their people.'

Canon Périer's 'case of conscience'. They remained unaware of their false position. Clement XI had sharply reproved them in January, 1706, because they set themselves up as judges of the papal Bulls. But the bishops held fast to Gallican doctrine and praxis and would never have relinquished examining the Bulls, even though by this time they ended by agreeing with the Pope, and, in any case, they and the Court had often urged him to a pronouncement.

The Bull *Unigenitus* had been finally accepted as law of the land, but since there were many who, under cover, opposed it, the Bishop of Amiens in 1746 ordered that priests, summoned to the deathbeds of those whose attitude was doubtful, should demand their explicit assent to the Bull before giving them the Viaticum and Extreme Unction; the eventual refusal of the Sacraments meant also refusal of ecclesiastical burial. Similar measures were taken by many other French bishops, and by the Archbishop of Paris, Mgr. de Beaumont. The Jansenists were profoundly stirred and the Parlement took their side to the point, in April, 1752, of forbidding priests 'to make any public refusal of the Sacraments under pretext of absence of certificates of confession'—(this certificate was required when the priest who gave the Last Sacraments was not the priest who had confessed and absolved the dying man and who hence would have asked for assent to the Bull). This was not enough. In the following month a general assembly of the Chambers of the Parlement, summoned over the same question, denounced the Archbishop of Paris to the King as a promoter of schism. The Archbishop hastened to exculpate himself to the King, but the King forbade him to publish his defence.

The Parlement's action continues without mitigation; priests, whole chapters, are tried and sentenced; the Archbishop of Paris is banished; the publication of the circular letter of the Bishops' assembly of 1755 is prevented. The King, who had always kept a middle course between clergy and Parlement, ended by backing the Parlement. Finally towards the end of 1755, Pope Benedict XIV intervened, with a Brief ruling that only those 'notoriously refractory' should be asked for explicit assent to the Bull *Unigenitus* before they were given the last Sacraments. Moreover, he restricted such cases of 'notoriety' to the point of making the demand for such a declaration a very rare exception.

Thus implicitly he repudiated the zealots. But even this did not satisfy the Parlement, which refused to register the Brief; Louis XV confined himself to sending it on to the bishops, forbidding them to make public use of it. The succeeding Pope, Clement XIII, insisted that Benedict's Brief should be followed, but in vain. In the meantime there had been many priests banished or publicly whipped, bishops deprived of their temporalities, their supporters persecuted, in all the French provinces. This melancholy phase of religious strife in France coincided with another, wider and fiercer struggle against the Jesuits, which may be considered the epilogue of the resistance they had maintained openly against Jansenism and secretly also against Gallicanism. This, in spite of the declarations they had been forced to make, they could not but combat, supporters as they were of the papal rights.

§ 39.—The Jansenist character of the struggles that had been going on in France for a hundred years must not make us forget that the sub-tratum of the disputes between Catholic States and the Church was of a more general nature and concerned the post-Tridentine structure. These disputes bear different names; in the last century and recently writers like Hinschius, Scaduto and Ruffini have characterised them as struggles over jurisdiction; hence the name, which has become general among students of ecclesiastical law, of *Jurisdictionalism*. It is a legal and formal standpoint rather than a sociological and substantial one, but it helps to bring out many structural elements of State and Church and to show the reason for the respective positions they assumed. Jurisdictionalism in the wide sense is not a phase special to the XVIII century, but may be said to come into being the moment State and Church assume reciprocal juridical positions, to be held by each both in defence of its autonomy and in assertion of a right to intervene in the sphere of the other. The type of relations, however, between State and Church in a jurisdictionalist system is distinct from (and in certain respects opposed to) that of cesaro-papist and theocratic systems. Whereas in these we find an absorption and systematic confusion either to the advantage of the secular power or to the advantage of the spiritual power, a jurisdictionalist régime implies co-ordination, with clearly defined spheres of competence and separation of activities and ends. This, however, is theoretical; in historical fact we may note the tendency towards co-ordination, but this tendency can work only as part of an historical complexus in which the past, with its theocracy and cesaro-papism, forms the very substratum of the jurisdictionalist conflict. And since claims to jurisdiction were mostly made in the name of the State, jurisdictionalism is often identified with regalism and Gallicanism, while the claims of the Church of Rome are characterised as Curialism.

This notwithstanding, jurisdictionalism is not always the same; it varies according to the epoch, for the theories on which it rests and the claims it seeks to make good vary likewise from century to century. Such a conception emerges in so far as the State seeks to cast off its cesaro-papist caparison in favour of a less theocratic and more juridical conception; and in so far as the Church disengages herself from feudal and international political positions, falling back upon the legal interpretation of her spiritual and temporal rights. From this point of view, a certain jurisdictionalism is to be found towards the end of the Middle Ages, and gradually assumes different aspects both in the period immediately prior to the Reformation and in the period following.

During the Counter-Reformation the Catholic princes sought to obtain from the Papacy as many rights and privileges as possible, the while they vigorously defended the traditional rights of their Houses or their States, in order to form politico-religious unities that would better consolidate their thrones and dynasties. But they possessed a religious sense that made them zealous champions of the Catholic faith, haters of Protestants, mistrustful of the Pope, whom they believed weak, and of those bishops whom they suspected of uncertain orthodoxy. For Spain, Naples, Milan, Sicily, Portugal and for Toulouse, the Inquisition, with its mixed character, ecclesiastical and political, so completed the system, that the King could truly repute himself an 'External Bishop' in his own right, and a Legate Apostolic in perpetuity, and hence independent. Such a conception, attacked by curialists and maintained by regalists, who were most of them ecclesiastics, was tolerated by the Papacy, both for the sake of ensuring the valid co-operation of the secular power in the extinction of heresy, which entailed a risk of wars and revolts, and in order that the clergy of each nation should remain united to the centre, in such manner as was then possible, through the ecclesiastical departments of the several monarchies and subtle Roman influences in appointments and promotions. We have already more than once shown the confusion of powers that ensued. The jurists of both sides had their work cut out to avoid a hair's breadth of trespass over the traditional demarcation of rights and competences; hence volumes upon volumes over the most trivial and insignificant disputes.

The theories that grew up in support of the positions of the Curia and the monarchies, although they reproduced medieval theses and based themselves on the most ancient documents, could not fail to take on the character of the age and feel its influence. Not for nothing had the waves of Protestantism passed over the Catholic world and seemingly engulfed it; the jurisdictionalist theories that were taking shape show no small traces of Protestant influence. In reaction, the curial theories accentuate the medieval claims. And though the Roman Curia was actually on the defensive, theoretically it remained inflexible. Its practical weakness in the face of the monarchies was increasing, for the Papacy found no support for its theses either in general culture, which was becoming secular, nor in the national clergies (with a few exceptions), but only in a well disciplined diplomatic corps, the Roman clergy, trained in the study of law and juridical controversies, and a part of the religious Orders, among them the Jesuits, in the forefront as polemists, organisers and men of culture.

The anti-curial theories which prevailed up to the beginning of the XVIII century can be broadly distinguished as 'Regalism' and 'Gallicanism'. The first based itself on the function of kings as protectors of the Church, custodians of discipline, chastisers of heresy and schisms —a function integrating the spiritual authority of the bishops and of the Pope, and, judged necessary to the welfare of the Church and of the State, as such in certain respects autonomous. Gallicanism included all this, but added a strictly concomitant position on the part of the episcopate. The Gallican clergy had adopted a position of its own, nominally autonomous, of co-operation with the Pope in dogmatic questions and with the King in practical and disciplinary questions, so that the Church of France was under a threefold authority. Therefore the Gallicans upheld the theory that the Council was superior to the Pope, and that the Pope had no right to depose bishops, and that papal Bulls had to be discussed by the Clergy Assemblies and obtain their assent before the King could supply them with Letters Patent. Such was the substance of Episcopalism. Bossuet, after the condemnation of the Four Propositions of 1682 and the retractation ordered in 1693, wrote that all this was as it might be, but that this doctrine of the Parisian theologians remained 'unshaken and free of all censure'. —*manet inconcussa et censurae omnis expers illa sententia parisiorum.* Regalism outside France held to the greater part of the Gallican theses, but there were differences in respect of the organisation of the clergy and the theories of episcopalism. For a certain period there was disagreement over the question of the popular origin of the royal power, till the Gallicans ended by adopting the thesis of monarchy by divine right, which already prevailed in the rest of Europe.

The jurisdictionalism of the XVIII century in the religious field felt the influence of Jansenism, and in the juridico-political field that of jusnaturalism. The result was a hybrid jurisdictionalism, of which the extreme wing had an anti-Catholic substratum. Leaving out of count its slow and equivocal historical evolution, we can distinguish between the jurisdictionalism that seeks to attribute to a still confessional State a predominance over the Church even in religious and disciplinary matters, and the jurisdictionalism that seeks to set the Church under the control and vigilance of the State for purely political and police reasons. In this second phase the State is changing from the confessional type to the jusnaturalist secularising type. No one who fails to grasp this slow process of break-up of the past and of transformation towards another term in which the State is the central objective, can understand the significance of the struggles between Church and State in the XVIII century, or the crisis that was preparing. Otherwise the jurisdictionalism of this period will be confused with that of the period before and immediately after Trent.

Among the most famous juridictionalist churchmen we must note Zeger Bernard van Espen of Louvain (1648-1728), whose *Juris Ecclesiastici universi hodiernae disciplinae* had a wide circulation and great influence; and Nicholas Hontheim, better known under the name of

Justinus Febronius, (hence the name of *Febronianism* given to his theory), who in 1743 published his *De presenti statu Ecclesiae deque legitima potestate Romani Pontificis*, which became a standard work. Episcopalism, of which the Council of Trent had clipped the wings, had never ceased to creep forward and to assert itself under various aspects. Of these Gallicanism was the best known in that it had been able to formulate itself as a doctrine, to which the name of the Sorbonne gave authority. There was indeed also an episcopalism in Spain, in Austria and in the other Catholic States, but since it had no marked character of its own, it was confounded with the tendency of national churches and with the thesis of the superiority of the Council to the Pope. Jansenism, in its obstinate and captious resistance to papal condemnations and in its struggle against the Jesuits, leaned now on the bishops, now on the nobles and on the courts; hence many of its writers were at the same time episcopalists and jurisdictionalists. Episcopalism was an endeavour to solve the constitutional problem of the Church, till then insoluble for those who wholeheartedly accepted the conciliar theory, because (as the Council of Bâle had shown) the direct government of the Church through a conciliar assembly had proved impossible in practice. Some Jansenists, during the dispute over the Bull *Unigenitus*, put forward the idea that before the acts of the Pope were binding on all the faithful they must receive the assent of the Church. But practically, what assent was meant? Some stopped short at the episcopate (the Gallican praxis), others went so far as the lower clergy, parish priests and curates, giving to the presbyterate an office of church government. There were also those, though very few, who under Protestant influences spoke of the assent of the faithful.

This point gave an impulse towards a democratic conception of the Church. There was a wish for a new reform; the electoral principle was put forward as a revival of the practice in the first period of Christianity, when the lower clergy and the people took part in the elections of presbyters and bishops, and when the local churches, while recognising the primacy of Rome, developed and governed themselves through an almost uninterrupted series of councils. All this might seem an anachronistic return to the period prior to the Reformation, if it had not been combined with other elements which bring out the jurisdictionalist character of the alleged democratic reform of the Church; above all, with the acceptance and defence of State control of ecclesiastical discipline, of the acts of church government and the administration of the Sacraments. This might be accepted by the Febronians as the traditional co-operation of the Monarch in building up the 'Christian Republic', but it was also admitted as a defence of the monarchy and of the State against interference from the Roman Curia, and against the influence of the episcopate itself and of the national clergy. Certainly a democratic reform and State control were not easily compatible, but the ideas, even if inconsistent, made headway. The specious explanations given by certain jurisdictionalists was that the people had lost its right of nomination and control in the Church by giving it up to the monarchs, who thus possessed it *jure proprio* and not by papal grant.

In the second place, the Febronians agreed with the regalists in accepting the reduction or even the suppression of the privileges and rights of the Church in respect of civil and criminal immunity, the administration of property, purchases, legacies and sales. And this with the double aim of concentrating in the State the greatest sum of powers, thus suppressing duality of competence, and of promoting unhampered the civil, penal, administrative and economic reforms that in this period were demanded on every side. To achieve this, the theory sufficed that such rights had been granted to the Church 'by the benevolent and revokable concession of princes'.

The episcopalist movement and the jurisdictionalist movement, though diversely inspired, gave each other mutual support; they had the common objective of reducing the power of the Papacy, which had emerged with new strength from the Council of Trent and had re-established its authority through the firm and decided enforcement of the Counter-Reformation, realising, in so far as was possible, a maximum centralisation in Rome. The XVIII century was not one of the happiest for the eight popes who succeeded each other from Clement XI to Pius VI. Only Benedict XIV was a broad-minded man who understood his age, but even he was weak, feeling it impossible to be strong. By now the defensive position was obligatory on Rome. The vindication of the traditional rights of the Papacy, like that of deposing kings and releasing subjects from their oath, which the curialists never ceased to record in their books, (as did the Franciscan Gian Antonio Bianchi of Lucca in his *Della Potestà e della politica della Chiesa*, 1743) had an anachronistic sound when popes were forced to give way to the European courts, whose pretensions increased from day to day up to the suppression of the Order of the Jesuits; and when the monarchs with impunity claimed rights of control over the sacramentary and devotional activity of the Church, even fixing the times and places of hearing confessions, or forbidding the introduction of the Feast of the Sacred Heart.

Such acts to-day seem to us absurd, but they were not judged so then. It was a case of consolidating, guaranteeing and perpetuating power in the hands of a class or category of persons, of given families, of traditional circles, centring round the Court or the various organs of the State. All outside interference, all signs of independence, all pretensions to autonomy cast a shadow, aroused suspicion and jealousy. The religious Orders in the dependence of Rome were too powerful and too wealthy to be left without check or control. One of the episcopalist aspirations was the complete subjection of the monks and friars to the bishops; this coincided with the governments' wish that no foreign subjects should become the provincial heads of the Orders, or that friars and monks in their States should not depend on generals living, as most of them did, in Rome or in other foreign cities. The ban on the devotion to the Heart of Jesus was due to Jansenist opposition, which exploited the resentment of the bishops against the Jesuits, or of the governments who were in quest of pretexts to assert themselves over the Roman Curia.

In that period when big industry was beginning and trade was developing with greater rapidity, the need for economic reforms was genuinely felt. The States had already their own finances and their own treasury, no longer confused with the private purse of the sovereign; a certain system was being introduced with more logical theories, built on experience. It was plain that this movement for reform would have to embrace the system of church property, which by Canon Law was inalienable and exempt from taxes and fiscal burdens. Mortmain withdrew lands, houses, rents, leases from commerce. The governments intervened to regulate and limit donations and legacies to churches and religious houses. There were innumerable friaries, monasteries and convents, thronged with the cadets of noble houses who, through the right of primogeniture, had no resource but to choose between a military or a religious career. The governments sought to take appropriate measures, but they should have abolished primogeniture while there was yet time, or brought a better regulation of the system of inheritance. They believed it would be enough to restrict the number of religious houses and of the monks or nuns allowed in each. Once embarked upon this course, government intervention reached the point of a supervision of the discipline and morals of the religious houses, especially when there was fear lest curialist maxims perilous to the rights of the State were taught there, or that they might harbour politically suspect elements. Religious houses were on occasion the centres of a web of interests of powerful families and intrigues of ambitious courtiers.

The monarchies always looked askance upon the fiscal immunity of Church property; the story of the controversies it created is a long and bitter one. In France the clergy often yielded to the King's instances over war contributions and other needs of the treasury; from time to time spontaneous donations were made to propitiate him. This system had become common in Catholic countries. When it was necessary, the assent or permission of the Pope was asked. This however satisfied neither the kings, who were made dependent on the clergy assemblies, to whom they had to give the reasons for their requests, nor the propertied classes, who groaned under the fiscal burdens on their possessions; public opinion and the reformist trend were contrary to the fiscal privileges of the clergy.

A vigorous struggle was waged against the immunity possessed by consecrated places; the State no longer tolerated the system of sanctuary in the churches of monasteries and bishoprics, often the hiding-places of factious men, brigands and thieves, or those politically persecuted. There was an endeavour to subject the whole territory of a country, without exceptions or privileges, to the supervision of the royal police. We must recognise that in those days the police system was rudimentary; citizens were insufficiently protected against arbitrary acts on the part of power or of the dominant families. Such exempt sanctuaries could still fulfil a certain social function, which would gradually diminish as the organisation of the State improved. The clergy for the most part did not consider the problem from the social angle, but from the standpoint of Canon Law and tradition. Therefore they resisted the governments, viewing their action as unlawful interference and an infringement of the privileges of the Church. A stronger resistance was made to State encroachments on the ecclesiastical courts, where these still flourished. In this period we find in France priests sentenced to be whipped or banished by the royal tribunals and the Parlements. In Spain and elsewhere the Inquisition was a mixed tribunal in the hands of the monarchs, having the right to deal with the offences of clerics, including bishops. But the ecclesiastical courts in all Catholic countries dealt not only with common crimes or indiscipline among the clergy, but also with certain offences committed by laymen, such as concubinage. The Church's resistance on this point was such that the Catholic States of the XVIII century did not accomplish the abolition of the ecclesiastical courts, but only certain particular reforms, limiting their competence.

By the system of the confessional State and through ancient regalist traditions, papal acts had to be authorised by the royal *exequatur* and *placet*. During the jurisdictionalist period this system was extended to cover acts that had no legislative character, and did not involve the revenues of the churches or benefices reserved to the Pope, but were merely grants of personal favours, ecclesiastical permits or disciplinary dispensations. These acts too had to pass under government control, which was becoming vexatious. It was common to forbid bishops, clergy and faithful, to communicate directly with Rome. There was an endeavour to centralise ecclesiastical business in government offices or royal councils created for the purpose. In order to avoid the effect, of excommunications and interdicts, threatened by the popes to protect their rights or to strike at undisciplined churchmen, the governments took their stand on the jurisdictionalist theories, which declared that such censures were not binding in conscience, but only of an external, legalistic or ritual character. In view of the disturbance to public and economic life brought about by interdicts, the jurisdictionalists contested this right to the popes and bishops in what were deemed political matters, and demanded the prior consent of the secular power in the case of strictly ecclesiastical matters. The jurisdictionalist struggle was juridical in form, but really political and economic in substance.

If the positions of the State in its disputes either with Rome or with curialist bishops were to be always and surely defended, it was necessary to have a clergy that was not only not hostile but convinced, from the canonical and theological standpoints, that the State was in its rights. Hence the care taken by the governments in the appointment of bishops and beneficed clergy, the strict supervision to ensure that books like those of Santarelli (of which we have already spoken) or of the Franciscan, Bianchi, to mention the most hated, should not be published or circulated in the kingdom; above all a control of the teaching not only in the universities but in the episcopal seminaries and monastic schools. The common doctrines were the Regalist, Gallican and Febronian. There might be attenuations (often formal) and controversies on the points most hostile to the Papacy and showing small conformity with the Tridentine decisions, but in general the education of secular and regular clergy tended towards State jurisdictionalism. In the dispute between Benedict XIV and the Venetian Republic over the decree of 1754, which, based on a strictly regalist conception, limited many of the faculties of the clergy, many ecclesiastics sided with the Republic. The Republic gave in to the Pope who succeeded, simply because he was a Venetian (Rezzonico, who took the name of Clement XIII), but the act rescinding the decree asserted that the Pope 'recognised the legislative faculty born with the Republic and always exercised by us'.

The situation that was being created constrained Rome to show indulgence towards the monarchs and heads of States, and to take advantage of diplomatic expedients and of such propitious occasions as might arise from dissension between the States and their need, in their continual wars, of papal support. But often the disputes with Rome assumed an ugly aspect, and ministers and even the monarchs themselves adopted an arrogant and contemptuous tone. The popes were placed in positions of increasing difficulty, driven back upon a ground that grew more and more confined. Their methods had become less effectual. The days of excommunications and interdicts had passed, and the feudal rights that they might claim had no longer the significance of once upon a time. When the Emperor Charles VI granted the title of king to the Elector of Brandenburg, Frederick III (1700), Clement XI opposed it, both in the name of the Holy See's rights over the Electorate and because the Hohenzollerns were Protestants. But the papal protest had no effect; what interested Austria was the friendship of Prussia and the eight thousand soldiers promised for the War of the Spanish Succession which was about to begin.

The same Clement XI was constrained by armed force to recognise to the House of Austria the succession to the throne of Spain, Naples and Sicily (1709); hence the wrath of Philip V and Louis XIV, which rebounded on the ecclesiastical questions then under consideration. In the meantime, through the Peace of Utrecht of 1713, Sicily had been given to Victor Amadeus II of Savoy, to the anger of the Pope, who had the right of feudal sovereignty over Sicily. The dispute reached such a pitch that Clement put the whole island under an interdict, and Victor Amadeus replied by driving out a good three thousand priests. Victor Amadeus's reign was brief, and in 1718 he had to abandon Sicily, accepting Sardinia as compensation, the royal title to which would remain to the House of Savoy till the unification of the Kingdom of Italy. But the question of Naples and Sicily was not yet closed. Innocent XIII in 1722 confirmed the investiture of the House of Austria, and, to re-establish the papal right that had been set aside, he revived the practice of the annual offer of the white mule, as feudal tribute. The House of Austria soon after lost Naples and Sicily through the Treaty of the Escurial in 1733, which bound together Spain, France and Savoy against it. The Bourbon Charles (later Charles III of Spain) became king, and Naples and Sicily were recognised as an autonomous kingdom. The question of the white mule on several occasions disturbed relations between that realm and the Holy See, till its suppression by unilateral decision. The old feudal right that had brought so much trouble to Rome thus came to an end.

It was in Naples that there arose one of the most representative writers of the time, who combined the jurisdictionalist conception of the State with a special hatred for the Papacy, Pietro Giannone, born in 1676, who may be called a Voltairian before his time. He wrote the *History of the Kingdom of Naples* as a polemical work (1723); it had a great success and in 1729 was translated into English, in 1738 into French, in 1758 into German. Forced to leave Naples, he went to Vienna, where he wrote another anti-papal book, *The Triple Kingdom*. Persecuted, he took refuge in Geneva, where he fell into the trap laid for him by the King of Sardinia, who had an understanding with Rome. Thrown into prison, he remained there till his death in 1748. Pietro Giannone, both for the jurisdictionalists and for the Encyclopedists and anticlerical currents of the time was a martyr, and one of the strongest champions of the Italian Enlightenment.

It was during this period that Benedict XIII, who was a weak Pope and had left political business in the hands of untrustworthy persons like Cardinal Coscia, thought to put Gregory VII among the saints; he may have been moved by devotion towards the great Pope and perhaps also wished to recall, in the midst of so many acts of weakness, a strong Pope who had vindicated the superiority of the Church over the secular power. But a general protest arose from the Jansenist and Febronian currents. The governments formally opposed the cult of the new saint and prevented the saying of his Mass and office. The Pope stood firm, and by an act of 1729 annulled all the decrees of the various States on the matter. (It was the time when kings did not wish the *Magnificat* to be sung because of the verse: 'He has put down the mighty from their seat and has exalted the humble'.)

During this period Rome was coming to the conclusion that it was far better to have recourse to Concordats with the Catholic States in order to fix the limits of reciprocal rights and concessions. After the Council of Trent only one Concordat had been made, that of 1640 between Urban VIII and the Emperor, Ferdinand II, to settle the ecclesiastical questions of Bohemia. Only in 1727, after the sharp disputes with the House of Savoy in Sicily and Sardinia, did Benedict XIII draw up what would be the typical form of Concordat of the period. But the disputes with the House of Savoy were so continuous that the first Concordat was followed by four others in 1741, 1742, 1750 and 1770. In 1736 Clement XII made a Concordat with Poland. The most important were those with Spain in 1737 (under the same Pope), and in 1753 under Benedict XIV, who in 1741 had regularised the new situation of the kingdom of Naples and Sicily and in 1757 would do the same with the Duchy of Milan, showing so much indulgence as to make his Cardinals murmur against him. It was hoped that by fixing the terms of the relations between the Church and the separate States motives of friction would be eliminated. Unhappily the legal formulation of such relations evaded the problems which arose from diverse and often antithetical conceptions and from the ferment of new ideas.

§ 40.—The struggle against the Jesuits for their suppression had a threefold character that came from anti-curialism, Jansenism and the Enlightenment. From its start the Company of Jesus had met with hostility, but the strife aroused by this new type of congregation had been either on the lines of the rivalry between religious Orders of diverse tendency, or on those of theological and ascetic controversy. Many ecclesiastics, bishops and cardinals and even an occasional pope were hostile to the Jesuits for one reason or another, into which it would be fruitless to enter here. Much hostility came from the princes, either because the Jesuits maintained the rights of the Papacy, contesting the regalist and Gallican theories, or because they supported the thesis of the popular origin of power and that more daring one of tyrannicide. There was also jealousy of them because of their growing influence, their methods of education, their enterprise and corporate spirit. They irritated not a few by their ardent and sometimes biting polemics against adversaries of the Church, real or so believed, especially by their unflagging war against Jansenism and the Jansenists. But what made the Jesuits redoubtable and detestable to certain people was their power in the Courts, as confessors, spiritual and political counsellors, channels of royal favour or disgrace. Hence envy, rancour, adulation and intrigues.

Up till now, however, apart from human weaknesses, errors and malice, on either side, no one in attacking the Jesuits meant to attack the Catholic Church as such. Indeed it was believed (and by many in good faith) that it would be good for the Church to reduce them to subjection, to keep them within due limits and even to send them away from places where they had raised tempests. Whether such measures came from the Pope or bishops, or from the monarchs and parliaments, had no importance in view of the current ideas on the exercise of the authority of the Church and the rights, real or otherwise, of the Catholic monarch. In the XVIII century philosophical naturalism, political reformism and the Enlightenment of the Encyclopedists for the first time gave the anti-Jesuit struggle an anti-Catholic colour. Not all perceived this background to the picture, through the weight of anti-Jesuit resentment that had accumulated in nearly a century of friction. Political pretexts were not wanting and not a few men believed they were defending religious interests that had been prejudiced by the ill-considered and overweening attitude of the Jesuits. The development of the Jansenist current among the Catholic clergy (not only in France, but elsewhere) and of anti-curial Febronianism obscured the anti-religious motives of this struggle, which was conducted with the utmost intransigence by the Catholic monarchies.

The dispute over the Indian colonies of Paraguay, founded and administered by the Jesuits under the name of 'Reductions' aroused violent resentment in the governments of Lisbon and Madrid. For some time the Portuguese and Spaniards of South America wanted to destroy the 'Reductions', which formed an obstacle to the lucrative slave trade and among the colonies were a 'scandal' through their economic prosperity, their incorrupt administration and the spirit of 'Christian socialism' before its time (it is a mistake to speak of communism), which had so widely developed and taken root there. A first attempt was made by inciting the 'Mamelukes' (a kind of native brigand) to assail some of the colonies. The Jesuits at first sought to remove the bordering populations, most exposed to the raids, to surer centres, but when they were again molested and assailed, they asked the King of Spain for permission to arm and defend themselves. This they did with much ability, with technical skill and fair armaments. Unfortunately Spain, wishing in 1750 to settle her frontier questions with the Portuguese colonies, ceded a part of Paraguay. This was a good opportunity to destroy the 'Reductions', which put up a well-organised armed resistance. Now the Spaniards, now the Portuguese had to retreat before the fire of the Indians, till both, uniting their forces, made a final assault and were victorious. As the epilogue of this romantic episode the Jesuits were accused on grave charges for rebellion, for failure to pay taxes proportionate to their commercial turnover, for making treaties with neighbouring tribes, for refusing obedience to the governments of Lisbon and Madrid, and finally for having coined money with the effigy of a certain Father Nicholas.

The Portuguese court had other charges against the Jesuits. They had become so powerful in this kingdom as to be reputed a State within the State. Bound up with the aristocracy, they had more influence than the ministers. The King, Joseph I, did not count; he was sickly and left the care of the State to his ministers, preferring amusement and women to business. His minister Pombal, a bourgeois by birth, despised by the aristocracy, imbued with the ideas of the Encyclopedists, was at odds with the Jesuits, who at the beginning of his career had protected him. In the beginning of 1758 he obtained from Benedict XIV, a little before the latter's death, the appointment of a Visitor for the Jesuit houses and Cardinal Saldahna was entrusted with this office. Thereupon they were forbidden to preach or hear confessions in the whole orbit of the Patriarchate of Lisbon (kingdom and colonies); the confessors of the King and of the court were dismissed and a more radical decision was awaited when Pombal found the occasion that precipitated events. The young Marquis of Tavora, angered by the king's illicit relations with the Marquise his wife, lay in wait for him on one of his clandestine visits and fired a shot at him from a carbine, missing his aim. At Court it was immediately presumed that behind Tavora stood the Jesuits, since he would not have dared fire on the King unless he had a strong backing. A case was made out against the fathers Malagrida, Matti, and Alessandro, who were tortured and put to death by the Portuguese Inquisition. Two hundred and twenty-one fathers were imprisoned on a ship anchored in the Tagus; all the rest, including those in the colonies, were expelled from Portuguese territory. In vain did the new Pope, Clement XIII, request that he himself should judge the guilty, and appeal for grace for the others who were held prisoner. On receiving a negative reply, he protested against the measures taken. Thereupon the Nuncio was expelled and diplomatic relations between Portugal and the Holy See were broken off.

After Portugal, France. Here the feeling against the Jesuits had been steadily growing through their two-fold clash with the Gallicans and with the Jansenists; to this was now added the hatred of the Encyclopedists and the resentment of the Court, especially of La Pompadour who completely dominated Louis XV. In those days the problem of the Paschal Communion of the King (a public adulterer) greatly troubled confessors: it was complicated by Court gossip over the refusal to give Communion to La Pompadour. Easter for such a world was a social convention rather than a religious duty that called for moral conduct. Great and petty causes fed the resentment against the Jesuits. The climax came with the case against Father Lavalette, director of the colony of Martinique, who, to assure an income to the Jesuit missions, had taken to commerce. When certain cargoes were captured by the English, Father Lavalette could not meet his payments. A house of Marseilles thereupon laid a suit against the Jesuit Order, but the Provincial replied that they were under no obligation to pay Lavalette's debts, especially since their rules forbade any act of commerce. The award of the Marseilles court went against the Order, which appealed to the Parlement of Paris. The Parlement obliged the Jesuits to produce their rules and, while dismissing the appeal, declared certain of the provisions of these rules to be immoral and dangerous to the State. In the polemics that ensued, and in the *salons* of Paris and the provinces, the old questions of the end justifying the means, mental reservation, laxist morals and tyrannicide were brought up again. The Parlement intervened, ordering that the books published by the Jesuits from 1590 onwards should be burned—a great bonfire of folios—prohibiting public lectures by Jesuits, and ordering families to withdraw pupils from the Jesuit colleges. The King summoned the bishops who at once started an enquiry into the moral charges against the Jesuits. These thought it opportune to issue a declaration of Gallican faith, not very unlike the earlier ones that we have already mentioned, but with the difference that in the past these had been forced from them and now they themselves came forward as though to propitiate the bishop. What was worse, they took the occasion to declare that they would always teach '. . . the doctrine established by the Clergy of France in the Four Propositions at the assembly of 1682', and that they would 'never teach anything contrary to them'.[1] —thus forgetting the papal condemnation of the Four Propositions and the obligation laid on the bishops to retract them.

But such declarations were out of date. The situation had changed. Although the bishops were in large majority opposed to the expulsion of the Jesuits, the Parlements (Paris first, then the provinces) decided that the Company must be suppressed, its members expelled, its property confiscated. Louis XV who needed the Parlement for new taxes, and who was ruled by La Pompadour and his minister, Choiseul, ended by signing the decree. Pope Clement XIII protested, but his Bull *Apostolicum pascendi* of January 9, 1765, was never published in France and did not come into force.

Spain soon follows. Charles III came from Naples, having renounced his crown there for the sake of the Spanish succession. He passed for an enlightened, paternalist but absolutist king; the celebrated Bernardo Tannucci had been his tutor and minister. He took umbrage at the immense power of the Jesuits and did not like their methods. At the time there was fear of a revolt, fed by the clandestine circulation of pamphlets and leaflets. The Court and the police saw in them the hand of the Jesuits. The incident of the hats had a catastrophic outcome. The police had noticed men wearing wide-brimmed hats and voluminous cloaks. This roused their alarm, and a decree was issued forbidding the suspect attire. But what did it mean? One day the streets of Madrid were filled by a crowd of wide-brimmed hats and voluminous cloaks. Was it a demonstration? The beginning of a revolt? The crowd would not disperse in spite of the intervention of the guards and the King's promise to dismiss the Minister of Finance, who was responsible for the 'hat decree'. Finally the Jesuits appeared and persuaded the demonstrators to go home. Their intervention had been too effectual, the acquiescence of the crowd too ready, not to arouse suspicion that the Jesuits were behind it all. There were those who accused them of preparing a plot. The Minister Arandha was of the type of Tannucci, Pombal, Choiseul; the example of Portugal and France gave courage for a similar *coup* in Spain, but Charles III wanted

[1]'La doctrine établie par le Clergé de France dans les quatre propositions à l'assemblée de 1682, et que nous n'enseignerons jamais rien qui y soit contraire.'

it to be without agitations, discussions or trials. In 1767 the Governors of the kingdom received an order to open certain sealed letters in the night of April 2–3, and to carry out immediately the royal commands they contained. By these commands the Jesuits were that very night expelled from their houses, taken to the ports, and finally embarked on a ship and driven out of the country. Where were they to go? Naples refused to receive them. Civitavecchia, a papal city, rejected them. They ultimately landed in Corsica, which still belonged to the Republic of Genoa. The Pope intervened, yet again without result. The example of Spain was followed by her satellites, Naples and Sicily, Parma and Piacenza, which likewise expelled the Jesuits.

In the following year the Franciscan Ganganelli ascended the papal throne, taking the name of Clement XIV. During the conclave the Catholic courts had ventilated their wish, or rather their will, to finish with the Jesuits. The choice of pope had been conditioned by this policy. The Pope delayed nearly five years, ordering enquiries and study, or trying to placate the courts. Several times he declared that he wanted the prior consent of all the Catholic sovereigns, and Maria Theresa of Austria would not give hers in spite of the insistence of her son Joseph II, co-ruler with his mother over the hereditary States. Mainz and Bavaria, which were at odds with the Jesuits for one reason or another, consented, and finally Maria Theresa herself gave in. The Pope had no further political excuse for retarding the decision which for five years had been hanging over the head of the Order. The Jesuit seminaries of Rome and of the Papal States were closed and on July 21, 1773, the Bull *Dominus ac Redemptor* was promulgated, which decreed the suppression of the Company of Jesus. All the Catholic States hastened to receive it in legal form, to the great joy of the Jesuits' enemies. The Prussia of Frederick II and the Russia of Catherine II wished to show themselves extraneous to papal Bulls and the hatreds of the Catholic courts by receiving the Jesuit refugees, but the Order as such legally ceased to exist.

Clement XIV is the last of the popes whose acts have been subjected even by Catholic historians to open criticism. From Pius VI onwards their attitude is rather that of apologists. It is fortunate that we find this precedent in respect of a recent pope, so that no irreverence can be imputed to anyone using the same historical method towards some of his successors. Actually, there are three points to be made against Clement—the first, that of having yielded in the conclave to the condition imposed by the Courts; the second, that of subordinating his decision to the consent of all the Catholic sovereigns; the third that of presenting the suppression of the Order as carried out to safeguard the interests of the Church and to assure the unity of the Spirit in the bond of peace. It is usual to attenuate Clement's responsibility by the melancholy conditions of the time and the conspiracy of the Courts; indeed no reasonable historian can take any other view. But what would have better corresponded to the nature of the crisis would have been a reform of the Company, to eradicate those evils that had arisen from its power and wealth. To accomplish this, apart from his qualities as a man of government, Clement XIV would have needed to be sure of a free and independent episcopate; he would have needed the courage to face the problem of a wider reform, to break through the bonds of jurisdictionalism, renouncing the defence of a series of rights that for the Church were so many fetters. There would then have been a repetition, in other circumstances, of the situation in the conflict between the Papacy and the Empire; it would have needed therefore another and more fortunate Paschal II to abandon the worldly interests that weighed too heavily upon the Church. St. Alphonse of Liguori, one of the most notable saints of the time, said: 'Poor pope, what could he do in the difficult circumstances in which he found himself, when all the Crowns in concert demanded the suppression?' And the Jesuit, Father Cordaro, wrote that in the Pope's place he would have done the same. Apart from such defence, which does not eliminate the Pope's responsibility, it must be agreed that not a few Jesuits had adopted a position that had become untenable, with their court confessors, their ties with aristocratic families, and their system of favouring or combating ministers and powerful men. A similar method, when it is practised not by a single ecclesiastic, be he even a Cardinal like Richelieu, Mazarin or Alberoni, but by men bound by discipline in a widespread, rich and protected Order, perpetuates itself beyond the brief span of one man's life and may assume the aspect of a State within the State, or a Church within the Church.

To their credit it must be recognised that in the whole period of the Counter-Reformation there were Jesuits of great sanctity, intelligence and heart, true apostles and martyrs, men detached from the world yet living in the world and fighting in the world. But there were also the narrow-minded, the intransigent and obstinate, and the harsh and satirical polemists; unhappily among many great and generous souls petty intriguers were not lacking. Their zeal was multifarious and extraordinary, like their iron and volitive discipline. It was impossible for them not to carry with them the defects of an activism that wanted the end at any cost, and not to magnify too much an *esprit de corps* that had been rendered acute by their power, their successes and their titanic struggles. All this, though without a pre-established aim, led to a displacement of the battlefield from the Papacy to the Jesuit world. The Papacy, made to unite about it the militants of all sectors, was weakened; the Jesuit world, because it took its character from a particular Order, led to the detachment of all those (secular clergy, religious Orders, institutions and groups) who dissented from its theories or its methods or the pre-eminent persons who directed and represented them. It is true that the Jesuits, in the spirit and intention of all their members, were an Order faithful to Rome, defending the rights of the Church. It is true that the popes trusted much to the Jesuits to obtain for them, either by open campaigns or by secret ways and by their influence in the Courts, what they were unable to obtain through their diplomats and through the bishops. But by this the popes were not seldom weakened—especially when they were constrained by events to repudiate them after having used them—and often also it led them to pursue methods and ways that were not the best from the point of view of a limpid moral rectitude and of respect for the supreme authority.

For the Jesuits, the period of suppression was a purifying trial, but for the Papacy it was a humiliation that did not help it to gain either prestige or the good-will and trust of the monarchies. These were set on a course of ever greater disengagement from Rome, towards the autonomy of the State and powers so full and absolute as to demand the complete subjection of the Church and her elimination from the political field. The reformist currents were moving towards this goal, but in Rome greater importance was still attached to relations with the sovereigns and their circles than to the new currents that were gaining ground and that sought to sweep away both monarchic absolutism and ecclesiastical authoritarianism. The authoritarian conception of society was so deeply rooted (and to this the Jesuits of the XVIII century had notably contributed) that it was inconceivable for the Church to do otherwise than to seek, by all methods and at any sacrifice, the agreement and collaboration of the princes.

§ 41.—Just as in the Protestant countries in the XVII century there had come about a new orientation and an inward change of which the ripples had reached the Catholic countries, so in the XVIII century there came about a transformation in the Catholic countries that was reflected in the Protestant ones. The centre of this crisis was France. Here the ferment of ideas was more active because the intellectual class was larger and there were continuous contacts with Holland, England and Germany. The *grand siècle* had left a fruitful heritage in letters and philosophy, Paris was the centre of European life, Versailles the leading court; whereas Rome, Venice, Florence on the one hand, and Madrid on the other, no longer had the international role that had once been theirs, and Vienna was only then beginning, under Maria Theresa, to emulate the great capitals.

There was a weariness among men of culture of strictly religious and dogmatic polemics, like those over grace and free will between Jansenists and Jesuits. The curiosity of the reading public was turned to the concrete problems of knowledge and of earthly life, to render it less dreary, to achieve a new order, with aspirations towards reform in every field, for everywhere there was a sense of the weight of an old world in conflict with general aspirations. The fascinating idea was that of Nature—a fundamental naturalism, which assumed now sentimental, now philosophical, now artistic aspects, which crept into all the recesses of the thought of the time, like the revelation of a happy world to which the contemporary system, based on dogmatic and authoritarian religion and on absolute government was in contradiction.

The conception of Nature, of man in the abstract as naturally endowed with all good qualities, arose out of that of reason as the sure light of truth and that of the Law of Nature as the basis of human sociability. Descartes and the rationalists, Grotius, Pufendorf and the jusnaturalists had contributed to make of nature an ideal and almost mystical element; the natural was tending to supplant the supernatural, reason was taking a more important place than faith, and indeed a growing opposition was developing between the two terms. The ideal of a nature endowed with reason and all the qualities that would make man happy was contrasted with real society, full of inequalities, injustices, bonds, oppressions and miseries. Men of letters, journalists and philosophers who had to fight the ecclesiastical and political censorship in order to publish their books or to obtain those books the circulation of which was forbidden, vented their wrath on the authoritarian system. The economic crisis, due to bad government, wars, the gross inequalities of taxation and the excessive proportion absorbed by the government, incited to the study of reforms. The judicial system, both civil and criminal, presented itself as illogical, barbarous, corrupt and unjust. The educational methods of the schools and colleges, based on authoritarian discipline and constraint, the dogmatic and classical teaching, made up of rhetoric and scholasticism, were reputed in contradiction to the naturalistic and sentimental conception that was taking shape. And since the whole world of the time presented itself under a predominantly religious aspect—from the power of the King, as coming from God, to education, which was in the hands of the religious Orders and bishops, and even to the allotment of taxes, over which the parish priest presided, while in the Sorbonne and the States-General and the royal councils there was not a place where the clergy were not present, wholly bound up with the régime and making one with it in the economic and political structure of the country—thus the formation of the naturalistic currents tended to be directed against the domination of the clergy, the content of Christian teaching, and faith itself.

In a police- and censorship-régime, anyone who wrote openly against the faith ended in the Bastille or in exile, and his books were burned by the public executioner. There were a thousand ways of evading these dangers, so long as criticisms were subtle and insinuating, and the satire refined and never direct, founded on analogies to be understood by all except the censor—whether the ostensible subject was the kingdom of the Persians, or the life of Mahomet, or the views of the English Quakers, or those of the ancient Greeks and Romans, or the study of hypothetical societies beyond the Ocean, Canadian or Australian. What mattered was to bring into light natural society, natural morality, natural religion, and to criticise the offshoots of the actual society of the time, its prejudices, superstitions, cruelties, tyrannies. Such insinuating and persistent criticism was on occasion judged as impious, contrary to faith and dangerous to the throne. But repression was not such as to prevent the clandestine circulation of those books and pamphlets, which were all the more sought after and appreciated, and excited the curiosity of supervised schoolboys and of wide-awake young women.

Controversy there was in plenty—weighty books of confutation and others in their turn lively and sarcastic, journals and reviews, libels and broadsheets; nor was there any lack of episcopal charges warning the faithful of danger and forbidding the more perilous books. Unfortunately the traditional writers were not among the most brilliant, either in ideas or art; they nearly all failed to understand the psychological motives favouring the naturalistic current, and for the most part they maintained so close a connection between the Catholic religion and the established order as to render, according to the point of view, either the cause of religion or that of order unpalatable. They did not understand that they were faced by a crisis of thought, by the quest for a new moral and political orientation, for a profound renewal of the social structure.

To certain modern Catholic writers it has seemed strange, to say the least, that while the Church and clergy, both upper and lower, through jurisdictionalist motives and political aims were treated by governments and Parlements in the most oppressive manner, they were attacked by the Encyclopedists as authoritarian dominators, as those on whom the hate of the innovators must discharge itself. Those who raise this question forget that while the jurisdictionalist disputes took place between the civil and ecclesiastical powers and between the Sorbonne or Parlement and the bishops, the moral, philosophical and juridical campaign of the Encyclopedists was directed against religious intolerance, against arbitrary power, against the judicial methods, against all that was or was deemed superstitious, against educational methods, the dogmatic spirit and intellectual authoritarianism. Philosophers, politicians, economists, historians, novelists, *literati* and polemists in setting their course by the ideal of a good nature, of a better earthly order, of a law equal for all, were whetting a spirit of research and criticism and dreaming of generous utopias and idyllic societies. Therefore, they despised the past, the whole of the past, even the religious Christian past which was rejected from incomprehension, whereas Greek and Roman history and an alleged pre-history were cherished. Their hatred of the Church, their resentment against the civil order, and their destructive satire lacked historical foundations.

One of the deepest reasons for the contrast between a logical rationalism with *idées simples et claires* and a pronounced utopianism, between the need for reforms and the demolition of the civil and spiritual order, can be found in a certain lack of historical sense in the Enlightenment. Those who have in prospect a palingenesis, a messianic transformation, no longer understand the past; they would start afresh at Year One. The repudiation of the past is the repudiation of history. This would come about with the French Revolution, but it is spiritually prepared by the Encyclopedia. This statement may sound strange about a period when the revival of historical studies had produced men like Leibniz, Muratori, Mabillon and Vico, the last the true creator of reconstructive and philosophical history. But Vico's work was known only later and the great philologists were then laying the rational foundations of historical construction, and had as yet no influence in forming the historical sense of their contemporaries. Voltaire, who had the qualities of an historian, wrote (as is done also to-day) with polemical aim and from extrinsic motives. History and philosophy were then separate and opposed; and therefore the Enlightenment could not understand the true spirit of history.

A history that ignores the reasons of the past and repudiates it is no longer history. A human reason that reveals itself to itself as a palingenetic novelty, denying the past that has led it to the point it has reached, is no longer human reason but a revelation, albeit a lay one, to be set against religious revelation. It will lack *continuity*, the historical law posited by Leibniz; it will be lacking in *inward process*, the historical law divined by Vico. On the other hand those who opposed the Encyclopedists in the name of the past, of tradition, of absolute power and of the Church, presented the historical resultant as something fixed, immutable, abstracted from the dynamism of reality, alien to the changing of men and the succession of events. It is true that Bossuet in his *Discours sur l'histoire universelle* did not omit to mention the 'spirit of the times or of the nations', in order to bring out that besides Providence there were the secondary causes, but apart from the general incapacity to explain the inward movement of such causes and the laws of their contingency and continuity, the reformist trend was met by an immutable stability, the need for liberty by an absolute authority, the impulse of reason by the application of an exclusive and non-comprehensive supernatural law. Thus the traditionalists too stood outside history and precipitated the clash of the two worlds, both conceived outside temporal relativity—the world of a rational and good nature and the world of an absolutist and ossified Christianity.

When Montesquieu's *Esprit des Lois* appeared in 1748, it had an immense success. The prohibition to introduce it into France was soon raised; the Sorbonne meditated a censure, but thought better of it. The book was appreciated not so much for its constitutional content and constructive value as for its reformistic spirit, the way in which it threw into relief problems felt in practical life—all elements that would polarise the keen attention and awakened curiosity of the great public. In the authoritarian conception, the law came from God and the King was its minister and manifestation; in Montesquieu's approach, the law assumed the relative character of a custom suited to the particular conditions of a people, an age, a climate, a culture. The idea of good and evil no longer referred to a complex of precepts and prohibitions that came from above, but to the utility a custom or law might procure for the social group. Montesquieu's criticism was founded on the idea of social utility. Intolerance, tyranny, slavery, serfdom are useless and dangerous; hence the necessity to reform or abolish them. His attitude remained one of reformistic pragmatism, which did not succeed in grasping either permanent values or the historical continuity of the life of peoples. If this was Montesquieu for his contemporaries, he would appear otherwise to the public of half a century later.

The same happens with Rousseau. To his contemporaries he is not so much the author of the *Contrat Social* as the author of *Emile* or *La Nouvelle Héloise*, and later of the *Confessions*. Rousseau's conception of nature is the same as that of the whole naturalistic literature of the time. The idea of a nature initially happy without need of laws is a pendant to that of a happy and harmonious society under the rule of reason—a mythical and static conception, to be raised as a counter-altar to the Christian conception between two paradises, Adam's Eden and the promised heaven. But the naturalists needed to eliminate not God (a vague deism and a so-called natural religion sufficed them) but Original Sin, the Redemption, Christ and the Church, the rewards and penalties of the next life. All this for them was bound up with dogmatic intolerance and tyrannical absolutism in the name of the supernatural. Rousseau drew entire attention to education; men were not evil by nature but corrupted by false education and by society; it was necessary to refashion education so that it should inform society; right feelings, love, fraternity, solidarity, would lead men to a happy life.

The Encyclopedists and Voltaire above all, with original works, studies, histories, criticism, works of popularisation, polemical pamphlets, poems, novels and satires, spread broadcast a spirit of revolt against the religious past, of deification of reason, of expectancy of a better future through the new methods of education and schooling, through social and political reforms, through the destruction of the might of the Church. The favourite image was that of the light of the new philosophy as against obscurantism and superstition represented by Christianity; hence men spoke of the *Siècle des Lumières*, while among the Italians the new trend was known as *Illuminismo*, among the Germans as the *Aufklaerung*, among the English as the *Enlightenment*. Voltaire's action was the most effectual for more than half a century of writings of every kind, tragedies, comedies, poems (he aspired to the title of epic poet with his *Henriade*, hoping to rival Virgil and Tasso), his letters on England, *l'Esprit des Moeurs*, and above all *Candide* and *l'Ingénu*, which satirised together the works of God and those of governments. But to his writings, which circulated throughout the world, through their mordant vivacity and limpidity of style, he added—and it was to his advantage and his credit—the defence and rehabilitation of those unjustly condemned. The case of the Protestant Calas, condemned to death on a charge of murdering his daughter who wished to become a Catholic, that of the Protestant family Sirven, condemned in contumacy on a charge of drowning their daughter in a well because she had become converted to Catholicism, that of the Chevalier de la Barre, condemned for sacrilege, these and other cases gave Voltaire the occasion of presenting himself as the champion of condemned innocence and as the accuser of the defects and crimes of the judicial system and of religious intolerance. The effect in France and elsewhere was immense, and gave fresh motives for the anti-religious struggle.

The publication of the Encyclopedia, which began in 1751 and was completed in 1765, in spite of all the difficulties from the Church and from the political authorities, marks the salient point of this movement of thought and orientation in the XVIII century. The furnishing of information, scientific and practical, historical and moral, literary and artistic, religious and political, by means of huge analytical and alphabetical publications was not new. There had been Cyclopedias, Encyclopedias and *Thesauri*, each more or less an indigestible hotch-potch. But the publication of the *Encyclopédie du Dictionnaire universel des arts et des sciences* was an unique event in the world of culture and was esteemed by many as a real war engine against the Church and despotic government. Clement XIII condemned it in 1759, during the period when its publication was suspended by order of the Parlement of Paris. The suspension was rescinded through the protection of La Pompadour, of the Minister Choiseul and of Malesherbes, during the phase of tension that preceded the expulsion of the Jesuits. The success of the *Encyclopédie* was international. There were translations and foreign editions, as well as imitations. The *Encyclopedia Britannica* started publication in 1768.

At the sight of so intensive a movement of ideas and events, undermining the foundations of the Church and the traditional order, there have been those who explain it by an occult cause, as a planned conspiracy working towards a definite goal. Freemasonry has been indicated, for precisely at this time was it developing in France, imported by the English refugees who followed Charles Stuart to St. Germain.

It appears that the first affiliations go back to 1736. Curiosity was aroused by the rule of secrecy. In 1737 Cardinal Fleury, then Minister of Louis XV, forbade the meetings of the Lodges that had already been founded here and there in France. Clement XII in 1738 issued a bull: *In eminenti apostolatus specula*, in which, on the rumours that had grown up round the new society, and 'thinking of the grave evils that might be brought not only to the tranquillity of the temporal society, but also to the spiritual health of souls', he called for proceedings against the Freemasons as 'vehemently suspect of heresy—*de haeresi vehementer suspectos*', with, eventually, the intervention of the secular arm. Clement's condemnation had no great echo. The government of Louis XV was very luke-warm about it; most were convinced of the harmlessness of Freemasonry, many of the nobility belonged to it, with a good number of priests and friars, while great ladies formed the women's lodges.

In 1751 there was a fresh condemnation, by Benedict XIV, who gained no better hearing than Clement XII. Indeed from now onwards proceedings against freemasons, always very mild, become extremely rare, and rare too the voices of bishops concerned about them. The Sorbonne intervenes in 1763 with a condemnation, but under the shafts of the Encyclopedists the Sorbonne was losing credit and authority. There is a certain dissension among the Brotherhood; the English rite and the Scottish rite do not agree—there are expulsions from the lodges, and the creation of the Grand Orient of France, which condemns and ends the Grand Lodge. In 1773 the Duke of Chartres (the future Philippe-Egalité) is Grand Master. L'abbé I. P. Lapanze, a much respected priest, is Venerable of the lodge of English rite of Bordeaux and in 1782 presides at the general lodge; freemason priests had no fear of declaring themselves such, indeed they held it as an honour. An occultistic current crept into French Masonry, imported from Germany or fermented locally, with a mingling of Catholic mysticism, of visionism (like that of the *illuminati* of Bavaria) and of Templarism and magical occultism. Later we shall find Joseph de Maistre 'Grand Orator' of the lodge of Chambéry, which followed the 'Martinist' type (called after Saint-Martin) of the Lyonese branch.

In the XVIII century the French Masonic movement like the English was deistic, 'enlightened', reformist and mysticising, and followed the prudent maxim: *nihil de principe parum de Deo*. To make it play the part of an active and propulsive element, the centre of a battle against the Church and Power, is to make a myth of it. In the whirlpool of the French Revolution, some began to think that Freemasonry had something to do with it, and little by little, after it had adopted an openly anti-Catholic attitude in the XIX century, it came to be considered the occult cause of all the upheavals. But historically it may be taken as proved, in spite of certain dissentient voices, that the role of Freemasonry then and even later was that of the *mouche cochère*, and even this was attributed to it *post factum*.

Freemasonry was then a sign of the times, the child of the age, animated by its spirit. If priests and friars and practising Catholics belonged to it, it was not that they shut their eyes to evil perpetrated, but because they did not see any harm in spreading what they considered to be wholesome ideas and honest sentiments. The secrecy, which aroused the suspicions of outsiders and of the authorities, gave a certain satisfaction to the cryptic instinct in the heart of every man, and to the wish to feel important. Many, in the want of mystical fervour and spiritual aspirations, contented themselves with symbolical surrogates, and those who sought a mysticism of none too pure alloy were often seeking to remedy the void left by the religious formalism of their upbringing; if they no longer believed in the mysteries of the Trinity and the Incarnation, they contented themselves with the fashionable deism and humanitarianism. To be able to communicate in secret gave them a sense of a kind of liberation from the vigilance of the political power, of the ecclesiastical power, of the Sorbonne, of the *parlements*, of the police. It was a slight evasion from a world of constraints into what seemed a world of liberty. Here were the obscure and subconscious motives which later would become transmuted into movements of rebellion and struggle.

§ 42.—The encyclopedist movement and the masonic conventicles did not belong only to France, nor did they come only from France. The flux and reflux of such ideas, tendencies, feelings, aspirations had a general origin in the two previous centuries of reforms and counter-reforms, of wars of religion, hegemony, succession, of absolutisms and intolerance; their outcome in rationalism and naturalism marked historically the bankruptcy of the close union or confusion of religion with the monarchic power, of the Church with the State, under the sign of political conformism and systematic authoritarianism. Therefore from England to Germany, from Spain to Italy, from Austria to Poland, with degrees of difference and according to the special conditions of each country, we find in the XVIII century the same currents as in France.

The typical British representative of this period was David Hume (1711–55), philosopher, historian and economist, who spent some time in France, and travelled in Italy, Austria and elsewhere. His philosophy, a radical epistemology and a fundamental sensationalism, led him to establish sympathy or fellow-feeling as the principle of morals, and to find the basis of religion rather in feeling than in reason. It is curious that in his *Dialogues on Natural Religion*, published after his death, he represented himself not in *Demes* (the man of mystical religious feeling) but in *Cleonte*, who advocates a rationalistic deism, with a certain inclination towards *Filone*, who is now sceptic, now naturalistic. Hume was also an economist, a free-trader, and the forerunner of his celebrated friend Adam Smith (1723–90), whose *Theory of Moral Sentiments* (1759) was influenced by Hume's thought. For Smith moral feeling arises only when man lives in society, on a basis of instinctive sympathy; he rejects the theses of morality as enlightened selfishness or as reason but he does not deny the importance of reason in the development of the moral sentiment. Reason co-operates in the generalisation, not in the perception of good and evil. Thomas Reid, the leader of the Scottish school (1710–96), in attacking Hume's philosophy takes his stand on experience, both from the psychological and historical standpoints; but experience he often limited to the definitive field of facts, without an integration in a religious and ethical complex, which also could have been experimental.

These philosophical trends explain the decadence of the Anglican Church, the lack of any serious theological speculation, and the abandon into which the churches and public worship had fallen; yet the Church enjoyed the protection of the monarchy, the support of Parliament and a privileged economic position. As a reaction, in 1729 a pietistic movement was started at Oxford by certain zealous students mainly inspired by Charles and John Wesley; through their anxiety to find a method of life they were known as Methodists. The groundwork of their religion they drew from experience and a devout and sentimental enthusiasm rather than from dogmas. They abounded in sermons and hymns. (Charles Wesley was their poet, and wrote over 6,000 hymns). The Methodists had their prophets and their convulsionaries, just as the Jansenists had in France at about the same time. They broke away from the Established Church, finding life in common with it impossible, and formed a church of their own; later they divided and subdivided into many other churches. Methodism spread widely in America. It gave its colour to Anglo-Saxon religious feeling of the XIX century. Another movement, that of the Evangelicals, grew up within the Church of England. In contrast to the liberal tendency, which reduced dogmas to symbols of natural truths, and simplified Christianity, reducing it to a natural religion, the Evangelicals sought a spiritual revival based on individual conversion to faith in the supernatural.

In Germany we find an analogous movement to that of the Methodists and Evangelicals in Pietism, which spread nearly everywhere and reacted against both the indifferentism of the official Protestant churches and against the rationalism and naturalism of the *Aufklaerung*, while it prepared the ground for the Catholicism of the Romantics. But the *Aufklaerung* was so widespread among men of culture that it allured the aristocracy, dragged the clergy in its wake, influenced the courts, and affected even the Catholics, who in that period had no outstanding personalities. This does not mean that resistance to the flood of the Enlightenment was wanting, just as it was not wanting in England or even in France, but opposition in the field of speculation and polemics was unequal to its task, while in the political field restrictive measures had often the reverse effect.

Christian Wolff (1678–1754) continued and popularised Leibniz; his clear, plain, systematic superficiality did more harm than good to his master. He was the first to write of philosophy in German, just as Thomasius was the first to write of law (it is to Wolff that German philosophy owes the formation of its terminology), and he divulgated

European speculation in Germany, becoming the most notable exponent of rationalism. He did not deny Christian theology; he wanted to explain it rationally by the Leibnizian principle of 'sufficient reason' (which in Wolff acquired a quasi-deterministic aspect), and by reducing the supernatural facts to natural symbols. The Halle Pietists raised the alarm, and when Wolff sang the praises of Confucius and of the purity of Confucian morality, a storm burst. Frederick-William I deprived him of his professorship and sent him away. Later, however, he recalled him to Halle, where he went on writing till his death.

It was not long before a reaction arose against Wolffian rationalism. The influence of British philosophy first, then that of Rousseau, sounded a recall to the problems of the individual and to the study of psychology and the appreciation of experience. Pietism, as a deviation from Lutheran dogmatism and a revival of religious feeling, might be considered a reflection of the psychologism that was becoming a philosophic theory. There was a recoil from Cartesian rationalism to experience of the concrete, but every experience implies a critical appraisement either of the instruments with which it is made or of the object experienced. Baumgarten in 1750 published his *Aesthetics*; the word would remain appropriated to the theory of beauty, in the philosophical and artistic vocabulary. He conceived aesthetics as an experience of obscure representations (lower cognitions) thus differing from logic which gives us the rules of clear perceptions (higher cognitions). His work was an index of the place that feeling was taking in philosophical speculation as 'a faculty of appraisement'—as Moses Mendelssohn defined it. Immanuel Kant (1724–1804) brought philosophical criticism to its highest point, and with it a reconsideration of all the positions of thought.

To outward appearances, and also in the conviction of many, religious and ethical problems were viewed in the light of a vague deism and Christianity was not an enemy to be overthrown, as it was for Voltaire and the French Encyclopedists, but an experience to be outgrown or an historical fact to be interpreted, or else a symbolical content to be deciphered. Therefore the naturalism of the Enlightenment, sensationalist psychologism and rationalist criticism led towards a kind of obscure and veiled pantheism, that rose from the depths of the mystically inclined Germanic soul. Lessing (1729–81), with the idea that the effort to attain truth was the reason of human dynamism, established an activist principle in the insatiability of the mind and will. It was impossible for him to conceive of a personal and perfect God; he preferred a divinity in immanent relationship with the All and in perpetual motion towards an unattainable completeness. Wolfgang Goethe (1750–1832) based his Faust upon a duality: nature, infinite and eternal, man immortal but not eternal, immortal in his spiritual essence, not in his shape or matter. Nature is unconscious, man conscious; nature is serene, man disquieted by his will to be himself; nature is innocent, man subject to error. Hence an inward conflict that is ever renewed and which tends to an appeasement (salvation) in the dialectic of good and evil or else in the complete surrender of man to nature. Goethe's is a poetic and symbolical pantheism, which expressed no indifferent side of the German thought of the time, wavering as it was between a rationalism *à la* Wolff and an immanentism *à la* Lessing.

In Italy after the group of Southern philosophers of the late XVI century, Telesio, Bruno and Campanella, and after Galileo Galilei who opened a new era in science, it seemed as if the whole force of speculation, poetry and art of the Renaissance had been exhausted, leaving it to be represented only by the great architects, painters and sculptors of the baroque period and by the musicians who were taking the first place in the expression of Italian sentiment and culture. The Cartesian influence was felt; the writings of the jusnaturalists beyond the Alps were read, English philosophy penetrated, and Leibniz was known by a few intellectuals. Above all there was a diffusion of the scientific spirit, of practical experimentalism and of historical and philosophical research; while the study of canon law and Aristotelic philosophy maintained their sway intact in the schools, which were for the most part in the hands of ecclesiastics.

Giambattista Vico of Naples (1668–1744) had not an environment able to appreciate his genius or to understand his profound intuitions, which should have created a new philosophical current in Europe. He had the fate, common to many geniuses, of being rediscovered over half a century after his death; it is then that he begins to be understood (neither wholly nor correctly), and his theories find an environment better prepared to receive them. He is anti-Cartesian. For him man does not acquire knowledge through 'simple and clear ideas', which may represent what is false just as much as what is true, but by becoming himself in a manner the cause of the fact into which the true is convertible. God knows things because He has the archetypal idea realised by His creative act. Man really knows what he makes (which is history) because he makes it. Man knows nature through what he is able to make or recreate of nature by his experience and activity. Man knows God through what he experiences of Divinity, either as historical consciousness (the common opinion of the human race) or as individual consciousness (we should call it to-day experience of the Divine), or as revelation (Primal, Hebrew, Christian). Vico, therefore, regards history not as a narration of facts and succession of dates but as a continuous creativity-cognition on the part of man. He does not consider the past (as the Encyclopedists would) as an accumulation of barbarities and superstitions to be overcome and forgotten, but as human wisdom itself clothed in facts, which may indeed be barbarous and superstitious. He does not conceive nature as a benign myth from which all good comes to man, but as an element of human conquest and creativity—we should say as a conditioning of the creative energy of man. Vico centres in the historical man the whole knowable and therefore conquerable universe, and only starting from this does he come to man's nature, his laws, his destination and transcendence.

From this focal centre Vico sheds beams of light on the whole trend of thought of his time, on philological history, on natural law, on the problem of natural religion and of revelation, on ethics and on politics. They are not always beams of light; both in his thought and in his style there are lacuna and opacities that leave the reader perplexed. In politics Vico tended to avoid any collision with the régime of his time, and to indulge a little in adulation, which in the reign of Charles of Bourbon corresponded to the paternalist and national euphory of the new independent kingdom of Naples. This notwithstanding, he did not fail to raise the problem of civil liberties and democratic systems, looking back to Greece and Rome.

Taken as a whole, Vico's speculation presented a potent aid for a vigorous reaction against the rationalistic abstractionism of Descartes, the sentimental naturalism of Rousseau, and all the anti-historical current of the Encyclopedic Enlightenment—but only on condition that an arid, formalistic and Aristotelising scholasticism were set aside, with the development of a robust Platonising philosophy of history and a renovation of the old instruments of legal and political science. All this demanded not only time to mature but also sympathy; the camp of Italian Catholic scholars was too rhetorical, tending to wordy apologetics and held fast by the fear lest in abandoning the traditional positions of general culture, they might fall into theological errors. Therefore, not only was the appearance of the *Scienza Nuova* (1725) not well received, save for a few superficial praises, but the attacks on it came from ecclesiastics of a certain intellectual standing, and precisely from the point of view of Catholic tradition. It must be added that in this period a philosophy, even that of Vico, would not have sufficed to set Catholic thought on a sound course; what was needed was a bold spirit of practical reform in every field. From this the clergy shrank, finding themselves under the pressure of Jansenistic jurisdictionalism and 'enlightened' reformism. They were so bound up with the world of the past, under the sign of the Counter-Reformation, as to have almost lost the initiative demanded by the growing needs of the cultural and political life of the day.

The spiritual movements counterbalancing the naturalistic currents were limited in Italy to the sphere of popular education and piety, in an effort to revive the religious spirit in the countrysides and to charitable assistance and the training of youth. Among the apostles and saints who had a great influence in Italy we must note St. John Baptist De Rossi (1698–1764), known as the Vincent de Paul of Rome; St. Leonard of Porto Maurizio, a Franciscan (1677–1751), the preacher of popular missions; St. Paul of the Cross (1706–73), founder of the Congregation of Passionists, which rapidly spread among the people, winning high consideration. Above all the Neapolitan, St. Alphonse of Liguori (1695–1787), stands out as theologian, apostle, and founder of the Redemptorists. He gave a decisive formulation to the problem of Probabilism, raised casuistry out of the discredit into which it had fallen, and fought the Jansenistic rigorism that was diffused among the Southern clergy.

Jansenism in Italy, indeed, if it was a belated and imported phenomenon, found there a certain rigorism in a latent state and made this its fulcrum. The discussions over grace remained within the camp of the theologians (not all the clergy was composed of theologians), but rigorism found motives for development in the contrast between the rigorous Jansenists and certain literary and dandified abbots, ambitious and wordly monsignori of the Curia, a lax and inert aristocracy (such as Parini satirised in his *Giorno*), in a society devoid of generous impulses. Italian Jansenism, however, in so far as it expressed itself in writings and as an active force, was a reformist, jurisdictionalist and anti-Roman movement, represented particularly by the Bishop of Pistoia, Scipione de Ricci (1741–1827), and by the Abbot Pietro Tamburini of Pavia (1737–1827).

It was not in this direction that the Italian thought of the time could develop, but under the influence of the French Encyclopedists. Montesquieu, Voltaire and Rousseau were much read by cultured people and by scholars. The Marquis Cesare Beccaria (1738–1794) was strongly influenced by the *Lettres Persanes.* He and the brothers Pietro and Alessandro Verri published *Il Caffé* in Milan, a journal that supported civil reforms and spread the new ideas. As the protector of the prisoners, in contact with the machinery of criminal justice, he conceived his book *Dei Delitti e delle Pene* ('On Crimes and Punishments') in 1764, which had an extraordinary success. In a short time edition followed edition. Translated into French it was printed three times in two years (1764–66); Voltaire wrote a commentary to it. The English translation was published in 1768. The book is mainly a searching criticism of penal systems, on the ground of the inadequacy and uncertainty of evidence, the abuse of torture, the barbarity of penalties, and above all the death-penalty, which Beccaria judges unreasonable and useless. The principle on which he based his work was essentially naturalistic, that is that the social contract is founded on the aim of achieving the greatest happiness for the greatest number. He attacked the death penalty on the principle that no man by the social contract would have granted to other men, even as representing all the contractants, the faculty of depriving him of his life as a punishment, for this was in contradiction to the very nature of the social contract, which is 'the sum of tiny portions of the private liberty of each'. But if this corresponded to the spirit of the XVIII century, the ethical substance of the book was superior to its formulation, and therefore remained as the starting point of modern penal law in all countries. If the death penalty, which up till then had been abused, came to be restricted to exceptional cases or wholly abolished, even though long after 1764, it is due to this first humane and enlightened outcry.

The naturalistic and reformist trend was not very widespread in Italy, but those who rose above the common mediocrity became its exponents and exerted an undisputed influence, like Filangeri and Romagnosi. Those who reawakened Italian poetry from its long sleep, the Abate Parini and Vittorio Alfieri, both of them by satire and Alfieri also in his tragedies, made humane feelings felt, with a disgust for moral servility and political servitude, and a sense of the necessity of moral and social reforms. At bottom, an old Italic stoicism united with the naturalism of the age, and the remoteness from Christian sources showed how deep a gulf was coming to separate the cultured element in Italy from the popular masses.

§ 43.—In order to meet a movement of thought and a wide and continuous propaganda against Christianity (which was identified, through error and *parti pris*, with the traditionalist positions, authoritarian and anti-reformist), the clergy called for secular intervention for the enforcement of the laws of repression. This was often forthcoming, where the breach of law was too apparent, or there was fear lest the new ideas should shake the throne, and when ecclesiastical influence or the advantage of clerical support to the secular authority created a closer bond between the two powers. But at other times it was not so; the complaints of the clergy remained without effect, and indeed the governments seemed allied with those who waged the most subtle war against the Church and her dogmas.

The State is not an abstraction; it is a resultant of the concrete forces of society. The State, in spite of its name, is not static but dynamic. It moves with the movements of ideas, feelings and interests in the country. Hence the oscillation which we note in the cultural, religious and reformist conflict of the XVIII century was due to the veering of the blasts released by the two conceptions, the traditionalist and the naturalist—the one seeking to sustain established social positions and to identify itself with them, the other seeking to uproot such positions, and to depreciate Christianity itself. As disaffection towards the Church increased, especially in the Catholic countries, there was increased resentment against the exercise of ecclesiastical rights and authoritarian methods, and hence the desire to limit and check them, and to abolish those rights that were in conflict with the proposals for civil, economic and cultural reform. Reformism was conceived as the panacea for all ills. It must be recognised that there was a real need for reforms. Those who opposed them, in the name of a static society, made a dangerous confusion between what was truly Christian and what was an historical superstructure, to be renewed or destroyed.

In this period all the kings, even the less intelligent, were reformers more or less tinged with the Enlightenment. The most famous would remain Frederick the Great of Prussia (1712–86) and Joseph II of Austria (1741–90), called by the curialists the 'Sacristan King'. Ferdinand VI of Spain, too, passed for an enlightened prince, and came into conflict with the Inquisition itself, of which he was the political head. Charles III who succeeded him, and even Charles IV, who was more a despot and imbecile, had the same leanings. Louis XVI, certainly *malgré lui*, under the pressure of events and also of the Queen, Marie Antoinette, who came full of the ideas of the Court of Vienna, had to start his reign with reforms. He began by restoring life to the Parlements which his grandfather in 1771 had dissolved. His new minister, Turgot, carried forward economic and financial reforms, arousing the discontent of many, till he and Malesherbes were dismissed. In Austria Maria Theresa had begun the great reforms that were a prelude to the transformation of the feudal régime into an administrative State founded on public law. Joseph II her son followed, who first as co-ruler with her, then as Emperor, directed all his activity to the renewal of the machinery of the State, shaping it according to the prevailing theories in finance, economy, administration and civil and criminal law. We have already spoken of his rigid, invasive and excessive jurisdictionalism. He sought to place the State above any ecclesiastical influence and to control the Church as a branch of its administration.

The reform that in France, Austria and the Catholic countries in dependence on Vienna, stirred the different currents for a certain time, was the introduction of religious toleration. A century earlier it had stirred England, Holland, North America and Germany, only in the interest of the various Protestant churches, with the exclusion of the Catholics who had always remained either in conditions of legal and moral inferiority or else in situations that already were consolidated, for better or for worse as the case might be. In France the impulse came from the situation in which the Protestants now found themselves. A declaration by Louis XV, in May, 1724, laid down the principle of a presumption *juris et de jure* that they were all to be regarded as *new converts*. By this legal fiction any act of Protestant worship was to be punished as the crime of apostasy. No one might contract marriage save before the Catholic priest; unions made without the Catholic rite were considered as concubinage, the children were registered as bastards and had to receive Catholic baptism, and legal inheritance was not recognised where they were concerned. The Protestant pastors continued to bless marriages in secret; such unions were known as '*marriages du désert*'. The moral and civil effects of such a state of things for about a million inhabitants were extremely serious.

To-day it seems astonishing that ministers and bishops could be unaware of the social harm produced by the declaration of Louis XV. In 1750, on the contrary, it was believed that to increase the penalties against the unfortunate Protestants would remedy the evil. What a chance for a campaign in the name of Natural Law! Montesquieu, as a pragmatist, confined himself to saying that such penalties were quite useless and ineffectual; he believed it a wise law that a government, if it could choose between admitting or not a new religion into the realm, should decide in the negative, but that if the religion was already established there, it should be granted toleration. Rousseau, on the contrary, starting from Natural Law, advocated complete freedom where religion was concerned. In the controversy that was aroused many intervened for and against toleration. Turgot, Voltaire, Marmontel, d'Holbach, Condorcet had greater effect than the Bishop of Agen and l'Abbé de Concirac and others of the traditional Catholic party whose names are forgotten. The trials of Calas and Sirven (to which we have already referred) served to rouse the interest of the public at large in the problem of toleration. The question of marriages was, by order of Louis XV, examined by the Council of State and by certain bishops, but without result. The Parlements before their dissolution in dealing with similar questions were inclined to be liberal. The movement for toleration went forward with fresh vigour in the new reign of Louis XVI.

The last uncertainties and hesitations in France would not have been overcome had not Joseph II promulgated his *Toleranz-Patent* of October, 1781, for Austria, and another, the following November, for Transylvania, besides extending these measures to Flanders and Lombardy. In May, 1782, Louis XVI decreed that the children of Protestants should no longer be registered as bastards, and finally, in November, 1787, he caused the promulgation of the *King's Edict concerning those who do not profess the Catholic Religion*, which regulated the civil position of the Protestants. In spite of the resentment both of the Catholics and of the Protestants themselves (who had not obtained as much as they hoped), the Parlement of Paris and then the other Parlements registered the edict, but by that time it was already the eve of the Revolution.

The patent of toleration issued by Joseph II was wider in scope than that of Louis XVI. In Austria it met with much favour and small opposition; the same in Lombardy and in the other countries subject to the Hapsburgs, save in Flanders. Here opposition was so strong that Leopold, who succeeded Joseph, in 1792 had to withdraw the Patent; it was only for a short time, for the French arrived, bringing the revolution. In Rome there was a sense of the approaching storm, but the reformist movement was often confused with that of jurisdictionalism, and the moral and social questions raised by the first were translated into legal terms. Pius VI, faced by the two-fold action of Joseph II—on the one hand reforms touching the traditional rights of the Church and introducing religious toleration, on the other a jurisdictionalism placing the domestic organisation of the Church herself and her apostolic and sacramentary activity under complete State control—decided in 1782 to make a journey to Vienna to persuade the Emperor to go back on his steps. The poet Vincenzo Monti celebrated this in his *Il Pellegrino Apostolico*, but the journey had no serious result.

The movement towards toleration in the Catholic countries had not grown up out of a religious conception, as was partly the case in the Protestant countries, but solely through the development of the jus-naturalist ideas. In the decree of Louis XVI it was stated that the concession to the non-Catholic was '*ce que le droit naturel ne nous permet pas de lui refuser*'. These ideas had been working in the previous century in Holland, England and Germany, though mingled with religious theories, which are not wanting in either Grotius or Hobbes or Pufendorf; but in the France of the end of the XVIII century the course was set towards the break-up of the confessional State, and hence natural law appeared not as allied to the Christian churches but as an adversary and as a competitor. In Austria, on the contrary, with the prevalence of the Germanic currents of jusnaturalism, and, among the clergy, of the theories of Febronius and van Espen, the State remained confessional even while anti-curial.

However, while the Catholic countries were now conceding toleration to their old adversaries, the Protestants of England and Holland still maintained the civil and religious disabilities of Catholics. In Ireland, which only in 1782 after agitations and revolts succeeded in vindicating the independence of her parliament (though the executive power remained subordinate to Westminster), Catholics were excluded even from the franchise. This was conceded to them in 1793 under the influence of the French Revolution. Only in Prussia, Frederick the Great from the beginning of his reign was inspired by the ideas of the Enlightenment to accord complete religious toleration. In a decree of June 15, 1740, authorising the Italian Catholic Antonio Rumi to accept the property left him by his brother in Frankfurt-on-Oder, Frederick wrote: 'All religions are equal and good in so far as those who profess them are honest men, and if the Turks and pagans came and wanted to populate the country, we should be ready to build their mosques and temples.' According to Frederick, the State should see that the various religions and sects 'lived in peace and worked together and in equal measure for the good of the State.' Thus he acted towards the Catholics in Berlin in 1746, allowing them to build churches and giving them the necessary ground; and, as we have noted, he showed good-will even to the persecuted Jesuits. When he conquered Silesia he left the Catholic religion as the prevailing one and granted toleration to the Protestants. It was, however, his successor Frederick-William II who, in imitation of Joseph II and of Louis XVI, by a decree of 1788 known as the *Religious Edict of Woellner*, established toleration in all his States, placing the various Christian religions on a footing of equality, and at the same time maintaining the privileges of the various churches. Apart from this, Frederick the Great was a forerunner of the modern State. Although his conception was that of an absolute paternalism, yet his reformism outstripped that of the other States, both from the administrative and judicial and from the religious and military standpoints.

In spite of the obvious resistance of the absolutist tradition and of its ties with the Christian churches, the political conception was little by little moving towards a broad constitutionalism, and already the first signs of the new democracies were making their appearance. The influence of English parliamentarism had been notable from the time men began to write about it, in France and elsewhere. Although there was no thought of drawing from it a motive for practical imitation, yet there was a confused yearning for the ideal, from the day that the divine right of kings ceased to awaken echoes in the common mind, and was merely left in the hands of the jurisdictionalists as a useful weapon in their disputes with the Roman Curia. Hobbes' absolutism, too, ceased to carry weight, once nature was no longer conceived as savage and bestial, but as good, idyllic and happy. The individualistic conception of Locke, the organic conception of Thomasius, the personalistic conception of Pufendorf held more significance, only they lacked a reformistic aim that would go beyond theoretical constructions and be practically concerned with individual rights and the limits of power.

Montesquieu was the first to define the separation of the three powers, legislative, judicial and executive, and although he does not harmonise them in a unifying element which, without invading their spheres or confusing them, would provide a synthesis into which they would resolve, he none the less represented an immense advance, both in regard to the technical principles and to the characteristics of the modern State. What is wanted, he says, is the elimination of the arbitrary factor in the concept of power. This is less present in the actual making of laws, because the legislator considers general cases, the customs and interests of the community for the future, and he establishes the requisite norms. But there will be other organs to execute the laws they have not made and cannot make, and these—that which applies the law, as administration and police, and the other, independent likewise, which gives justice between private individuals and assigns penalties for crime—become ministers of the law, subject to the law and not above the law.

The separation and independence of the three powers is the firm basis of the State *de droit*, a basis that up till then had been established only theoretically, as a metaphysical problem, in the study of the origin of power from the people, in the definition of individual rights and in enquiry into the nature of such rights. But so long as these speculations had not found a form of concrete expression, they remained as fluctuant factors even in countries where a parliamentary tradition existed. It was necessary not only to temper monarchic absolutism (for at that time no one in France, Austria or Spain thought of a republic) by a participation of the electoral bodies in political power, but it was necessary to create the inner logic of the State *de droit*, by which law would be sovereign, rights respected, the individual able to vindicate his rights, and no one would be able to assume arbitrary power without encountering a legal obstacle. Montesquieu's theory presented itself as a mechanism for establishing a balance on a plane of rights; therefore it could not fail to be alluring.

Immediately the problem of the synthesis of the three powers presented itself. Montesquieu did not succeed in solving it, for he did not solve the problem of sovereignty. The monarch must derive it either from God or from the people. An historical investiture is not enough; it has a pragmatistic but no theoretical basis, and thus is relative but not absolute. If the law is the custom and this, albeit relative to times and places, is expressed by the consent of the many, it is necessary to go to the many (that is, to the people) to find the law in their will. The sovereign people will be the new synthesis of the State *de droit*. The theorist of popular sovereignty was Rousseau. For him power, all the power, indivisible, inalienable, permanent, is in the sum of the wills of the individuals. It may be expressed through a common decision by the majority of individuals; it can never be delegated either to monarchs or to parliaments. Rousseau's *Contrat Social* (1762) was like a violent blow given to a pendulum, driving it to the extreme opposite point before it can return to its central and balanced oscillation.

The technical aspect of power in the *Contrat Social* cannot stand the test of experience, while that of Montesquieu was ideal and practical at the same time. But Rousseau provided a new absolute basis which in Montesquieu was lacking. Rousseau's style of popular sovereignty presupposed the goodness of nature and the free contract between men to live in society. The collective will being good and indivisible knows no limits to its power and is of itself intrinsically ethical. It becomes contractually legal, inasmuch as everyone has of himself entered into an obligation through the collective will. With this solid bloc the separation of powers became a technical question, as did that of delegation of powers which, denied in Rousseau's rigid conception, was felt to be a means of reconciling the principle with its practical actuation.

The churchmen and traditionalist Catholics did not perceive that with Rousseau, albeit in distorted and degenerate form, the old popular and contractual theory of society was returning, which had been upheld in the Middle Ages and the Renaissance, and which certain curialists still repeated, simply as the metaphysics of power, in their polemics with the regalists who put forward the divine right. Such Catholics, both then and up to our own times, opposed Rousseau's contractual theory because they confused it with his theoretical premises—the goodness of nature, which denied Original Sin; the absolute quality of the popular will, which denied objective ethical limits; the inalienability of power, which denied not only delegation but also the stability of sovereignty and of social institutions; the popular origin of power conceived as the antithesis of the derivation of power from God. Rousseau's theory corresponded to the naturalistic current of the XVIII century, to the struggle against the absolutism of the kings and against the Church, against the political, economic, religious and feudal bond-systems of the time. The fulcrum of the struggle and of the reforms was in the people, to which was attributed not an original sovereignty given only to be lost at once, according to Hobbes' conception, nor a kind of historical title of original sovereignty hard of realisation, according to that of the Counter-Reformation theologians, but a power actual, permanent, complete. At the time when the conception of the State was taking this course, the Church was fettered by jurisdictionalism, shaken by the Jesuit question, impoverished in men of thought and culture able to face the currents of the Enlightenment in every country.

PART III

THE SECULAR STATE AND THE CHURCH

CHAPTER XI

FROM THE FRENCH REVOLUTION TO THE HOLY ALLIANCE

§ 44.—With the recognition of the independence of the United States of America, by the Treaty of Paris of September 3, 1783, with the federal constitution of 1787 and finally, in 1789, with the nomination of George Washington as first President, the republican system reappeared among the great States, as representative government of the people without a monarch. After the fall of the Roman Republic and the inauguration of the Empire by Augustus, the monarchic principle had triumphed throughout the world. The medieval republics were of a civic character. Only the maritime cities rose to a state of military and commercial power—Venice, indeed, acquiring territory on the mainland and maintaining a closed and aristocratic system of government, for over six centuries was a first-class Power. Republican Florence had an exceptional grandeur between the Middle Ages and the Renaissance; politically and economically she outstripped the greatest kingdoms and held her own against popes and emperors, but the Republic several times collapsed and returned to life, perpetually undermined by internal strife and foreign wars.

The history of the Middle Ages and of the Italian Renaissance had no hold on the minds of the bourgeois, merchants and intellectuals of XVIII-century Europe; Rome and Greece meant more to them. For the Anglo-Saxon peoples the idea of parliament and of the free citizen took primacy over the monarchic tradition, which in regard to the House of Hanover might be considered almost meaningless. The American colonies were very far away from Great Britain, they liked their own methods and their liberties, and would not suffer the interference of London in their affairs. During the Seven Years' War they had become conscious of their military and political potentialities, which before that experience they were not aware that they possessed. The revolution and the War of Independence—helped by France, Spain and Holland, the traditional enemies of Great Britain—created a new political reality, the United States of America.

Towards the end of the XVIII century the conception of monarchy by divine right had had its day. Jusnaturalism had given it its deathblow; it subsisted only as a popular tradition, as a religious rite, as a legal title. In Great Britain the parliament shared in the monarchic sovereignty and this diarchy, if on the one hand it had subdued any pretensions to divine right after the Stuart fashion, on the other had immunised the monarchy from the corrosion of power. The creation of the transatlantic Republic therefore did not shake the British monarchy, but struck a mortal blow at the absolute sovereignties of Europe. Their right was challenged by that of the people to create their own régime, to give themselves a constitution, to appoint their own head.

The Declaration of Independence and of Rights, made by the Congress of Philadelphia in July, 1776, precedes by thirteen years the *Declaration of the Rights of Man and of the Citizen*, by the National Assembly in Paris, August, 1789. Both documents throw into relief certain jusnaturalist principles that were then everywhere diffused—the civil and political equality of men, their inalienable natural rights, independence and original liberty, the power or sovereignty of the people, direct or representative. All that had been maturing in this regard, for over a century, by both declarations was brought down, from the theoretical plane of university schools and debates between intellectuals, to the practical plane of political assemblies.

The differences between the two declarations sprang from the historical data which shaped the premises of their all but abstract formulas and from the practical aims they sought to achieve. The American Congress sought the liberation of a people from subjection to another, and accomplished the first act of colonial emancipation. The French Assembly sought to abrogate the feudal and political rights of the monarchy and of the privileged classes (nobility and clergy) and created the first public title of the Third Estate to emancipation. In America the republic was sought simply as a means of liberation from Europe. In France at that moment what was sought was to reduce the monarchy to a mere organ of the nation.

From the religious standpoint, the Americans for nearly a century had enjoyed the English régime of toleration established in 1689; only Catholics were treated as citizens and subjects of a lower order and often as undesirable. But at the moment of revolution the confessional distinction was swallowed up in the need for union in resistance and struggle. In France, on the other hand, the religious problem embraced many other problems, spiritual, political and economic. Between the Christian conception—whether Catholic or Protestant—and the naturalistic and rationalist conception there was a spiritual and historical antithesis, which in America was not felt at all. If in the Declaration of the Rights of Man there is only the faint reflection in Art. 10: 'No one must be molested for his opinions, even religious opinions, so long as their manifestation does not disturb the public order established by the laws', yet, in a short time, the religious problem, together with the monarchic problem, would become the most important for the French Revolution. Behind the monarchy were the feudal privileges, behind the clergy was mortmain property, behind both the authoritarian and intolerant system. Therefore very soon the French Revolution becomes anti-monarchic and anti-Catholic.

In every revolution the party that promotes it identifies itself with the nation. The Third Estate, treated by the other two like a poor relation, by a series of small events—they became significant through the spirit of reform, which was blowing from every side, and through the ebullition of the masses—succeeded in taking all initiative from the nobility and clergy as 'Estates' and spoke in the name of the nation. In a first phase the bourgeoisie, backed by the parish clergy, put the nobility and upper clergy in a minority, gave check to the king and asserted its authority over the turbulent mobs. This political success sufficed to create a propitious atmosphere for the abolition of feudal dues, with or without compensation as the case might be, and of the church tithes, at first declared redeemable, then suppressed without indemnity. Shortly after came the confiscation of all the property of the Church of France, with the formula that it was placed '*à la disposition de la nation*'. In compensation, Church expenses were set to the charge of the State budget. With the sale of the Church and Crown property, and with the liberation of lands subject to feudal dues, a mass of landed proprietors was formed, bound by stable and permanent interests to the revolution and to the régimes to which it gave rise. The new liberal class was created, reinforcing at the same time the old elements of the mercantile bourgeoisie and giving an impulse to industrial development.

It was necessary to bind the clergy, too, to the new régime. Though they had voted its laws, they could not be counted on, both because they were divided by various currents and because at bottom they were monarchic and reactionary. The suspension of solemn vows had restored their freedom to those religious who wished to become secularised (and they were not a few); the others were gathered together in a certain number of monasteries in order to leave the rest free for sale. The clergy did not resist this onslaught, which infringed the traditional laws of the Church; they were carried off their feet by revolutionary pressure and national feeling. It did not even occur to them that the Holy See might have a right to a say in the matter, for Gallican theories were still operative. The population did not see anything anti-religious in such measures. Nobles and clerics became purchasers of church property without remorse of conscience. There was no serious resistance to the laws on the religious Orders, on the part of the representatives of the Church, partly because of an unconcealed antipathy of the secular clergy towards the regular. The suppression of church property had the political consequence of depriving the Estate of the clergy of its basis and *raison d'être*, just as the abolition of feudal dues had so deprived the Estate of the nobles. The class revolution had already been accomplished.

The political position had fallen; there remained the ecclesiastical position in regard to relations with the 'nation': on the one hand, a State clergy, the budget for religious purposes on the other. The idea came within the criteria of the Gallican Church. It was a logical step for those legists who attributed the totality of powers to the State, but not for those who professed the universality of the Church. On the one hand, the Jansenist current prevailed, which still nurtured resentment against Rome for the unforgotten bull *Unigenitus*, and on the other, the heirs of the Encyclopedists, who expressed themselves as Mirabeau: '*Il faut décatholiciser la France.*' The bishops, placed in conditions of inferiority, could do nothing against the *Comité Ecclésiastique* of the National Assembly which was entrusted with drawing up the 'new charter of the clergy'. By this Civil Constitution of the Clergy (July–November, 1790), not only were the dioceses reduced by an act of authority, without the Pope's consent, to correspond to the civil *départements*—with the two-fold aim of administrative centralisation and financial economy—but it was established that bishops and parish priests should be elected like the deputies and officials (decree of December, 1789), as corresponding to the new system; this had the absurd effect that Protestants and Jews were among the electors of the Catholic bishops. The bishop-elect, if the metropolitan and the other bishops of the province refused to accept him as unsuitable, had the right to appeal *ab abusu* to the tribunal of the Department, which would judge the motives of the refusal. To subject the upper clergy to the electorate meant separation from the monarchy and nobility; to place it under State control meant separation from Rome; the only concession was to communicate the appointment to the Pope as 'visible head of the universal Church in witness to the unity or the faith'.

The bishops at first refused to discuss the project and proposed the summoning of a national council. When this proposal was rejected, opinions remained divided. The King, on the advice of the bishops themselves, signed the Assembly's decree and begged the Pope not to condemn it; the papal Nuncio, too, was of the King's opinion. But among the bishops who were deputies in the Constituent Assembly the opposite view prevailed. Thirty of them in October, 1790, published an *Exposition des principes sur la Constitution du clergé*, to which all the others except four assented, denouncing the points contrary to Catholic doctrine. To this act, the Assembly replied by making it compulsory for bishops and priests, as State functionaries, to swear allegiance to the Constitution. The King hesitated, but ended by signing the new decree. The clergy speedily split into jurors and non-jurors. In March, 1791, Pius VI condemned the Civil Constitution of the Clergy, declaring it schismatic and heretical, and making it obligatory on the jurors to retract within forty days, under pain of suspension *a divinis*. The orthodox clergy rallied round the Pope, the constitutional clergy round the State. From April, 1791, till the Napoleonic Concordat, for ten years, the Church of France was officially schismatic. But the greater part of the clergy remained in orthodoxy, taking the road of exile, going into hiding, ministering to the faithful at the cost of innumerable perils, facing imprisonment and death in thousands.

The persecuting phase of the French Revolution, if it is to be understood, must be seen within the frame of events. These are too well known for it to be necessary to treat of them here. The fear of a return to the past and hence of losing the benefits of the abolition of feudal dues and tithes, and of the liquidation of Church property, bound the bourgeoisie and a part of the country nobility to the Revolution. This fear was rendered sharper by the rumours of an armed offensive to restore order by the nobles who had fled to foreign Courts. Such rumours had an appearance of truth; the German princes possessed of feudal rights in Alsace, basing themselves on the Treaty of Ryswick, demanded the intervention of the guarantors, Austria, Russia and Sweden; while Louis XVI had turned towards Vienna and Marie Antoinette was urgently begging her imperial brother for help.

To-day historians can ascertain the facts and, up to a certain point, give them their true value. But in the white-hot atmosphere of the Revolution, in the midst of suspicions, ambitions, angers and hatreds, it was, if not impossible, very difficult to discern truth from falsehood. The Pope's condemnation, coinciding with the question of the Comté de Venaissin and Avignon, the resistance of the clergy to the second oath imposed on all, the refusals of the King to sign new laws combined with the efforts to ally the Powers against revolutionary France and to subdue her by force of arms. In the meantime all were manoeuvring for the outbreak of war, each thinking, after his fashion, that war would cut the knots which the Revolution had tied so inexorably about the court, the *émigrés*, the parties and the men who worked through them. Even a part of the clergy looked to war for salvation, for them salvation meant a return to the past.

In spite of the ill-advised manoeuvres of the courts and those of the *émigrés*, war would not have broken out had not the revolutionaries of Paris wanted it, and had it not been for the death of the prudent

Emperor, Leopold of Hapsburg. To the French ultimatum of March, 1792, Vienna sent a very firm reply (the young Francis II had just ascended the throne): they must restore the imperial princes to their rights in Alsace, give satisfaction to the Pope for the occupation of Avignon, reorganise the Government so as to avoid dangers of disorder in neighbouring States. Louis XVI on April 20 proposed war on Austria. The mob was delirious and only seven Deputies had the courage to vote against it. But for the allies, Austria, Prussia, Piedmont, war was rendered difficult both by the lack of true political objectives, and by the intrigues of Catherine of Russia and Frederick-William of Prussia over Poland, intrigues which Vienna sought in vain to thwart. Thus France had time to reorganise her armies as best she could, and to countermine the manoeuvres carried on by Court and nobles under cover of the war. This drove the monarchy towards ruin and the country towards the Terror.

Thus arose the French Republic, historically the First Republic. The word *republic* was not then understood precisely as the government of a people without a King, but more as a mixed government, independently of the form it might take, with the participation of the various citizen orders. Jean Bodin towards the end of the XVI century had written his *Libri sex de Republica*. The revolutionaries in order to avoid ambiguity did not say that they wanted to establish a republic; not one of the orators of the Convention of September 21 pronounced the word. They demanded the 'abolition of the monarchy', they said they wanted 'the nation without a king', or else 'the sovereign nation'. The word *republic* was imposed by the people, which likes clear ideas and precise formulas. With the abolition of the monarchy, decreed by the Convention, the new form of popular republican government arose in Europe, on the eve of the fall of Venice, the senile aristocratic republic, by this time without strength or ideals or life.

§ 45.—The experience of the French Revolution in regard to the problems of State and Church and their interference, may be considered in relation purely to the revolutionary period, or in a wider sense in relation to modern times up till our own day. The first aspect interests us only in order to define the motives that inserted themselves into the historical process, and to bring out their connection with the past. Just as Humanism was not a breach with the Middle Ages but their historical outcome, so the Revolution was the historical outcome of the *ancien régime* rather than a breach with it. All agree that the accumulation of economic crises, due to the enormous inequalities of property, a fettered commerce, the extension of mortmain, the burden of feudal dues that still survived, the continual wars, had brought a sharper sense of the moral and political crises. Rationalism and jusnaturalism had placed the moral conception of life and the political conception of the State on a new basis. Catholicism as a dogmatico-ethical system was undermined by Jansenism, as hierarchic discipline by Gallicanism, as a canonical system by jurisdictionalism. The Revolution like a whirlwind shattered the frail equilibrium of the old social structure. From the overthrow of the established orders, the assured economies, the traditional theories, there emerged certain elements which, denied in principle or in practice, survived the injustices, revolts, wars, slaughters, horrors of an unprecedented ten years.

The Church passed through three stages: that of the official cults (1789–95), that of separation (1793–1801), that of the Concordat (1801–14). In all three phases there were persecutions against the clergy as refractory, or non-patriot, or non-imperial. In all three phases the popes had their share—the occupation of Avignon and Rome, the imprisonment of Pius VI at Valence, of Pius VII at Savona. Schism was no novelty for the Church, nor was persecution of the clergy, nor the occupation of Avignon and Rome, nor the exile and imprisonment of popes. Nor was there novelty in the affirmation of a national church and the decrees on the Constitution of the Clergy, which were in the Gallican tradition, from the Pragmatic Sanction onwards. What was new for the Church was the laicization of the power of the State.

Jusnaturalism had separated, in principle, the idea of State from the idea of Church. Jurisdictionalism maintained them united, State and Church, in a traditional monarchy of sacred character. The Revolution first reduced the King to a functionary of the nation, then eliminated him. No more would there be that 'external bishop' of the Church, forming the bridge between the spiritual and secular powers. The ecclesiastical rights of the Catholic monarchies, whether they were privileges granted by the Church, as the curialists held, or whether they originated with the royal power, as the regalists maintained, could not be vested in a voluble and factious popular assembly, in which believer and unbeliever, Catholic, Protestant and Jew had the same rights—in which often the miscreant, the man of passion and blood, a Danton or a Robespierre, prevailed over all the rest.

On the other hand, these assemblies, made and unmade under the pressure of the revolutionary movement, were all founded on the conception of natural equality—no more privileges, only rights, all coming from the People and from its will as interpreting Nature. The practical triumph of the theory of popular sovereignty and the fall of the monarchy carried the foundations of the State on to a new plane; the laicizing of the political power was inherent in the new conception of the State, and would have come about even if the persecutions and massacres had been averted. This did not mean that the French people meant to break away from the Christian religion or that even the leaders of the revolution meant to create a State without religion. There was a quest for a religious arrangement corresponding to the new conception of the State. This arrangement was the Civil Constitution of the Clergy, which could not become final through the papal condemnation and the struggles of the refractory clergy. The two episodes of the cult of the Goddess Reason and the cult of the Supreme Being, to be substituted for the Christian religion as the official worship of the nation, were historically ephemeral and were inset in the struggle with Roman Catholicism, which was resisting. They had no other meaning than that of the quest for a religious symbol to represent in a period of passion the novelty of a political State founded on nature. The Goddess Reason and the Supreme Being were the symbols of the laicization of power; the symbols collapsed at once, but laicization remained, for it was part of the logic of the new experiment.

The successive phases of the struggle between State and Church, first separation then the Concordat, confirmed its advent. Separation, from 1793 to 1801, was an expedient. The surrogate religions had collapsed, the position of the sworn clergy was rendered difficult by the passive resistance of the faithful; there was a desire to find some way out of the *impasse*, and separation seemed the best path. It was not.

The measures of protection for the sworn clergy and the persecutions of adversaries at once mark a return of interference by the State, which in the midst of so many difficulties found it hard to cope with the continual recrudescence of religious questions. As events tend towards the Directorate, and at last a firm hand is felt at the helm, the idea of a concordat awakens. But a concordat with whom? No longer with 'the Catholic nation', as those of 1418 made by Martin V; no longer with 'the Catholic sovereign', like that between Leo X and Francis I of France.

The laicization of the sovereign power meant the end of the confessional State, even though the State continued to claim jurisdictionalist rights over the Catholic Church. Here is the second novelty produced by the Revolution in relations between Church and State. We have already referred to the second phase of jurisdictionalism which in the XVIII century made the State tend to disengage itself from the Church, while accentuating its control. This disengagement showed itself in two ways: in religious toleration, though with the maintenance of a State religion, and in the laic character given to legislative reforms. The Revolution (after the attempts at official religions) went a step further. It abolished State religion and the remains of canonical legislation, making its own Civil Code. But if the confessional State vanished, jurisdictionalism survived as the intervention and control of the secular power in the Church, under the guise of police supervision.

From the point of view of the Catholic Church, the Revolution had two great effects. First, the liquidation of Gallicanism, which was bound up with the monarchy and the *ancien régime*. Once the scaffolding of the Estates had collapsed, and with it the economic basis represented by church property, only the episcopalist conception of the Church remained. But this (and here is the second effect) received a grave blow both from the fact that the bishops rallied to the Pope to defend the Church of France during the revolutionary persecutions and the schism of the sworn clergy, and from the necessity of a concordat between Paris and Rome. The most serious blow to Gallican Episcopalism came from Pius VII, when in execution of the concordat he obliged the legitimate bishops to resign, and, in the event of refusal, held them as deposed *ex officio*. The episcopalist theory would no longer have a basis. Gallicanism and Episcopalism would persist in France for some time yet, but as incoherent elements of outworn theories, while henceforth there would be a development of Ultramontanism and papalism.

What we have been saying might be challenged in the name of various passages in the Concordat, but the letter counts for little when the spirit has fled. The expressions of the preamble, that 'the Government of the French Republic recognises that the Catholic, apostolic and Roman religion is the religion of the great majority of the French', justifies the concordat but does not re-establish a State religion. The other phrase in the preamble, that the Catholic religion may expect the greatest good from the restoration of public worship and 'from the particular profession of it by the consuls of the Republic—*de la profession particulière qu'en font les consuls de la République*'—does not mean that the power of the consuls was not a laic power, simply because the Pope recognised that the actual consuls were Catholics (as they certainly were by baptism), especially since the same Concordat in Art. 17 provides for the case of a First Consul who might not be Catholic.

On the other hand, we must not believe that the Gallican Church was restored because in Art. 4 it is said that the canonical institution of the bishops would be made 'according to the forms established in regard to France before the change of government'. The whole structural basis of the State had changed and the Holy See by Art. 13 acquiesced in the abolition of church property, undertaking not to disturb the consciences of those who had purchased it or their heirs and assigns. Bishops, parish priests, and other clergy ceased to constitute an economico-political order, and became functionaries of the State, paid out of public funds, subject to the discipline of the new system. This system became harsh under Napoleon. To counterbalance bureaucratic and police interference the only resource was to lean on Rome, and through the influence of Rome to regain a lost personality. The other bishops and priests who, remembering the old monarchy or still imbued with Gallicanism, put themselves at the service of the autocrat, suffered all the consequent humiliations.

The Napoleonic Concordat was the first of modern type between Rome and a laicised State, on a jurisdictionalist basis and in contractual form. It was natural that the Pope (and many with him) should think that this was a first step towards a return to the old system. This the Restoration seemed to confirm, but it was an illusion. The concessions made by Pius VII to Napoleon and the measures wrung from the Pope by force and trickery showed instead how no other idea than political policy had inspired the framing and actuation of the Concordat. The 'Organic Articles' annexed to it were framed in order to re-establish the rights of the absolute kings over the Gallican Church—such as (among the best known) the 'verification' of the acts of the Holy See and of the decrees of Councils; the prohibition to bishops to gather together in councils or leave their dioceses, even to go to Rome, without government authorisation; the revival of appeals *ab abusu*, to be settled by the Council of State; the obligation laid upon seminary professors to subscribe to the Four Gallican Articles of 1682, and similar measures. Here was a rebirth of Gallicanism out of season. Pius VII protested against Bonaparte's duplicity, then tried diplomatic ways, but he obtained nothing.

On becoming Emperor, Napoleon wanted to use the Church to consolidate his personal power, employing promises and intimidation. Fearing lest the name *Pères de la Foi* covered the fathers of the disbanded Company of Jesus, he prohibited them, and the same with any other non-authorised religious association. To these, criminal proceedings gave the character of unlawful associations. In the meantime, he sought to lure the Pope to Paris. To make of him an instrument of the Empire, to confront the courts and peoples of Europe with the moral support of the first religious authority of the world, was an idea not to be despised, even by Napoleon. Pius VII after many hesitations agreed to come to Paris in the hope of obtaining the withdrawal or modification of the Organic Articles, of the decree against religious congregations, and of the recognition of divorce in the Civil Code. But he obtained nothing. Having crowned the Emperor in Notre-Dame, he himself only with great difficulty was able to leave Paris after a five months' stay which might be considered a gilded imprisonment. Government control over the Church of France and of the other countries annexed to the Empire became ever stronger, and reached the pitch of a systematic and legalised persecution and at the same time a domination of the church schools, clergy and parishes. In the official catechism for French Catholics we find the following question and answer: 'What do we owe to our Emperor? We owe to Napoleon love, respect, obedience, military service. To honour and serve our Emperor is to honour and serve God Himself.'

Rupture with the Holy See was inevitable. It came about over a political event, the anti-English blockade. Pius VII refused to follow out the orders that in January, 1806, Napoleon sent him from Munich, in his quality of 'Protector of the Holy See and Emperor'. Napoleon, crowned Emperor by the Pope, had adopted the Carolingian title of Protector of the Holy See, but he was not the stuff Christians are made of and to his Empire the faith of the IX century was wanting. His might be considered a laic-Gallican Empire. Nor, for his part, did Pius VII believe that by lending himself to the coronation he was restoring Christendom and making of Napoleon the Charlemagne of the XIX century. That improvised and ephemeral empire (though this could not then have been foreseen) was based on the principles of the Revolution, already propagated throughout Europe and rendered actual by the French victories. Glory and the dictatorship of arms gave Napoleon a personal international power, which he turned to his own advantage just as he wanted to turn to his advantage the power of the Church.

If Pius VII lent himself to the religious act of coronation of one who, according to the theories of the Curia, must be regarded as the usurper of the throne of France and of other thrones, he did so to avoid greater evils which, it was feared, would follow a refusal. Also, perhaps, because many were then grateful to Napoleon for having put an end to the bloody anarchy of the dominion of the Assemblies and for ending the schism by making the Concordat. At a distance of time we may say that Pius VII was weak, but in a period when the world trembled before Napoleon and the clergy of France showed, by continued adulation and complete subjection, that it had lost the courage of the days of the Revolution, the oscillations, hesitancies, weaknesses and discouragements of Pius VII are understandable. He partially redeemed his act in crowning Napoleon, both by his resistance to him over the anti-English blockade, when he would not drag the Holy

See into war, and also when, after the annexation of the Papal State to the Empire, he replied by excommunication. Napoleon laughed at the excommunication, made the Pope prisoner, continued to harass the Church, and, posing as religious head, himself directed church committees and councils, obtained the annullment of his marriage from a diocesan church court—thus avoiding judgment by the Holy See—wrung consent to his proposals from the imprisoned Pope and obtained additions to the Concordat. When he understood that the Pope repented of this and would withdraw his consent, as he actually did in refusing to ratify the new text, Napoleon promulgated it and brought it into force by his own authority. Pius VII, his moment of weakness past, continued his resistance, declaring the nominations made by the metropolitans to be null and void, the bishops appointed intruded and the bishops who consecrated them schismatic. Events were precipitated: the Pope returned to his States when Napoleon abdicated at Fontainebleau.

These historically tragic events would not be unlike others in the Middle Ages if there had been the same faith and if the Napoleonic Empire had had something of the religious character of the Holy Roman Empire of other days. But this new Empire, (apart from its caducity, through the lack of a solid structure and tradition), was purely military and personal and could not assume the character either of that of Charlemagne or of Louis XIV. Napoleon falsified the historical process by creating religious quarrels that did not fit the rhythm of the time and by bringing back theories that no longer had any real significance. What would survive of the Napoleonic experiment, in relations between Church and State, would be on the one hand the laicization of absolute power, following upon that of democratic power—in spite of the parade of the coronation at Notre-Dame and the other superficial religious manifestations that Napoleon himself voided of meaning—and, on the other hand, the achievement of a concordat that lasted nearly a century, and a system of perfected police control of the Church, which future laic-jurisdictionalist governments would find useful.

On the disappearance of Napoleon it was believed possible to wipe out the First Republic, the Directorate and the Empire, to put everything back as it was, frontiers, privileges, rights, politics, economy, culture; as if from 1789 to 1815 twenty-five years counted for nothing, and could be cut out of the historical process and remembered only as a long and dreadful dream between the evening watch and the new dawn that rose on Waterloo.

§ 46.—The State that was taking shape through the bloody experiences of the Revolution and of the Napoleonic wars could no longer mould itself either on the absolute monarchies or on the reformistic State of the second half of the XVIII century. In spite of everything, a new democracy had been born. It must not be thought that democracy sprang ready made from the brain of the French revolutionaries like Minerva from the head of Jove. Democracy in the concrete is itself experience, and its process is still in course; a century and a half cannot suffice to change the political history of thousands of years, in which democratic forms appear as rare oases in a vast desert. After the popular republics of the Middle Ages, and, in certain respects, after republican Rome, the French republic may be considered the first experiment in democracy; we must go back to Athens to find any term of comparison, but neither Rome nor Athens, with their slaves and helots, nor the medieval republics with their serfs and guilds, can provide conclusive models for the first French republic or that of North America. It is from these that the experience of contemporary democracies takes its origin.

Practice alone would bring to light the nascent problems of democracy and the various attempts to solve them. The endeavour to abolish the past led the France of the Revolution to destroy all the organic social forms, which had become ossified, producing breaks and voids that impeded the circulation of life in the body politic. But when the estates, guilds and other particular organisms had been demolished, there remained only the individuals face to face with the State. The struggle was polarised between the two terms—on the one hand the individual, who, craving omnipotence, transformed liberty into licence; on the other the State which, in order the avert an individualistic disintegration, transformed its democracy into tyranny. If it were possible to regard this period as a physico-mechanical phenomenon, we might say that the breaking down of the old social dykes let loose warring natural forces, which fought for an equilibrium only gradually attainable. It was not a physical phenomenon; the human mind and will entered into it far more than has been believed, but they had to feel their way in the new experiences that had found realisation in social life in the midst of seething passions.

A mediation between the State and individuals was wanting. And since social life cannot develop without a progressive articulation, there arose a spontaneous crop of factions, clubs, directorates, parties—variable, unstable organisms, since they were born of mob passions and precarious situations, and also because they lacked economic and juridical bases such as property, the corporation, the social estate. These temporary and passion-inspired groupings acted as mediators between the individual and the State, but in the absence of a tradition everything was created *ex novo*. Only slowly could a unitary consciousness be formed, binding citizens together in a common aspiration. The variability of groups, the creation and dissolution of parties, the practical difficulties to be overcome led to a constant remaking of constitutions, an ever-changing series of representative men, the elimination, even by the guillotine, of those who at a given moment seemed a danger to the State. This instability led to an accumulation of powers in the hands of a few, and thus, as outcome or solution of the successive crises, the way was paved for the Directorate, the Consulate and the Empire. The first experiment in an inorganic and individualistic democracy was doomed to collapse between demagogy and tyranny.

But if democracy failed because it was inorganic, its elements remained to fecundate new forms, to enter into fresh experiences and to overcome the practical difficulties. The reawakening of the popular consciousness and the proclamation of the Rights of Man and of the Citizen remain as the substratum of all the new State régimes of civilised countries. Criticised, denied, trodden under foot, the basic rights re-emerge because the consciousness of possessing them and of the duty of exercising them survives. Formulas apart, which suffer the corrosion of history and adaptation to events, the idea of the equality of individuals and that of political rights as inherent in the person of man as a citizen persist. Napoleon would be inexplicable save through these two basic ideas—individual equality (the civil code) and political rights (the popular origin of power), which persist even when, through his victories and his genius, in practice he transformed his power from popular into personal and from free into the authoritarian power of a police régime. This phase was not the negation of the principles of the popular origin of power and of equality, but the counterpart to the excesses and degeneration of democracy.

From these two phases there emerges now the idea of Nation, now the idea of State, as something above and beyond both the uncertain and fluctuant collective will and the transient personal will of the autocrat of genius. The administrative and military structure of the State, which forms a depersonalised whole, working through a higher and lower bureaucracy, responded to the need of replacing the organisms and social hierarchies that had been suppressed, and of providing a new articulation to collective life. There would be no more mercenary and professional armies, no more royal guards, whether Swiss or of other nationalities; the army belongs to the nation, the army is the nation. All who are able must bear arms, conscription will be compulsory, there will be permanent standing armies. This transformation is not simultaneous or identical in all countries; history is not made by passes of a magic wand. There are countries, like England and the United States, where even to-day permanent compulsory conscription has not been introduced; through geographical and political conditions it has not been necessary, though they have their regular armies and their fleets. But apart from differences between one country and another, it is no less true that the conception of the modern State leads towards a national army and, in a general way, towards compulsory conscription.

This State centralisation has two causes—personal power and democratic individualism. The personal dominion of Richelieu and Louis XIV had broken down the resistance of vassal princes, independent cities, clergies and autonomous bodies. The Revolution and Napoleon did the rest. France henceforward would be the most centralised State imaginable, not only in administration but politically, ecclesiastically, culturally. Paris dominated and overwhelmed the other cities. A centralised and perfected police force and a State spy-system had been wanting; Napoleon supplied them and made them the most effective nexus of a centralisation at once statal and personal. Once the individual had become the basis of society, once all the intermediate nuclei had been destroyed or reduced to mere forms, once the origin of power had been attributed to the people (even if such an origin was inconvenient), there was nothing left but to centralise and control the life of the State and social life, and to summon the people to express the collective will by plebiscites or electoral vote, so as to give a kind of effectual title (though without intrinsic value) to the power won or usurped. Napoleon's example would be followed.

As part of the picture of such a centralised State comes control of the autonomous, private, religious school. Under the *ancien régime* no one challenged the Church's office of instruction and education. The States, or rather the monarchies, sought to guarantee themselves against papal encroachments by prescribing the theories to be taught on regal rights; the universities enunciated the official theories in ecclesiastical matters and prosecuted theories contrary to religion and morals. The prohibition against the Jesuits of France, who might not teach or have schools, was an exception, due to their clash with the Sorbonne. Democracy was bound to bring compulsory education. The State school was a consequence; Napoleon turned it into a school for the State. The school system was centralised. The old Sorbonne became a State University; under it were all the schools of France, down to the elementary ones. Methods, programmes, classes were unified, stabilised, arranged so as to form the citizen-soldier and subject.

The State of the *ancien régime* had rested upon the ethics of the Christian religion and on Canon Law, according to the prevailing or official confession. The school therefore was always definitely confessional. The conception of natural law as autonomous, antecedent to the Christian religion and independent of it, gave the motive for a cultural parting of ways. The democratisation of the laicised State rendered this parting of ways effective through the State school. Napoleonic authoritarianism added a finality—*for* the State. The Church under Napoleon aimed at collaboration in a confessionalised State school—a servile collaboration which continued under the Restoration. Historically, the educational monopoly would be the starting point for a new struggle between Church and State for the vindication of educational freedom—a struggle still in course, and the end is not in sight.

The State or the Nation, alternatively or conjointly, could not affirm their autonomy and laicity save through a philosophy in which they were recognised as realities. Such a philosophy, if it were to be reconcilable with the Church, would have had to admit a duality; this very fact would have attenuated the autonomy of the Nation, whereas on the contrary the tendency of thought and of the social fact was towards the Nation monistically conceived, with the State as the realisation of its potentiality. The French Revolution conceived the nation as a common will, a sovereignty of the people, a collective solidarity as opposed to the will of a few (oligarchy), to the sovereignty of one (monarchy), to division into 'estates' (hierarchy). Napoleon consecrated this national ideal with his victories, and it outlived him. Although there were those (they are always present) who sought to monopolise the idea of nation, assimilating it to their own political and economic group, yet the idea remained as something above and beyond even the State, a kind of hypostasis of the people as a whole, with its characteristic genius, race, language and history.

It was possible to talk of a nation not only in respect of France, which was a political unity, but also in respect of Germany and Italy, which were divided into various independent States. Even for the peoples of different race and language subject to foreign powers there was talk of nations from the moment a consciousness of national personality began to take shape. Little by little two feelings developed, which became theories and political movements, that of nationality as a personality to be vindicated against foreign governments, and that of the nation as a political order in which the people, a living and united community, was the constitutive and finalistic factor.

F. G. Fichte in his letters to the German people, then subjugated and reduced to impotence by Napoleon, not only incited them to a political rising in order to win their civil independence, but saw in the nation a characteristic vitality, a unity of living thought as participation in a single soul, that of 'Germanity'. This was conceived as a pantheistic entity in which and by which the phenomenal existence of the individual found consummation. Up to Fichte the current conceptions such as liberty, equality, fraternity, nation, people, parliament, sovereignty, division of powers, religion, church, had been those worked out by jusnaturalism and by the Enlightenment of the XVIII century. Fichte introduced a new element which gave a synthesis to the collective or popular will of Rousseau. This, taken as implicit will, would have no means of making itself understood; taken as explicit will it would become the will of an oligarchy or of a tyrant. Rousseau led first to the Convention, then to Napoleon. Fichte instead created a mysticism that gave the nation its basis, as the idea-force of a people that had yet to find its unity and to achieve its moral and political unification. Fichte conceived the nation pantheistically, whereas the French revolutionaries had conceived it rationalistically. The two ideas could not be amalgamated. The nation rationalistically conceived was integrated by the international and humanitarian idea, while the nation mystically conceived had no further integration than in itself and in its own exaltation.

The nation rationalistically conceived became an active principle not so much of external differentiation as of internal assimilation. International policy was to set its course by the new irenic conception. Wars would be waged not for the magnification of the dynasty, for between nations there could not be struggles and wars born of occult interests and the jealousies of reigning houses, nor of the spirit of conquest and domination, but only in defence of national integrity. In declaring war on Austria, the National Assembly of Paris on April 20, 1792, proclaimed that 'conformably to the maxims consecrated by the constitution, which forbid France to undertake wars for aims of conquest or to employ her forces against the liberty of any people, the French nation takes up arms only for the defence of its independence; the war into which it has been forced is not a war between nation and nation but the just defence of a free people against the unjust aggression of a king'.

It is true that this magnificent label covered damaged goods, that is, a war provoked by the various parties and by the Court, for purposes of domestic policy. But it is also true that France in that war had no aim of conquest, nor did she seek to deprive any other nation of freedom and independence; in certain respects she was safeguarding her own independence. Apart from this, there are historical moments when words signify far more than the men who utter them, and indeed assume an objective character that transcends the intentions with which they were uttered. The case is comparable to the prophecy of Balaam's ass. It would have been impossible for an absolute monarch to have spoken such words; he was obliged to think of the good of the country in function of the good of his House. The new international conception appeared in the world in practical (and no longer theoretical) form precisely at a moment when in practice it was being violated by its very exponents. It was no rare happening (the Holy Alliance would be another example), but such as to create possibilities for the future.

Immanuel Kant with his *Essay on Perpetual Peace* (1795), published at three years' distance from the declaration just quoted, gave a liberal basis to the international organisation he had in mind. As yet the word *liberal* (as the adjective of liberty with a political significance) was not born, but the liberalism of the XIX century would find in Kant its first and greatest philosopher. The separate States which, according to Kant, would form a federation would each have its free popular government, and accept the principle of the non-intervention of one State with another; an international *status quo* would be guaranteed by the popular will to make no war for greed of conquest or in violation of rights. It was then believed that the motives of war sprang only from the ambitions and jealousies of the reigning houses and from their absolutism.

Kant's international construction derived directly from his conception of the State. This was to be a State *de droit*, in which the bond of law renders possible the co-existence of free and equal individuals, based on the principle: 'to act outwardly so that the free use of the will can accord itself with the liberty of each in harmony with the general laws'. This presupposes the other Kantian principle, that 'right consists in the possibility of accord between general and reciprocal compulsion and the liberty of everyone'. Such principles throw light on the conception of the liberal State, in which wellbeing is sought by the initiative of individuals, which can be developed not only in so far as there exists a legal order which the State can use coercion to enforce, but also in as much as the individuals know that they must enjoy their liberty in such wise that their use of their own liberty can accord with that of others. The inner conception of duty coincides with the rationality and liberty of the man-noumenon; realisation on the juridical plane of the State *de droit* brings the co-existence of individuals, that is, the possibility of an accord of coercion with freedom.

When this conception was carried to the international plane, the federation of States was no longer conceived on a basis of egotistic interests to be vindicated one against the other, but on a basis of the right and liberty of individuals reciprocally recognised and respected. Kant's plan demanded above all a transformation of the domestic régimes of the separate States; the American Republic and the French Republic then appeared as the first beginnings of such a transformation. But the liberal conception of the State *de droit* would need time to ripen it; it would have to overcome the triumphant demagogies; perpetual peace could be only its crowning outcome. Kant was not a dreamer or a mystic, but at the moment when all the barriers limiting human activity were falling and the popular-national spirit was coming into being, the concept of liberty presented itself in a mystical guise as a liberation from the political, civil, ecclesiastical and economic suffocation of the past. Liberty assumed the aspect of a good in itself, liberty for individuals, liberty for States, not as a gift from without but as an inward development of personality, whether the personality of the citizen in the face of public powers or that of the State in the face of other States. It is the vision of the individual and humanity together, which in its binomial form sums up the whole social fact and reduces it to liberty and law. Within this vision had arisen the gigantic shadow of Napoleon, who seemed to destroy it. He wrote at St. Helena that his ideal was to form a confederation held together 'by unity of codes, of principles, of opinions, of sentiments and of interests'. Whether true or not, Napoleon passed, the vision remained.

§ 47.—The Napoleonic Empire, the thrones he had assigned and the kingdoms improvised under his lightning victories, could not form a lasting edifice in the political field, national and international, for two necessary factors were absent. One was a tradition responding to the feeling and interests of the populations, as a basis for the new order; the other an international equilibrium in which to find stability amid the clash of European forces and egotisms. As it had arisen through fortune of war, with misfortune of war it collapsed. Historians and philosophers question what would have happened had Napoleon emerged victorious from Waterloo? The question, in the realm of facts, is as idle as the others, what would have happened had Caesar not been murdered, or if the Crescent had won at Lepanto, or if Germany had won the Great War. Yet from the sociological standpoint it may be answered that even had the opposite of what actually happened occurred (which would have been the opposite only of what was considered a decisive episode), the social factors were such that neither a man of genius nor an acquired situation would have turned aside the historical process to any great degree. By another series of events which we cannot trace and with other men in command, a sociologically analogous solution would have been reached. With or without Waterloo, Napoleon's international edifice, either speedily or gradually, was bound to collapse or to become transformed.

What Napoleon's victors ill-understood and all the restorers of the past failed to see clearly or to grasp with foresight, was the necessity of utilising the constructive elements that had accumulated through the revolutionary experience. The period between the American Revolution and the Congress of Vienna was a forty years of elaboration of politico-social theories in the harsh soil of experimental fact, and to this task all had been called, kings and popes, nobles and clergy, bourgeoisie and masses, generals and soldiers, politicians, literary men, philosophers, courts, universities, clubs, parties, in a terrible and tragic melting-pot. To think that after forty years of such compass it was possible to return tranquilly to the past with the idea of a restoration was to admit the reversibility of history, to cut short a process in course, to make what had been done undone, to wipe out events from the memory and heart of nearly two generations. The responsible men of the Congress of Vienna were more or less aware of what had happened, but as gathered together to solve political, dynastic and international problems, they brought to bear upon them an attitude of mind unequal to the situation. They were thinking in terms of a Europe of courts and dynasties, of balanced alliances, of State hegemonies; the Europe of the nationalities and the Europe of the people escaped them.

The basic principle laid down at Vienna was that of the *legitimacy* of the sovereigns. The idea of legitimacy is inherent in that of power. It is impossible to conceive a power that is not legitimate; if it is not so, if it is a case of usurpation, it cannot be considered as power; there will have to be either a restoration of the old power or a legitimisation of the new. The problem consists in the criterion by which a power can be considered legitimate or able to be legitimised. For those who hold that all sovereign power resolves itself into the will of the people, apart from the theories in support of this thesis, legitimacy and legitimisation are two aspects, the one regular and the other irregular, of the proclamation of the person invested with power. In the first case he is legitimate in accordance with the traditional laws which are, at bottom, laws of the people, having its actual or presumed consent. In the second, legitimacy is achieved because the people ratifies the usurpation that has taken place, giving it value.

At Vienna there was no room for this thesis. What was affirmed was the historic right of the European dynasties as inherent in the sovereign families, independently of the popular will. The historic rights combined, in actual fact, with rights of conquest (the case of Poland) and with the interests of the victors—all titles of a dynastic character and of traditional law adapted to the circumstances. Invocation of the accepted principles was made only when they coincided with the interests of the great victorious powers and of their allies, and not in other cases, like those of Venice, Genoa and Saxony. When it was discussed at Vienna whether the kingdom of Saxony should be preserved or not, and Alexander I observed that the Saxons wished to remain united, Francis of Hapsburg replied that 'a prince can, if he will, cede a part of his country and all its people; if he abdicates, his right passes to his lawful heirs. He cannot deprive them of it and the whole of Europe has not the right to do so'. Talleyrand, on the basis of the principle of legitimacy, defended the rights of Louis XVIII, King of France.

The historic rights of legitimacy and heredity, the rights of conquest, when all popular consent was ruled out, on what principle should they rest? In default of popular sovereignty, there was no other principle than the sovereignty of God, with which the princes felt themselves to be invested. The three signatories of the Holy Alliance, the sovereigns of Austria, Prussia and Russia, declared that they considered themselves 'as delegated by Providence to govern three branches of the same family . . .' The manifesto of the Holy Alliance was called the Declaration of the Rights of God, as against the Declaration of the Rights of Man. There was no other choice—either a sovereign laic power, finding its origin in the nation or people, albeit through an historic right, or else a sovereign power rendered religious as founded on the authority of God and supported as such by the official Church.

The scholastic contractual theory that reconciled the two tendencies had been buried in silence even by its traditional and keen supporters, the Jesuits, before their suppression. Others, through fear of Rousseau, dared not advance it. Nor in those days would it have been understood by men who wanted to wipe out the memories of the Revolution and re-establish the absolute power of the kings. The Pope, who in the case of Napoleon, by crowning him had recognised the principle of a *de facto* government legitimised by the will of the nation, now could not but rejoice in the open recognition that sovereign power was derived from God. At the same time he was on his guard lest all the injustices that men were about to commit should be laid to the account of divine authority, including those towards the Holy See, whose historic rights were challenged through an understanding between Vienna and Murat, then King of Naples. When the quarrel with Rome had been settled, the map of Europe remade, while certain parliaments were permitted, with restricted powers and as a sovereign concession (apart from the traditional parliament of Great Britain, which was likewise passing through a reactionary period), the practical result was the affirmation of the absolutism of the kings, based on the religious principle of divine authority and maintained through the close union of Throne and Altar. Here was an historic variant of the old Divine Right, no longer counterposed to Church and Papacy, but as opposed to the right of the People and of the Nation.

Legitimacy, absolutism and the religiosity of the monarchic power were conceived at once as the basis of each separate State and as a common element of an European union or League of kings. In order to guarantee the maintenance of the new political and international system springing from the Treaty of Vienna, the Treaty of Paris and the Proclamation of the Holy Alliance, coercive methods were required, both against pact-breaking sovereigns and against rebellious populations. Hence the constitution of the four great victorious States as heads of the new Europe—Austria, Great Britain, Russia and Prussia. After a qualifying period, France was added to their number. The small States were set in the second rank, dependent on the great ones. Austria built them into a system of political balance of power and had the lion's share—the Germanic Confederation on the one side, the Italian States on the other.

To this system the mystical impulse was provided above all by the need for peace, which was keenly felt after twenty-three years of continuous warfare all over Europe and in America, carried on by large forces on sea and land. An organised peace, whatever its nature, always finds a sentimental acceptance on the part of the masses. With peace was combined the return of the dispossessed sovereigns, traditionally associated with paternal methods, in the midst of peasant populations as in the German principalities. Exiled nobles and priests were coming home, churches were being opened or restored, traditional worship was reinstated; even in England the Government took to building or restoring churches and to improving the conditions of the Established Church. The open union of the churches with the sovereigns gave many a sense of stability and social security, which transformed itself into a kind of ideal conception. The principle of authority, re-established in its twofold character, natural and supernatural, to those who had suffered by the revolutions and wars was a reason for faith in the future.

All this constituted the necessary premise for the development of a mystical sentiment, were there anyone or anything to awaken it. The Holy Alliance presented itself as a divine message, a word inspired from above. Here was a document of kings speaking of God, of Jesus Christ, of love, of justice, of peace. Alexander I of Russia was its prophet (before he too turned tyrant), wavering between humanitarianism, the Gospel, liberalism, and the Divine Right of Kings. Nor was a prophetess lacking, to inspire it—Madame de Krüdener. Goethe judged that act 'the most beneficent thing that has ever been tried by humanity', and many were of Goethe's opinion. But Great Britain had not given her signature. Castlereagh wanted to deal with affairs not to proclaim principles. The Pope had refused to put his signature side by side with those of two religious heads, the one Lutheran, the other Orthodox, in an appeal to the Gospel. All the other States were considered as minors or of the second rank, and were not invited to sign. Moreover, the Minister of the Austrian Empire counted far more than the Emperor; Metternich was of Castlereagh's mind rather than that of Alexander I. For him the manifesto of the Holy Alliance and all the propitiatory festivals that accompanied it meant much less than the military agreements and international police system on which the new authoritarian order would be founded, so as to impose on Europe the will of the four great victorious Powers and above all of Austria.

The Holy Alliance, idealised and felt as an aspiration that was coming to fulfilment in spite of historical contingencies, diplomatic intrigues and the incomprehensions of the men of *realpolitik*, could be believed to be a step forward and not a return to the past, a mystical motive touching the peoples, not a mere calculation or red herring on the part of the sovereigns. It contained a necessary principle for the salvation of Europe—that of international solidarity based on ethico-juridical foundations. Seeking as it did to be the negation of the immediate past, it yet contained certain of its elements. The necessity for finding a common ground, over and above the interests and egotisms of the dynasties, led to the establishment of moral principles of a general character. On this plane the opponents of dynastic absolutism and the champions of the nationalities found motives for polemics and a real basis for their antithetical constructions. Two mysticisms confronted each other on a political and sentimental plane—that of the champions of the Holy Alliance and that of the supporters and vindicators of liberties. The latter tended to revise the democratic positions with a view to a greater insistence on personal liberties, which were more appreciated now that they were lost; the former, insisting upon the value of the traditional authority, wanted to re-establish it, as a principle of order and of salvation. Freedom and authority were conceived as antithetical; Catholics as such allowed themselves to be dragged in the wake of the idealists of authority.

One of the most notable, and certainly the most interesting, representative of the period was the Savoyard, Joseph de Maistre (1754-1821). He passed as a kind of secular holy father of the Catholic absolutist revival and reaction, but he was more than this; he played a considerable part in the elaboration of the anti-rationalist, historicist and romantic thought of his time. He fought popular sovereignty and the contractual theory of the origin of power, upholding a kind of mystical transmission from God to the monarchs by providential participation. This thesis must not be taken in isolation; it was part of the system of philosophical traditionism, or fideism, which taught that our natural knowledge is not autonomous but is derived from a primordial revelation; thus just as society is a divine institution, power is likewise a divine participation. The value of such traditionism is indestructible through the direct action of Providence. If Providence permits evil, it does not fail to intervene to chastise the authors, making use of the devil or of the evil men themselves; if the chastisement is delayed it is in order that its effects may be more salutary. Under this aspect the Revolution was an instrument of Providence. Christianity, perfecting the primitive traditionism, is a perennial element of unification of human societies. This task is fulfilled by means of the Catholic Church. The other churches no sooner broke away from Catholicism, than they lost the characteristics of integrity of faith and apostolate. Only the Catholic Church preserves and increases them because at the centre stands the Pope. The national churches, such as the Gallican, have degenerated from true Catholicism because they limit the powers of the Pope and contest his infallibility. The Pope, in De Maistre's thought, is a vital principle of social conservation and renovation, for he incarnates in the highest sense the authority of God. The Pope, not this or that pope with his defects and the human insufficiencies of his government, is the active principle of the religious unity that must become the active principle of the unification of the world. De Maistre in his exceptional and prophetic form, while exaggerating traditionism at the expense of reason, performed a constructive work, for he restored to its place the sense of historical contingency, which the Encyclopedists under certain aspects had despised; he gave a motive to the historical process, interpreting it in an apocalyptic sense, and he centred it in Catholicism and hence in the Pope, as the maximum organisational expression and supreme authority of the Church. The idea that a new Christendom was emerging from the chaos of the French Revolution, permitted by God for the purification of society, for its re-creation by the sacrifice of so many, forms the mystical, historical, romantic substratum of De Maistre's thought.

He did not stand alone. The Count de Bonald, who had much the same outlook, had many followers in France, and he and De Maistre inspired a large band of writers, literary men and philosophers of the pre-romantic movement, the greatest of them being Chateaubriand. A place apart and one of very high order was occupied by Maine de Biran (1776-1824), who, abandoning the sensualism of Condillac, reknit in philosophy the interrupted line of thought of Malebranche and Pascal. In his spiritualism, understood as experience of a higher life, grace in the Christian sense fulfils and transcends nature, the irrational potencies of which cannot be subdued by pure reason and the simple training of the will. The historical experience of Christianity coincides with the inner experience of the Christian. Maine de Biran, as often happens, had no great influence on his own time, but later, when a new spiritual revival was preparing against the flatness of positivism, his psychology entered into the stream of modern thought.

What was then of import (and Maine de Biran's contribution was here precious) was the historical, psychological and literary restoration of Christianity as an integrating element of society, whereas rationalistic and naturalistic thought of the XVIII century (which was still in the ascendancy) had conceived of society as dissociated from Christianity; and at the same time the historical reconciliation of nature with grace, instead of the breach between humanism and the supernatural life. To this movement de Lammenais dedicated the first part of his literary activity, becoming famous with his *Essai sur l'Indifférence en matière de religion*. By misfortune this movement was largely authoritarian and reactionary, denying any right to the people. Society was looked upon from the gregarious standpoint, the individual conceived as an eternal minor. According to de Bonald, man is born to be taught and led; his teacher and leader, that is, the Monarch, is considered as belonging to an almost extra-human order like the Church. The monarchy is pre-existent to society since it constitutes society; its title is exclusively a divine title, its basis is divine tradition. An anti-rational authoritarian and religious traditionism is the soul of Bonaldian thought. His philosophy of knowledge is expressed in the proposition (which Catholics cannot accept): 'For all knowledge, even profane, faith precedes reason to form it and reason follows faith to affirm it'. The origin of society is analogous. Thus this mysticising and historicising movement of the pre-Romantic Catholics attenuated or denied reason for the sake of faith, attenuated or denied liberty for the sake of authority, attenuated or denied historical initiative for the sake of traditionism. And just as the Holy Alliance very soon threw aside a mystical fervour which had no solid basis, and showed itself for what it was, a reactionary and utilitarian political policy, so the movement of the Catholic traditionists lacked mystical nourishment, and, once the prophetism and lyricism of its pioneers had passed, became for many a reactionary and utilitarian conception of religion as the instrument of the absolute monarchies.

CHAPTER XII

LIBERAL, NATIONAL AND SOCIAL MOVEMENTS—POLITICAL AND RELIGIOUS REACTION

§ 48.—From 1815 onwards political reaction raged. Institutions created and measures taken in the preceding period were abolished wherever possible, even where this was useless or dangerous. Although certain prudent men at Vienna had recommended that the princes should use moderation in making changes, nearly all, and particularly the least intelligent, thought that the best way of governing was a return to the past, even in the fashion of clothing. Court calendars and aristocratic privileges were restored to honour. In Rome the Jews were driven back into the ghetto. Ferdinand of Spain restored the Inquisition and ordered the surrender of property formerly held by the religious Orders, taking it from its purchasers and possessors.

The European situation was then assuming very marked features. In half a century of experiences various factors had changed the basis of society, among them, with far-reaching effects, the abolition of the privileges of landed estates and of commercial and occupational restrictions and the establishment of the equality of citizens before the law. This was leading to the development of nascent industrialism, to free interchange, to the reinforcement of the bourgeois class and to the proletarianising of the worker. To attempt to reduce these movements to impotence was a desperate enterprise; of this the princes became aware only when it was too late.

This civil and economic substratum of the situation presented itself under a political aspect, for in the political field reaction against the past was in full swing on the part of absolutist sovereigns, court nobles, and novelty-hating clergy. Battle was engaged for the preservation or reconquest of the political constitutions and liberties. In Spain where absolute government had been restored there was a demand for the

Constitution of 1812; of the two parties involved the authoritarian party was called *servil*, the constitutional party *liberal*. Thus the adjective liberal and later the noun liberalism were introduced into Europe, creating in certain spheres much the same impression as the words bolshevist and bolshevism to-day. The liberals of those days were constitutionalists; the bourgeoisie wanted to share in power so as to limit the absolutism of the monarch, to prevent the return to class privilege, to protect themselves against dispossession of the property obtained during the revolution, or to regain it, as in Spain, and to ensure civil and religious liberty and equality.

Was there any possibility of a constitutional system in which the people would share in power, without freedom of opinion, of association, of speech and of the press? That is to say, without the direct and congruous means for the vindication of rights and interests? These liberties were demanded and defended all the more vigorously in that they were precisely those that the reaction denied or so limited as to make them useless, deeming them the cause of the disturbances, instability and revolts. Hence an irremediable friction both with the absolute governments and with the Church, who opposed such liberties as implying freedom of worship and the spread of theories contrary to Christian faith and morals.

Pius VII in a letter to Mgr. de Boulogne on April 29, 1814, had protested against the draft Constitution prepared by order of Louis XVIII, because Art. 22 allowed 'freedom of religions and of conscience'. He wrote: 'By the very fact that the freedom of all religions is established without distinction, truth is confounded with error, and the holy and immaculate Spouse of Christ, the Church outside which there can be no salvation, is placed on the same footing as the heretical sects and even as the perfidy of the Jews.' Further on he added. 'Our astonishment and our grief were no less when we read Article 28 of the Constitution, which maintains and promises freedom of the press, a freedom that menaces faith and morals with the greatest perils and certain ruin.' Louis XVIII did not accept the draft Constitution as it stood and introduced various modifications. The Charter granted proclaimed the equality of citizens, freedom of the press (with the corrective of government censorship), and freedom of worship, while at the same time declaring Catholicism the State religion. In France it was then impossible not to concede this minimum, and it was necessary to repeat yet again (after the Napoleonic Concordat) that the sale of national property was irrevocable. It was also added, in order to tranquillise the country, that it was forbidden to enquire into opinions expressed or votes cast by any citizen under the revolutionary régimes. It was thus hoped to achieve appeasement, while leaving public opinion a certain if limited vent through the press and parliament.

The most active and intransigent current among the Catholic clergy and hierarchy declared itself against all constitutionalism, rallying round the absolutist courts and especially the Court of Vienna. For Rome and for intransigent Catholics, Vienna was assuming a new aspect in the defence of Catholicism. For three hundred years it had been considered the most stalwart defence against Germanic Lutheranism, against the Islamic peril and against the encroachment of Slavonic Orthodoxy. Now Vienna, no longer the reforming and enlightened court of Joseph II, had become the centre of anti-liberalism. Vienna was thus playing a fourth role in European Catholic politics.

The Company of Jesus, reconstituted by Pius VII in 1814, showed at once so much vitality that it could be said never to have ceased to exist—so rapidly had it regained the spirit and discipline of its founder. In the struggle the Jesuits were for the most part with the intransigents, with the *ultras*, with the reactionaries, as they were called in the various countries, and, as was natural, they became the most hated. They were persecuted by the constitutionalists and at the same time looked upon askance by the absolute governments and national clergies, who fostered memories of a not very distant period. The monarchies wished indeed for the support of the Church, they were disposed to restore the confessional State which the Revolution had overthrown, but they wanted bishops and parish priests to be in the service of the Government, with a State monopoly of education even in respect of episcopal seminaries, and in general the privileges of the jurisdictionalist system.

Where, as in France, there was a modicum of constitutionalism, the governments sought to propitiate the liberals and those of revolutionary tradition by restricting the activity of the clergy where it might be troublesome, whether in the realm of religious and moral defence through the press and associations, or in that of education and even in the preaching of religious missions. These, on the other hand, were not always confined to religious matters, but with an often excessive or ill-considered zeal, turned into a campaign of intransigence and political reaction, now in accord with the bishops and government, now against them. No position could be more uncomfortable than that of the Church of France. It was officially bound to the Bourbon monarchy under the device of 'Union of the Throne with the Altar', and in certain respects was hampered in its ministry or embarrassed by the reactionary policy of the day. Hatred for the Government rebounded on to the Church that supported it, and the intemperate attitude of the *ultras* was undermining the system of constitutional monarchy. Thus irreligion and indifferentism spread among the cultured classes, in the bourgeoisie and even in the mass of the people whom, it was believed, the support of the political power would have brought back to religion.

Conditions in the countries under absolute government were no easier than in France. Rome sought to restore the hierarchy where it was lacking, to resystematise relations with States by means of new concordats—as with Russia, Bavaria, Poland, Naples and Sardinia—or else by other forms of understanding, like the *modus vivendi* Bull with Prussia and other German States. Rome facilitated in every way the return of the religious Orders, reopened seminaries, schools, colleges, and gave full support to the new religious institutions. But all this was at the price of a revival of the jurisdictionalist bond of the Church to the State, and of the support of the Church to the monarchies in order to keep the subject peoples under control. The political aims of the Holy See then coincided with those of the absolute governments, and although Rome sought to limit her intervention to religious questions, she did not fail to favour the governments in their ungrateful task of suppressing revolutionary movements; all the more so in that the Papal State did not lack its malcontents, conspiracies and liberal propaganda. The condemnations of the *Carbonaria* and the other secret societies corresponded to the tradition of the Curia and to the aversion of Catholicism towards any sort of cryptic and ritual mysticism. The Carbonari were denounced not only as enemies of Throne and Altar, but as men reared to crime, who did not shrink from use of pistol and dagger. Cardinal Consalvi, experienced in politics as he was, had dissuaded Pius VII from repression, especially since in Vienna the princes themselves were concerned at the line Rome was taking, under the direction of the Cardinals Rivarola and Pacca. He succeeded partially in promoting a political amnesty, but he did not succeed in checking the *sanfedisti* (a kind of clerical Fascists before their time), who were terrorising towns and villages with the idea of fighting liberals and freemasons. It was now that the Catholic reaction attributed to Freemasonry an extraordinary potency, beyond what the facts warranted (though in certain countries they were not inconsiderable), stirring the imagination and feelings of the people.

The Bavarian Catholics were forbidden to take the oath to the Constitution without an explicit reservation safeguarding divine rights. Consalvi, in order to find a way out and faced with the threat of conflict, obtained a declaration from the King of Bavaria that the oath to the Constitution concerned only the civil life of the country, not the law of God or Catholic doctrine. Apart from this episode—which showed a just anxiety not to confuse civil liberties with the naturalistic theories with which they were usually associated—any aspiration towards constitutional forms, towards political independence and the emancipation of the subject classes, even if promoted or favoured by Catholics and priests, was spied upon, delated, repressed. The Inquisition was again functioning in Rome and in Spain, while in the other Catholic States the Holy See gave the governments the support of its authority for the repression of liberal propaganda. In many countries and with not a few bishops political concern overshadowed even the pastoral ministry and the defence of principles.

At that time Rome believed that a return to the confessional State was possible, indeed, that it had already been effected; and that by methods of religious repression and police repression the factious element could be eliminated, tranquillity, order and a benevolent paternal régime installed, and little by little the very concessions granted in the matter of parliaments and popular liberties pared away. This increasingly rigid attitude on the part of the Holy See and of many bishops, bound to the monarchy and imbued with the old absolutist and regalist theories, combined with the anti-liberal campaign of the

Jesuits and other religious Orders, led to a confounding of a lawful constitutionalism and morally acceptable political liberties with the naturalistic and revolutionary theories. This helped to bring a still deeper cleavage between the Church and those aspiring to liberty and who, as liberals, passed for anti-religious and anti-Catholic when many of them were no more so than the very reactionaries who leaned on the Church to make of her an instrument of power or a means in the political struggle.

The confessional State as revived in the Catholic countries was formalistic and equivocal. The monarchs and the men of government might be inwardly more or less religious than those of before the Revolution, but the cleavage between religion and politics had already come about, nor could it be healed by the so-called union of Throne and Altar. The old structure of the confessional State had collapsed, the new structure was wobbling without sound foundations. Legitimism hampered the Church by binding her to determined dynasties. Absolutism meant a revival of the tendencies of the national churches towards Episcopalism and Gallicanism, and strengthened the position of laicising jurisdictionalism. The consecration of Charles X of Bourbon at Rheims was intended as symbol of the monarchic-Catholic revival of France. Rivers of rhetoric flowed; many old priests, in good faith, wept for joy and dreamed, some of Louis IX, some of Louis XIV. There were those to whom this sacred rite gave a sense of a reparation for the sacrilege of the execution of Louis XVI. And this notwithstanding that the papal coronation of Napoleon had intervened; at twenty years' distance this could not be forgotten by friends or foes of either Napoleon or the Papacy.

In this embarrassing union of State and Church a connecting link was wanting to bind the peoples to the absolute and religious power. The Church was now no mediatrix between the people and power, nor did the State mediate between people and Church. The two together widened the gulf between them and the people by coercive laws, police methods, repeated condemnations, (even though interspersed with amnesties), without reckoning with the exigencies of the middle and popular classes that were agitating. The series of revolts and repressions throughout Europe and the revolts in Latin America, which had been going on since the Napoleonic period, taught the rulers nothing but to fear the future and to aggravate repressive methods. The papal State was one of the most affected because its administrative methods were out of date, its legislation incoherent, while the system of entrusting civil and political offices to ecclesiastics was inadequate and dangerous through its mixed character, sacred and profane, paternal and inquisitorial, sacerdotal and based on police-methods. Brigands and *sanfedisti*, freemasons and liberals, ravaged the tiny kingdom which should have been a model for other States. To so many evils was added Austria, whose policy weighed on the Pope-King, or better, on the Pope and on the King of Rome. Vienna under Metternich was in the period of the Restoration what Madrid had been under Philip II at the time of Trent, with the difference that Metternich did not resemble Philip either in his faith or in his mysticism, but only in his method of imposing on the Church a particular policy, that of Austria, which he believed coincident with the salvation of Europe.

The religious situation was no better in the Protestant and Orthodox countries. Here the official churches had not suffered the crises of persecution and separation of the countries dominated by the Revolution and by Napoleon; they maintained the old privileges of union with the State and their dependence on the monarchs as religious heads. Yet the dissident movement was increasing day by day, presenting itself here and there as a political and religious liberal movement. Indifferentism had gained the upper classes and the working masses, and was such as to rouse the anxiety of the governments. The latter in the twofold exercise of spiritual and temporal power used every kind of repression and oppression. They, too, feared revolts. The police system was triumphant in Prussia, terrorism in Russia, tyranny in Turkey and over the other populations subject to Constantinople. Great Britain too, where Parliament was still in honour, was passing through a very difficult period of distress and agitation. The economic crisis, the sequel to the Napoleonic wars, was interlocked with political and social agitation of a very marked character, in favour of reforms with democratic aspirations. The monarchy was in decay, with the madness of George III and the dissolute life and unpopularity of the Regent. The aristocracy was incapable of coping with the agitation, and feared the people. An organised police force was lacking, especially in the big cities, which were liable to become the prey of exasperated mobs and peasant risings at a time when agricultural prices and especially the price of wheat were falling. The demonstrations in which the Phrygian cap and the tricolour were carried in triumph then aroused far more fear than those of our own post-war period with the Bolshevist hammer and sickle. The outcome was bloody repressions and blind reaction symbolised by Peterloo and the Six Acts.

Fortunately a group of men of worth and initiative, among them Robert Peel, William Huskisson, and George Canning, understood that it was necessary to return to Pitt's earlier tradition and to face courageously the problem of domestic reforms, among them that of the electoral system, penal reform and financial reform, as well as to change the course of foreign policy, till then, with the usual oscillations, bound to the reactionary policy of the Continent. Thus the British Government refused to intervene in Spain, which had revolted in order to win back the Constitution of 1812, and encouraged the resistance of the Spanish colonies; it supported the revolt of the Greeks against Turkey, and broke away from the concert of Great Powers that went under the now tarnished name of Holy Alliance. With Canning begins a liberal policy in foreign affairs.

§ 49.—In 1830 it was fairly clear that the policy of 1815 had failed, both in the international field and in that of the separate States. By then Metternich was no longer in a position to create a new European system. Charles X fell and the crown of France was assumed by Louis-Philippe who laicised it. In Spain Christina and Isabella had gained the upper hand through the support of the liberals. Belgium was breaking away from Holland, winning her independence and giving herself a constitution. Ireland, led by O'Connell, had won the fight for Catholic Emancipation, while Great Britain was on the eve of the political reform of 1832. In Italy revolts had broken out in Bologna, Modena, and Parma, with the constitution of provisional governments, soon overwhelmed by the Austrian armies. In Piedmont Charles Albert had acceded to the throne. In Warsaw the revolt had broken out which would lose the Poles the liberties they had possessed since the Congress of Vienna. Greece had already fought her war of independence. In America Bolivar died after winning the independence of the Spanish colonies; Brazil had been declared an independent State, though its emperor came from the House of Portugal; the Argentine had its republic and Mexico its dictators.

The aspiration to independence of the peoples subject to foreign governments—like the Greeks under Turkey, the Italians of Lombardy and Venetia under Austria, the Latin-American colonies under Spain and Portugal, Belgium under Holland—presupposed two principles: that of nationality and that of self-determination. These principles drew their life from that of popular sovereignty. At a distance of time the connection between the three may seem non-essential, but then it was in the logic of the historical process. The idea of popular sovereignty, as a generic right of the people and as its consciousness of personality, did not necessarily spring from a particular theory, like that of Rousseau, but it could not be isolated from the jusnaturalist tradition and from contractualist reminiscences, which had so many centuries behind them and had received three far-reaching historical confirmations—the victory of the English Parliament over the Stuart Monarchy in 1688, the independence of the British colonies in North America in 1783, the triumph of French democracy over the monarchy in 1792.

The Restoration which, denying the right of the people, gave everything to the sovereign, even the faculty of disposing at will of kingdoms and provinces, in striking the pendulum to one extreme provoked a swing to the other. The idea of nationality, which in the XIV century had found concrete expression in the autonomous monarchies as against the idea of the Empire and in the national churches as against the medieval Papacy, at the beginning of the XIX century returned to life as personality and popular will in the face of the absolute monarchies. Already nationality was shaping a theory of its own, disentangled from rationalistic and abstract jusnaturalism, and based on an historical, national concrete fact that was emerging from the consciousness of each people. The Encyclopedists had conceived a rationalistically *a priori* society founded on the idea of a wholesome and good nature as source of rights and on this they built up individual rights, forms of governments, the features of society. The idea of nationality, on the contrary, was based on the historic past of each nation or people, with its particular character, its language, literature, religion, mythology. Thus history was no longer looked upon as a sequence of facts and dates, external as it were to the people, but as the very life of the people, its soul, its mental formation, its feelings, its needs, its aspirations and achievements. Giambattista Vico's theory returned spontaneously to life; the many had never heard of it, but the psychology of the time was ripe for theory and facts to find an unexpected convergence. Before there could be consciousness of the value of such a theory, thought, under the impulse of Romanticism, had to take a plunge into the irrational, into intuitionism, into mysticism, with a confusion of ideas and a passion of feelings that showed a new and spontaneous, and by that very fact incomplete, phase of the general orientation.

Romanticism was not merely a literary movement. It found its expression and its name in literature and as such was known, loved, worshipped, distorted, extolled, attacked, belittled. But Romanticism was something deeper and more interesting than a literary movement. Literature cuts itself off from the currents of thought and art when it is cramped within aesthetic or academic circles and becomes a refined and cryptic exercise. True literature mingles with events and with the vital currents, feels their influence, and shares in the pathos of history. Then it is no longer literature in the narrow and sometimes even contemptuous sense of the word, but poetry, music, art, history, philosophy, politics, all that man thinks and expresses in a given manner, under given impulses, with ends that may or may not be clearly divined and expressed.

From the literary aspect, Romanticism was the movement of liberation from the classical rules of composition, from the logical order in speech, from the restricting unities of tragedy. It meant a free rein to fantasy, escape from the present, worship of the past, a leap into the unreal. It was the irrational turned towards the sensual, the mystical bordering on the orgiastic, the substitution of the passional for the lyrical, the abandon of the idea for experience of the concrete. All this brought confusion, but it gave a means of renewing the material and technique of poetic and artistic expression and marked, after its fashion, a step towards a conception of art that might in its turn be called national and liberal; national because it sought in the national sagas and myths, in the traditional, religious and political sentiments of a people, for inspiration for poetry, romance, history, painting or sculpture; liberal because in casting off classical bondage and the academic style and in emancipating itself from ecclesiastical and political censorship, it idealised the free and independent people, with its passions, its feelings, its history of sorrows and glories, like a being awakening after long lethargy to the intoxication of a sunny morning.

All the literary and artistic excesses of Romanticism, sentimental, liberal, fantastic, anti-religious, over-religious, corresponded to the political excesses of the revolutionaries, that is, to a negation, through excess, of the very motives that had impelled them to act, through the lack of inhibitions that is felt when the social environment is in upheaval. The underlying exigencies of the Romantic movement were sound: a return to historical, traditional, ethnical, religious and popular values—not a return such as some, in their exaggeration, wanted, to even the style and incongruencies of a Middle Ages that could not be brought back to life, but taking such values as permanent values of the historical process, successively realised by the culture of the various ages. Such a balance between past and present could be achieved only through a violent eruption, which in its impetus would overthrow established and crystallised positions.

The national and political passions already aroused in the bourgeois masses and in literary circles by forty years of upheaval, were quickened by the works of thinkers, poets and artists. In spite of the censorship, of the police and of customs barriers, the rebel writings had a large diffusion. It was impossible to confine this seething of minds and imaginations within closed circles and under strict supervision. 'Liberty!' was the cry of literary Romanticism, 'Liberty!' echoed the middle classes, 'Liberty!' was the demand of the merchant and traveller. The slogan was again directed against the tyrant and the oppressor, against the police and the priest who was bound up with them; a slogan no longer in the name of an abstract Humanity, as at the end of the previous century, but in the name of the reborn nation, of a history inspired with new life, of oppressed minorities, of peoples languishing under the foreign yoke.

The Romantic movement was at bottom a movement of Catholic liberation, albeit with an immense confusion of ideas and sentiments and with an unloosing of passions and signal deviations and distortions. In France the pre-Romantics, De Maistre and Chateaubriand, were followed by de Lamennais, Victor Hugo, Alfred de Vigny, Lamartine, Montalembert. In Germany Catholicism found a new force of attraction, both as the medieval church and as liturgy and living tradition. To the names of Stolberg, Schlegel, Werner, all converts, are united those of Görres, C. L. de Haller, Adam Müller, who took up the position, new for Catholics, of fighting the egotistic and absolutistic principles of the Restoration in the name both of the Germanic Middle Ages and of a Catholic conception of the State. Rationalism was then the flag of the Protestants, held high by Voss, while the revival of the Germanic soul came through the Romanticism of the Catholics.

There is kinship between English Romanticism and German, but Romanticism in England assumed a form of its own, more intimate and more mystical, in an endeavour to represent everyday reality as '*romantic and supernatural*' (Wordsworth) and the romantic and supernatural as '*expression of reality*' (Coleridge). The effort to escape from the flatness and formalism of social life and from a puritanism that for many had become exterior led towards the *fantastic* and *symbolical*, coloured by historical reality (Scott), towards passionate and frenzied denial (Byron), towards mystical idealisation (Shelley), to aestheticism (Keats), or apocalypticism (Coleridge), or the moralistic critical philosophy of Carlyle's first manner in *Sartor Resartus*.

The religious substratum was submerged in the pantheistic excess of aesthetic, philosophical and passionate elements. Coleridge's *Apostolic Church* had no foundations. Emerson came from America, bringing a message of spiritual elevation. It was in this period that the Oxford Movement was developing, with Pusey, Keble and Newman, as a true breath of spirituality, a religious revival which, without merging, enters into the romantic spirit of the time and becomes coloured with Catholicism. Newman actually passes over to Catholicism and would be for many years its intellectual and moral leader. At the same time there is a development of the ritualistic and dogmatic movement that became known as Anglo-Catholicism.

In Italy two great Romantics, among a large band of writers, attracted general attention; they would have an immense influence on the thought and trend of the *Risorgimento*—Alessandro Manzoni and Giuseppe Mazzini. The first gave expression to Catholic and political Romanticism, the sanest, most balanced and loftiest that could be conceived, in works of genius such as the *Promessi Sposi*, the *Tragedie* and the *Inni Sacri*. Mazzini envisaged a new religion, synthesised in the device 'God and People', a kind of popular theocracy, in which the people expresses and actuates the divine will. This religion for him was not torn out of history but was the historical continuation of Christianity, in accordance with humanity's movement of indefinite progress, which would end by forming a family of all nations. The principles of liberty and nationality are closely connected with the moral reform of the individual and with human brotherhood, all derived from God and from the divine idea mystically vivified. Mazzini's was a kind of secular prophetism in which, together with intuitions of genius and profound, optimistic convictions, there are irremediable contradictions and historical and religious incomprehensions, due to his anti-Catholicism. But Mazzini's influence came chiefly from his personality, through which his ideas inspired the most ardent ethical and political feelings.

Political and social life was becoming permeated with liberal Romantic thought. The great currents of reform were two, the one liberal, of the middle classes, the other collectivist or communist or socialist, of the working classes. The first movement aspires to take over the command of the State, the other to transform the economic conditions of labour. Both develop with more or less utopian ideals and with improvised theories, and through various experiences and social convulsions arrive—the liberal movement first, then the workers—at concrete results.

The bourgeois class, seeing the unrest of the working classes and remembering the unloosing of the mobs during the Revolution, sought to limit the scope of so-called popular sovereignty, even while they needed to lean on this in order to correct the sovereignty of the monarchs. Benjamin Constant (1767–1830) was the theorist of French liberal constitutionalism, and his theories passed the frontiers. Under Napoleon he had fought against the popular sovereignty which served to justify dictatorial power, through the expedient of a delegation of power by the people. After 1814 he maintained that the theoretical basis of power was indeed the sovereignty of the people, but understood not as an actually operative sovereignty but as the source of power; no one could arrogate to himself sovereignty unless he received it from the people either as its delegate (the parliamentary deputy) or as its highest representative (the monarch). Benjamin Constant took care to limit the scope of political power: it is not a social totality, for individual rights limit it. These must be vindicated against any sovereignty that might infringe them, whether that of the people or that of the sovereign. Hence, to the separation of powers (Montesquieu's theory) must be added the principle of the separation of the power of the king from that of his ministers. The formula was fixed by Thiers in 1830 in the famous sentence: *The King reigns and does not govern.* Just as the people is sovereign and does not govern and its sovereignty expresses itself at the polls, in plebiscites, in referendums, so the monarch (or president) becomes the symbol of the State, the element of balance between the powers divided into legislative, executive and judicial, the active element in the crises of public life; at the same time he is above the political responsibility with which his ministers are invested, and these at the same time are answerable both to him and to the people, as represented by parliament or summoned to the polls.

Louis-Philippe in granting the new Charter of 1830, to the words 'King by grace of God' added 'and by the will of the Nation'. Thus the legitimist theory collapsed and the contractual theory triumphed. In the Belgian Constitution the words 'by grace of God' were omitted, not through any wish to ignore the authority of God, but because no reigning house could claim an historic right that could be presented as a mission received from God. It was the representatives of the Belgian people who chose the new monarchy.

In the France of Louis-Philippe as in independent Belgium and in the England of William IV, and wherever parliaments existed, the constitutional basis was provided by the tax-paying classes with a varying property qualification. It was an *élite* that represented the people. The working classes had no political rights and their social agitations roved among the experiments of utopian theorists like Saint-Simon, Fournier and Robert Owen, and humanitarian and practical enterprises such as working-men's fraternities, friendly societies and other educational associations which corresponded to the ideals of Mazzini, or abortive revolutionary movements to which Karl Marx gave his theoretical and practical prophetism.

Between the two wings, the liberal-conservative and the revolutionary working-class movements, the democratic current was making headway. Tocqueville, in his *Démocratie en Amérique*, sought to prove to the French bourgeoisie—which still had lively memories of the Constituent Assembly and the Directorate and which had already forebodings of the movement of the working masses—that it was possible to organise a democracy on a rational basis, without falling into anarchy or tyranny. Democracy in order to be a vital government would have to be achieved in a régime of freedom; then the rhythm of the parties, as in England, would be effectual in avoiding mob demagogy. A party cannot be improvised; it must grow gradually, gathering strength as little by little it is nourished by the aspirations, interests and needs of groups, families and currents of thought and action, which it expresses on a parliamentary and electoral political platform. Only thus can a party survive the blows of fortune, create a tradition, insert itself into the life of the liberal-democratic State. The idea of party alarmed many, who saw in it the condensation of villainous ambitions of dominion, a means of dividing the country. Abate Rosmini, who looked forward to a free Italy, wanted parties to be excluded from its ideal constitution, just as Plato wanted to exclude poets from his republic. But reality is stronger than prejudices. From political, religious and social ideals diverse currents and conflicting forces arise, which in order to express themselves in the political field have need of parties. The better these are organised the better they correspond to that organic mediation between the individual and the State that is a sociological necessity.

Modern democracy starts from an equalitarian and individualist conception; the régime of liberty is based on the free expression of the popular will. The isolated individual would have no potentiality for making his needs felt; the popular will would not be able to express itself as a whole save by passing through different stages of its formation. If these are established *a priori*, mechanised, without sufficient elasticity, they do not correspond to popular mobility and may lead to violent crises. The same is true of parties when they become closed consortiums or rigid directorates. On the contrary, in the French Revolution the organised party was lacking, and instead there was the rapid and factious movement of the clubs, groups, and meetings; this could not but degenerate into anarchy and tyranny.

1848 was the historic year for revolutionary movements in Europe, in nearly every country. From 1830 onwards there had been sporadic agitations, conspiracies, revolts, showing the unrest of the peoples and the instability of governments and of monarchies. England had overcome the agitation of the middle classes, who obtained the Reform Bill with the Whig victory of 1832, and the campaign of the Chartists (1835–41), who failed to obtain the universal suffrage they demanded. But discontent was still rife among the workers, and was fed by news from the Continent. America, having separated itself from Europe, by the Monroe doctrine had signified its right and will to defend itself against possible claims upon it; at the same time the Europe of the Restoration met with its defeat. The independence of the nationalities, where it is not yet won (as in Greece) is proclaimed, willed, demanded. Where there are no constitutions, these are obtained or won by revolts. In France the monarchy falls and the democratic Second Republic is proclaimed. Everywhere the political and social movements are permeated with Romanticism. The liberal currents among Catholics assert themselves with originality of thought and moral vigour; in France, in Italy, in Germany, the best history, philosophy and poetry comes from the men of these currents. Even England has its Catholic revival, and there are similar movements among the Protestants of every country.

In the same year, 1848, international Communism asserts itself with the celebrated Manifesto drawn up by Karl Marx, in which three fundamental points are fixed, which would later form the basis of the international socialist movement—the class war as the reality and history of society; capital as the product of the labour of the many for the benefit of the privileged few; the abolition of private property as the means of eliminating class conflicts and wars between nations.

Each particular movement had its own causes. The political and social movements were not on the same plane; there was no similarity between the civil war of Spain, the insurrection of Russian Poland, the risings in the various States of Italy, the republican revolution in France. But everywhere the aspirations for liberty, national exaltation, working-class movements and romantic ideals intermingled with the various interests of the several groups and peoples, producing a whole such as to cause the enthusiasm of hope and the despair of illusion.

1848 was not and could not be resolvent; it was an eruption, an affirmation, a warning. As such it marks an unforgettable historical date, which accentuates more strongly than ever the principle of nationality and independence, the political system of freedom, the democratic aspirations of the bourgeoisie, and the social demands of the workers.

§ 50.—Among Catholics the movements based on civil and political liberties, in favour of national independence and at the same time demanding religious liberties, were followed in Rome with a mixture of favour and concern. There was then a lack of comprehensive vision of a social and historical character. Naturally concern for religious interests predominated, with the fear of introducing pernicious novelties into the traditional theories and Catholic praxis. Thus the various movements were judged in their particular individuality. The first, historically, was the Irish. The demand for religious freedom in the name of civil rights, as maintained by O'Connell, corresponded to St. Paul's *civis romanus sum*; and though Rome was inclined to grant the British Government such a right of interference in the appointment of Irish bishops that it was inaccurately termed a veto, yet she followed with increasing favour O'Connell's vigorous campaign under the motto 'God and Freedom'.

The word freedom had a different sound on the hither or farther side of the Channel, and therefore it rang with a different timbre on the banks of the Tiber, all the more so in that local reverberations among the traditional Catholics and bishops had planes of refraction of a character quite their own. In France Lamennais, abandoning monarchic traditionalism, had revived O'Connell's watchword, making it the motto of his paper *l'Avenir*; in its pages the young Lacordaire and Montalembert were fighting their first battles in a relentless struggle against the adversaries of the Church and the adversaries of liberty. Among the latter were many of the clergy, those of Gallican tendency, bound to the traditional power, who looked askance on the July Monarchy and were therefore ill disposed towards Rome which had recognised as King one who, for them, was the usurper Louis-Philippe of Orleans; as well as the Ultramontane clergy, who were engaged in an anti-revolutionary and anti-liberal campaign, in accord with the Jesuits.

Lamennais, addressing himself to such clergy, had written: 'You tremble before liberalism. Make it Catholic and society will be reborn.' *L'Avenir* had accepted the July Monarchy, but demanded the recognition of religious freedom on the part of the Government, which was playing with Gallicanism. It therefore preferred the separation of Church and State, the abolition of all jurisdictionalist bonds, and fought the prejudicial and embarrassing alliance of the Throne with the Altar. Montalembert's formula of *a free Church and a free State* anticipated that of Cavour. The young Montalembert had asserted himself vigorously in the Senate, as a Peer of France, over the question of educational freedom, a question that had then become one of the gravest to be raised in France, as later in Belgium. His speech was one of those successes that mark a date. He had concluded: 'I shall rejoice all my life that I have been able to consecrate the first accents of my voice to demanding for my country the one liberty that can strengthen and invigorate her. And I shall rejoice equally, always, at having been able to bear witness in my youth to the God of my infancy . . .'

Rome, which had greeted with enthusiasm the emancipation of Catholics in England and Ireland in the name of liberty, which had welcomed the separation of Catholic Belgium from Protestant Holland, even through a revolution, and which yet had not approved the insurrection of the Catholic Poles against Russia, was much concerned at the *Avenir's* campaign—all the more so in that there was no lack of complaints and remonstrances from the Paris Government and from the bishops to the Holy See, and journalistic controversy was very heated. Before then Lamennais, young and ultramontane, had been held in high consideration in Rome and his activity had been followed like that of an apostle. The subsequent liberal phase bewildered many. Father Gioacchino Ventura, philosopher, orator and political figure, already known as a liberal and in relations with Lamennais, had sent warning that in Rome the campaign for liberty seemed excessive. Under these circumstances, Lamennais' decision to go to Rome and to leave in the Pope's hands the decision whether *l'Avenir* should continue or not, was untimely and imprudent. O'Connell—as later Windthorst—avoided such appeals, which embarrass the authorities and are not favourable to bold particular enterprises, since they confuse responsibilities and embroil situations. The three 'pilgrims of liberty', Lamennais, Lacordaire and Montalembert, went to Rome in 1832 and were kindly received by Gregory XVI. They soon perceived that the Roman world was not that of Paris, and that problems were there seen in another light and under more characteristic aspects. Confidence of approval turned into fear of repudiation.

On August 15, 1832, the Pope published the encyclical *Mirari vos*, which held in substance a condemnation of the theses defended by *l'Avenir*. The act of Gregory XVI was on the traditional lines of the Catholic Church, and aimed at a general affirmation of doctrine with clear references (though without mentioning names) to the theories of Lamennais and the others, and in general to the theses of those who would later be termed Liberal Catholics. Gregory takes the idea of liberty in its negative aspect as the abolition of all bonds and checks, and applies it to Church discipline, to marriage, to the civil and political order, to relations between State and Church. He makes liberty of conscience derive from the indifferentism that will not discriminate between error and truth; hence, he adds 'the quest for an absolute and unbridled liberty'. Elsewhere he speaks of 'a liberty that dares everything', or 'the most uncontrolled liberty'. Papal documents never speak against liberty in general, but against liberty thus qualified or in some similar fashion. Gregory, even while referring to it as 'unbridled', meant the liberty that the liberals were then demanding and of which Lamennais and the others were unreserved champions. Turning to these, who maintained that freedom of the Press would benefit the truth itself, which could more easily be defended and propagated if it did not encounter civil obstacles, Gregory, after calling such liberty 'the most disastrous' and 'execrable', appealed to the tradition of the early Church, to the V Lateran Council and to that of Trent, in order to reaffirm the Church's right to censor books and printed matter and prevent their diffusion.

Lamennais' other thesis, the separation of the State from the Church, is treated very decisively by the Pope. He denies that it would be useful to either, and reaffirms the necessity and duty of the closest agreement between the two, which, he says, has always been most salutary and happy for both. In an earlier passage he had reprobated the doctrines that undermine the loyalty and submission due to princes 'kindling everywhere the torches of sedition', and he had inculcated the duty of obedience to the powers established by God. 'Thus divine and human rights rise up against the men who, by the blackest manoeuvres of revolt and sedition, strive to destroy the loyalty due to princes and to overthrow them from their thrones.'

The conservative wing greeted the Pope's words with relief. The 'pilgrims of liberty', who were at Munich (the centre of the liberal-Romantic current among German Catholics), while not concealing their distress, submitted and ceased the publication of *l'Avenir*. Their adversaries were jubilant and raised a cry of victory. Unfortunately Lamennais fell away and left the Church. *Les Paroles d'un Croyant* revealed his inner tragedy, which found its chief source in a false notion of contingent problems; he inclined to transport the relative into the absolute. Lamennais believed at first that the monarchic principle would save France and society and was its foremost champion. When he saw that neither for Napoleon nor for the Restoration had such a task been possible, he turned to Rome, to the Pope of De Maistre, who would restore society from its ruins—generous ideas but of hybrid conception, so that the religious plane was confused with the political, the supernatural and mystical with the natural and realistic, with no differentiation between the inner virtue of Christianity and of the Papacy and the human acts of papal policy; hence a kind of unrealisable theocracy.

The ideal and Christian Rome clashed in him with the earthly Rome as his critical and disillusioned spirit saw it, and he forsook it. He turned to the people; democracy was his third vision. Of democracy he demanded, as Mazzini did, the palingenetic virtue that he had found neither in the monarchic principle nor in Roman policy, and he failed for the third time, asking what the human, the contingent, the historical, could never give.

The encyclical of Gregory XVI, occasioned by political events, was not inspired by contingent ideas, and in the political realm it did not contribute much to arresting the trend towards liberty. It would serve to orient Catholics towards considering such problems with the traditional outlook. As was natural, Catholics continued to be divided in the political and social field. The traditionalists became still more closely bound to the absolutist forms and the reactionary monarchies. The so-called Liberal Catholics were more cautious in speaking and writing, avoided confusing their philosophy with that of the liberals, gave better study to constitutional and social problems, and suffered in patience and humility the blows that fell on them from above—like the generous Father Ventura, then general of the Theatines, who expiated his ill-repayed friendship with Lamennais by banishment from Rome (taking refuge with the Duke of Modena) and, later, when he was recalled, was even forbidden to continue his beloved studies in philosophy; or that other great soul, Abate Rosmini, who submitted immediately to the decree of the Index, condemning his pamphlet *The Five Wounds of the Church.*

A pause, a phase of discouragement, of reflection. Events were tending towards the liberal movement. Catholics were concerned in them and it was impossible to leave the problems of religious, educational, political and social freedom in the hands of the enemies of the Church, and to remain tied down to the defence of authority. Bands of Catholic writers, historians, thinkers, politicians, contributed to the new orientation. In Italy alone with the famous names of Manzoni, Rosmini, Gioberti, Ventura, Silvio Pellico, Niccolò Tomaseo, were combined those of the historians Cesare Balbo, Cesare Cantù, Carlo Troya, Abbot Tosti, and still others. Here the problem of political unity, of independence from Austria, united with that of liberty. The current that would be called 'Neo-Guelf' would have wished for a confederated Italy led by the Pope. Gregory XVI believed that severity would check the political movements, while Vienna kept watch that new ideas should not infiltrate into Italy and that their exponents, especially among Catholics and priests, should be firmly dealt with.

In Italy the national problem was coming to maturity, and the neo-Guelfism of the Catholics brought a potent contribution, preparing the atmosphere for the independence and unity of Italy. (It was in 1843 that Gioberti published his *Primato morale e civile degl'Italiani*, and Cesare Balbo his *Speranze d'Italia*.) In France the Catholics, led by Montalembert, were fighting for educational freedom and defending the Jesuits against the threat of fresh expulsion. The Restoration had inherited from Napoleon the system of a school monopoly organised for the benefit of the State. Mgr. Frassinous, elected Grand Master of the University, had emphasised this monopoly with the slogan 'for God and for the King'. Lamennais had come into collision with the powerful Monsignore, who sought to impose the Gallican ideas with which he was imbued. Montalembert's first speech in the House of Peers had been on freedom of education. In 1840 the Minister Villemain placed the seminaries under the strictest State control, and this irritated the bishops who protested on grounds of Canon Law. Montalembert carried the struggle into the political field, not only in regard to the seminaries but to the whole of education in schools and colleges, urging Catholics to organise and fight. In a pamphlet that had a wide resonance he wrote: 'Catholics have nothing to hope from either the Chamber or the Crown. For too long they have been in the habit of counting on everyone save on themselves . . .' And he added: 'For us Catholics who in so many modern States are in a minority, and who, even where we are in a majority, derive from it neither rights nor strength, freedom of the Press is a need of the first order. It is freedom of criticism; criticism is the lever that overthrows the walls of citadels and of prisons.'

The government and the pseudo-liberals of the July Monarchy struck back. The *Journal des Debats* wrote: 'It is true that the Charter envisages freedom of education, but the Charter has been made not for them (the Catholics) but against them.' To Montalembert, Ozanam,

Lacordaire, Froisset, Veuillot, de Parisiis, Dupanloup, who were fighting and urging the bishops to assert themselves, the hostile Press dissertcd on the themes of obedience, submission to the laws, respect for authority, as principles that should be inculcated by Catholics according to the papal encyclicals. And when they realised that on their lips such arguments rang false, Villemain in 1844 brought in an education bill which increased the fetters of State monopoly while an anti-clerical offensive was unloosed in the shape of legal proceedings. Montalembert replied by a powerful speech in which he adopted the motto of the Poles against Catherine II: 'We love liberty more than anything in the world, and religion more than liberty', adding, 'we do not conspire, we live in the light of the constitutional liberties and liberty is our sun, which no one shall take from us.' The anti-liberal law was passed, though not with the majority that the Government expected. Lamartine commented: 'Strange! For fifty years we have been giving liberty to everyone, God excepted!'

This conflict put the seal on what had been coming to a head since 1830, and which *l'Avenir* had advocated in an absolute form (and in this lay its mistake)—the separation of the Church of France from ties with the Monarchy. In 1838 Frederick Ozanam (the generous-hearted founder of the Conferences of St. Vincent de Paul, which have now spread all over the world, including the Mission countries) could write in a farseeing letter: 'For us Frenchmen, slaves of words as we are, a great thing has been done: the separation of the two great words that seemed inseparable, the throne and the altar.' This corresponded to a statement by Dupanloup, in a letter to the Princess Borghese (November 2, 1843): 'Gallicanism is inevitably dying; there are not eight moderate Gallican bishops in France.'

On June 16, 1846, Pius IX was elected Pope. The enthusiasm in Italy and in Europe generally was immense, and together with just hopes there was a romantic excess, due to the atmosphere of the time. The anti-religious or none too religious liberals were more enthusiastic than the rest. Guizot hailed 'Pius IX accomplishing the reconciliation of the Catholic Church with modern society.'

Assuredly, more than a little had changed in the general trend of Catholics and the Papacy. On the one hand there were those who sought to reconcile liberty with the Church, on the other those who claimed to reconcile the Church with liberty as they conceived it. Father Ventura, who had gone to visit his family in his native Sicily and had remained there nursing a broken arm, was at once recalled to Rome and became the trusted and intimate political adviser of Pius IX. He was entrusted with the task of setting forth the Catholic ideas on liberty, and he did so in two addresses at St. Andrea della Valle, taking the occasion of a panegyric on O'Connell, on June 28 and 30, 1847. His addresses had been revised by the Pope, and could be taken as authorised ideas, though the Jesuits of the Church of the Gesù (between whom and the Theatines of the neighbouring St. Andrea there was a certain rivalry) had criticised them vigorously in a public sermon.

Father Ventura, living in a revolutionary period, emphasises a first distinction: *active resistance, no, passive resistance, yes*. The first means for him violent revolt against oppression, 'but the drama of oppression is nearly always the same. The slave becomes tyrant and the tyrant becomes slave.' The second, accompanied by what he calls *active obedience*, is, for him, resistance to laws contrary to God and conscience and at the same time the task of moral and political transformation of the State: 'Catholic teaching does not proscribe action; in forbidding forcible resistance it does not forbid protest by the paths of legality and justice...

These principles are for Father Ventura the necessary basis of liberty. He added, with a certain lyrical sweep, that it was the Church that had upheld the *metaphysical* freedom of the soul, the *domestic* freedom of woman, the *civil* freedom of the slaves and helots—'in the same way, the Church alone will be able to proclaim *political* freedom in establishing the just and veritable limits of obedience and command, the just and veritable rights, the just and veritable duties of the people and the government.' He passes on to *freedom of conscience*. In the *absolute* sense certainly it is indifferentism, impiety and the denial of divine revelation, but in the *relative* sense, 'that is to say, in regard to the civil power which has not received from God the mission of preaching and interpreting the Gospel, it is a Catholic principle which the Church has professed, has defended . . .' What then is to be said of the union of the Altar and the Throne? That it is right to think that they have collaborated for the common good and may do so again, but it would be a grave error to think that if the throne fell the altar would have to fall with it. That would be to make the faith of the people dependent on 'the good or evil will of the prince', which would be 'to destroy the last vestige of human dignity'. He concluded: 'Let us unite love of the people with love of the Church and love of liberty with love of religion.' Father Ventura's addresses crossed the frontiers and for some years were the most authoritative utterance for the Catholics of Europe, who were then looking towards Rome in the hope of the greatest events that history had ever seen. They thought the Middle Ages were returning, in a new and gentler guise, to regenerate modern Europe.

In 1848 the Italian insurrection took place to the cry of *Viva Pio IX!* In France priests were blessing the 'trees of liberty' and the Second Republic came to birth with the participation of Catholics. In Germany it was Mgr. Ketteler who demanded liberty in the name of the Church. 'The liberalism of 1848,—so he wrote a few years later—'was a declaration of war on the old despotism born in the XVI century, which had spread over the whole of Europe. It fought loyally for the liberty of all. It had, it is true, only an imperfect idea of true liberty . . . the young liberalism of 1848 was honest enough to recognise the liberty of the Church.'[1]

The idyll of liberty and Church, as presented in the Romantic period of 1848, was soon over. The experiment of Pius IX in liberal policy was not a happy one through a series of internal and international difficulties, which could not have been met save by men of the requisite ability, with sure vision and swift decisions. The national war against Austria could not fall within the wishes of Pius IX. Nor could he compromise the rights of the Papacy to religious independence for a situation in which its sovereignty became merely nominal or might be wholly suppressed. To-day, at a distance of time, we may say that his flight to Gaeta was ill-advised, and still more so his return to Rome with a French army. Then events were precipitating, and international policy weighed heavily upon decisions. The Catholics of all countries, especially of France, were stirred by the happenings in Rome, all the more in that Pius IX in two years had become the most popular man

[1]*Das Kulturkampf* on *La Lutte Religieuse en Allemagne.*

in the world. With the changed political orientation, which follows the repression of the risings of 1848 in nearly all the capitals of Europe (save Turin), last of all including Paris, with the *coup d'état* of 1852, there comes a reconsideration of the problem of liberty and the system that had taken the name of *liberalism*.

§ 51.—What was precisely meant by liberalism, for and against which there was so fierce a fight towards the middle of the XIX century, is not easy to say; both those who supported it and those who attacked it were driven by theories, prejudices and events, to complicate its meaning. This, indeed, always happens with words that in given historical periods are coined to indicate a tendency, an ideal and a system to be achieved.

In England liberalism presented itself primarily under the economic aspect. The *Petition of Merchants* of 1820 is a kind of economic catechism. Commercial liberty is claimed in its whole range, against any and every system of the bonds and privileges, which represented a tradition still operative in all countries. Freedom was demanded not only for commerce, but in the whole economic field of production and labour. No more mixed corporations of workers and masters, nor free associations of workers, nor market prices, nor customs duties, nor protective measures: everything must be free and left to private initiative. Cobden and the Manchester School represented a necessary phase in the transition from small to big industry, from a monopolised commerce to free commerce. This the conservative opposition did not realise, and it was overwhelmed by the combative force of the early liberals; in 1846 the British Parliament voted the abolition of the Corn Duty and embarked upon the great policy of Free Trade.

Economic liberalism contained within itself its terrible adversary, the socialism of the workers, who were becoming what was later called *proletarians* in opposition to owners. The abolition of the guilds had been rendered necessary by their atrophy; they were, indeed, of a nature suited to crafts and home industries, and not to big industry. It was impossible for them to survive, given the need for economic reforms better suited to the new rhythm. But the worker, isolated in the face of the master, became a mere chattel, to be offered on the market under the empire of competition. Low wages, long hours and night-work, abuse of female and child labour, unemployment, inadequate dwellings, crowded work-rooms, were the immediate consequences. There could not fail to be a reaction.

The liberty invoked by the masters could not be separated from the liberty invoked by the workers against the Manchester School. The worker took part in the Chartist movement, accepting for his claims the political platform offered by the People's Charter, which demanded universal suffrage and annual parliaments. Chartism was unsuccessful. The workers, in order to obtain recognition of their rights, needed to be able to combine in associations of their own on a two-fold platform, economic and political.[1] There was hence the need for a compromise between the liberal theories and State intervention—liberal, inasmuch as the workers demanded the right of free association, interventionist inasmuch as they demanded from the State legal protection against the abuses of economic liberty. In the United States of America the problem of liberal economy was complicated by that of negro slavery, which still held out against anti-slavery propaganda. The Southern States claimed for the whites the freedom to keep slaves and there were facile theorists to declare that slavery was not contrary to either natural right or Christian law. There would come a moment when, in the name of freedom, England was on the verge of entering into the conflict on behalf of the Southern States, who were putting up armed resistance against the enforcement of the Act of Abolition. Fortunately Gladstone and others understood that the principle of freedom could not be invoked for freedom to keep negroes in slavery, any more than for freedom to make British workmen work sixteen hours a day, or (as had actually been done) to force the Chinese Government to allow free trade in opium.

English liberalism was establishing itself under its economic aspect and was triumphing over various opposition, while seeking to hold its own against the ferment of the working classes and to limit State

[1] Workers' organisations were not only considered as coming under the common law on conspiracy, but had been forbidden by the series of Combination Acts of the XVIII century, and in spite of mitigations (notably by the Acts of 1822 and 1859), strictly speaking trade-unions were unlawful associations till the Acts of 1871–6.

intervention. In France liberalism was establishing itself under a political aspect, as a system of guarantees for the bourgeois class in the face of the Monarchy, as a liberation from the impositions and privileges of the Church, as a means of defence of individual interests. The right of property, with the individualistic character given it by the Napoleonic Code, was at the centre of the politico-economic conception of French liberalism; hence the limitation of the suffrage to property-holders, the iron discipline against the right of association of working men and resistance to their claims, the State monopoly of education and the ecclesiastical jurisdictionalism put forward against the movement of the Liberal Catholics and the Ultramontanes. The fall of the July Monarchy, the proclamation of the democratic Second Republic, sponsored by Catholics, universal suffrage, the working-class revolts, the election of Louis-Napoleon as president were logical consequences.

Just as economic liberalism had not an absolute character, but was merely one of the transitory and alternate phases of modern economy between private enterprise and State intervention, neither did political liberalism have an absolute character. Given the right to vote, why limit it to property-owners? Why only to men and not to women? Granted the faculty of forming political parties (which could not be prevented save by denying freedom of vote) why and how should the formation of workers' unions and parties be prevented? Economic liberalism called for the trade-union; political liberalism called for the Socialist party. So long as the bourgeoisie denied one and the other, so long did it suffer mass risings, anarchic disturbances, or else it had to renounce the benefits of freedom and seek a dictator. The *coup d'état* of 1852 in France was a bourgeois revolution, while in England the alternate government of Conservatives and Liberals followed a line of resistance and compromise in respect of the working classes.

Ethical liberalism, likewise, could not stand the test if it were conceived on absolute lines. Freedom of speech and of the press could not extend to apology for crimes that cut away the foundations of social life, to obscene and impious propaganda, to private slander and libel. The necessity for legal limits was recognised, for self-limitation could not be the conduct of all citizens nor could public education be the work of a moment. Should such laws be preventive or repressive?

Theoretical liberalism admitted only repressive legislation; the governments of the time experimented with various systems, producing a continuous succession of laws and decrees on the press. These had not always an ethical intention behind them. In most cases they had a political or partisan purpose, to guarantee the government in office or to protect the bourgeoisie against the proletariat, the conservatives against the radicals, the anti-clericals against the clericals.

Religious liberalism, too, as proclaimed by the laic State with the separation of State from Church, has never been completely and absolutely achieved. The State has assumed a laic character, and in spite of the Restoration and the successive phases of union of Throne and Altar, in spite of the maintenance of official churches, of concordats, of budgetary expenditure on public worship, the State of the XIX century has never abandoned its laic basis. The legal or *de facto* separation of State from Church has come about in particular cases for partial periods, and in several countries has had an anti-religious or anti-clerical character. In the United States a neutral and respectful separation has been accomplished and maintained, with a background of Christian ideas admitted by political men who, in general, have never either repudiated or combated their respective churches. But in the American case, separation was concomitant with the birth of the Confederation, under a régime of freedom of conscience and of worship. Moral relations between the Federal and State Governments and the various churches have always existed, contributing to the maintenance of a religious atmosphere which only the spread of philosophical positivism and practical atheism among the cultured and ruling classes has to a certain extent modified.

Historically the liberal movement in Europe of the XIX century has three features. The first is negative, directed against the system of political, economic and religious bonds that came from the *ancien régime* and had either survived the Revolution or been brought back with the Restoration. The second is positive, of a practical character: the constitutional sharing of citizens in the life of the State and the limitation and control of the sovereign power. The third is theoretical, the quest for true individual liberty in a philosophy founded on the autonomy of reason from faith and of the human personality from every external power. Man in virtue of freedom not only acquires the habit of self-determination, overcoming the bonds that practical life imposes on him, but becomes autonomously an authority and law unto himself, for he conceives himself in universal form.

The Catholic Church, and also the other Christian Churches, relatively to the particular conditions of each, were opposed to the liberal movement, whether negative, positive or theoretical. The Catholic Church more than the others was opposed to negative liberalism because it struck at her juridical and economic structure by the laws suppressing the religious Orders, ecclesiastical courts and the legal competence of the bishops and the traditional rights regarding church endowments and the papal powers, for which she had been fighting for two centuries. She was also opposed to positive political liberalism, because it presented itself as subversive of the established order and based upon the exercise of liberties, such as those of conscience, worship and the Press, which were deemed either anti-Catholic or pernicious, or which implied philosophical and theological theories that the Church could not approve.

The experience of 1848 and in the years following, in countries where forms of liberal government remained in operation—as in Piedmont up till the unity of Italy, in France till 1852, and elsewhere, with the various vicissitudes of the time—had made Rome wary and suspicious of the liberal movement even among Catholics and of its leaders. Of these the most noted were Father Ventura (now in exile in France through the part he had played under the Roman Republic of 1849), Rosmini, on whom the Jesuits looked askance because of his philosophy and what they considered his liberalism, and Montalembert, from whom Veuillot broke away in order to follow an increasingly anti-liberal and intransigent line. It is the period when Italian liberal priests under Austria are tried and condemned to death, among them the celebrated Abate Tozzoli, Professor at the Seminary of Mantua, and Bartholomew Grazioli, Archpriest of Revere (1852–53).

Events were advancing rapidly. The liberal experiment was in operation, with all the difficulties of the hour. A part of the Catholics, while loyal to Rome, felt its necessity and the political and religious advantages to be derived from it. The nonconformists or reformers of protestant countries were canalised in this movement of liberty. Many did so in order to resist the wave of anti-religion, which brought with it a movement of rationalistic origin. The year 1859, which saw the publication of Darwin's *Origin of Species*, saw also that of Mill's essay *On Liberty*.

The religious problem, which had seemed to have become negligible, to be ruled out of the political contest, again became central either as a premise or as a goal, and both for the faithful and their adversaries.

In France and Belgium it presented itself in acute form as a question of educational freedom, but one liberty never stands alone; it must form part of a system or it is not liberty. In Switzerland, where the civil war had ended in the defeat of the *Sunderbund* of the Catholic cantons and in a constitution in the unitary sense desired by the victorious radicals, this gave Catholics a motive for taking their stand on a platform of religious and cantonal liberties. The Catholics of England and Holland wanted liberty for the revival of their episcopal hierarchies, and those of Germany in order that the clergy should be empowered to supervise religious teaching in the schools, and in order that the *placet* in the appointment of bishops should be abolished and the Jesuits and Redemptorists admitted.

In Italy many Catholics took part in the movement for independence from Austria and for national unity. Neo-Guelf confederalism had collapsed; there was a desire for unification with the suppression of the separate States, and Catholics were attacked in the name of particularist legitimism on the one hand and the unitary ideal on the other. What was to them a tormenting problem was that of the Temporal Power; they recognised the Pope's right to independence yet they could not be reconciled to the idea of an Italy divided into two portions. In the meantime in the Subalpine parliament there was no lack of Catholics who, while accepting the liberal constitutional basis of the modern State, sought to restrain the anti-clericalism and anti-Catholicism developing in Italy. In both the Parliament of Turin (1848) and in that of Florence (1861–70) there were farseeing men worthy of the name of Catholic, such as Manzoni, Cantù, Balbo, Lampertico, the Sicilian Baron Vito d'Ondes Reggio, the philosopher Augusto Conti, and others, who longed for an understanding with the Papacy to bring religious peace with a free and united Italy.

But whereas the active Catholics were few and divided, and the ecclesiastical hierarchy was mistrustful of all the forms of liberalism, the adversaries of the Church, in every country, increased in number and boldness, carrying the struggle into every field. In this the reactionary Catholics found arguments for supporting absolute powers and the use of repressive means; the others, of liberal and democratic tendency, for a more courageous action in defence and conquest of freedom. In order that there should be an understanding and common programme among the active Catholics of all countries, a congress at Malines in Belgium was promoted in August, 1863. Among those who took part was Mgr. Manning (not yet Cardinal), one of the most convinced of the higher ecclesiastics engaged in social action. The promoters wanted Montalembert to be present, although he was ill, and he went. His two speeches at Malines are comparable to the two addresses of Father Ventura in 1847. In the first he dealt with a free political régime and Catholics. 'Public life,' he said, 'that glorious appanage of adult nations, that régime of freedom and responsibility that teaches man the art of self-confidence and self-control, that is what is lacking, outside Belgium, to modern Catholics. They excel in private life, but they succumb in public life. They are trucelessly and everywhere dominated, surpassed, vanquished or fooled by their rivals, by their antagonists and oppressors, whether unbelievers or Protestants, democrats or despots.' He added further on: 'The new society, democracy, to call it by its name, exists . . . in half Europe it is already sovereign; in the other it will be so to-morrow . . . I look before me and I see nothing but democracy everywhere . . . In the new order Catholics will have to fight but will have nothing to fear.' His idea was to correct democracy by liberty and to reconcile Catholicism with democracy. Therefore in his second speech he faced the problem of liberty of conscience. He begins by rejecting as absurd and censurable the doctrine holding that 'all religions are equally true and good in themselves and that the spiritual authority of the Church is not binding in conscience'. He distinguishes between dogmatic intolerance and civil toleration: 'the one necessary to the eternal truth, the other necessary to modern society.' For him liberty of conscience is to be vindicated not against the Church but against the State. Hence Montalembert deduced that the Church may come to an agreement with the modern State that is founded on religious liberty, and that each Catholic is free to find the modern State preferable to its predecessors.

The success of these two addresses was extraordinary, but at once an offensive was launched by the reactionary Catholics. These transferred to a strictly theoretical plane what Montalembert had proclaimed on the historical plane, and they gave a theological character to what he had asserted as political. Pius IX believed that the moment had come to give a clear guidance to Catholics, publishing the encyclical *Quanta Cura* (1864), followed by a list known as the Syllabus of eighty propositions which, citing from his earlier letters, allocutions and acts, he declared erroneous and to be condemned. The clamour aroused by the Syllabus was enormous. The opposition on the part of Liberals, Protestants and certain sections of Catholics was of exceptional range. The word 'Syllabus' became for many an object of hatred. Neither then nor later did any great number of persons read or understand the Syllabus, but they viewed it with an obscure resentment, to the point that on many occasions Catholic writers devoted to the Church have felt and feel, even to-day, the duty of exculpating Pius IX, of justifying him, of explaining the document, for among Catholics discomfort in talking of the Syllabus has not yet wholly subsided.

The eighty propositions may be divided into three categories. In the first are those contained in the first section, which concern the supernatural principles of faith, the existence of God and Providence, the constitution of the Church, with the relevant errors, pantheism, naturalism and absolute rationalism. In the same category we may place the propositions condemning errors on the spiritual power of the Church, as limited or denied by jurisdictionalism, ancient and modern. In the second category are the propositions concerned with modern errors due to Protestant infiltration, among them indifferentism, latitudinarianism, and the like. In the third category are the propositions condemning errors or erroneous statements in regard to the modern State as then theoretically conceived, on a basis of philosophical theses prejudicial to the traditional rights of the Church and to the subordination of the temporal to the spiritual. In formulating the propositions there was a cautious care to maintain the condemnation on a theological plane, but in substance, besides pantheism, rationalism, naturalism and indifferentism—old errors in modern dress—there was a condemnation of the modern conception of the State and of the errors upheld in the name of what were then the vague terms of liberalism, socialism, progress, and the like, which had a different sound in different climates and environments.

Faced with the outcry of public opinion, the *Civiltà Cattolica*, the well-known Jesuit review which had been transferred from Naples to Rome after the return of Pius IX from Gaeta, and placed under the protection of the Vatican, put forward the distinction of *thesis* and *hypothesis*. This distinction was no novelty, but it had not previously been so clearly and authoritatively proclaimed. In this way, as a thesis, the conception of the modern State as an ideal to be pursued is erroneous and censurable, but if in the concrete, as an hypothesis such a State comes or has come into being, it cannot be rejected as an evil, but is to be tolerated, case by case and with the necessary reservations, with the employment of the legal means it allows for the achievement of the moral and religious good, besides the political and economic good, of the country. The terms of compromise with the modern State must not prejudice principles; therefore it is necessary to start from the *rebus sic stantibus* for the subsequent vindication of the rights of the Church in a régime of liberty. Mgr. Dupanloup, the bishop of Orleans, held fast to the distinction of thesis and hypothesis in his pamphlet *La Convention du* 15 *septembre et l'encyclique du* 8 *decembre* 1864. He examined the various articles of the Syllabus, comparing them with the context of the documents from which they were taken, in order to establish their true sense without the polemical distortions that were in vogue, and he concluded that it was the duty of Catholics, taking their stand on the *de facto* situation, to adapt themselves to the conditions of the moment and to fight with the modern arms of freedom of conscience, of the press and of the vote. Pius IX sent him a brief of approval and over 600 bishops all over the world associated themselves with his attitude.

Bishop Dupanloup's explanations of the Syllabus of Pius IX were more or less in the same spirit as those of Mgr. de Parisiis on the encyclical *Mirari vos* of Gregory XVI. But both papal documents were in substance the condemnation of the laic State which was establishing itself and would wholly supplant the old confessional State. The laic State came in the name of liberty and of democracy; the condemnation did not touch either liberty in its true sense or democracy as one of the types of State régimes, but it certainly struck at the liberal system and the democracy of the sovereign people. On the other hand, the confessional State presented itself as historically bound to the monarchic and to the authoritarian régimes. This did not mean that the Church sought to bind the two terms indissolubly together, only that she was defending them on the earthly plane in order to prevent the overflow of the anti-religious and revolutionary currents that were steadily rising. The position of those who were known as Liberal Catholics, in spite of the distinction between thesis and hypothesis, became progressively weaker, while the intransigents gained in influence and combativity, all the more so in that there was a passage from the political field to the religious field with the two questions that were now raised of the papal infallibility and the temporal power.

CHAPTER XIII

FROM THE VATICAN COUNCIL TO THE CONDEMNATION OF MODERNISM (PIUS X)

§ 52.—On June 28, 1868, Pius summoned an Oecumenical Council to meet in the Vatican on December 8, 1869. A special invitation was sent to the Eastern dissidents (Orthodox), another to all the separated Christians, i.e. the Protestants, and indirect approaches were made to the Anglicans. None of them accepted or showed any desire to be present. The German Protestants, in order to assert their own personality, held a great festival at Worms. The heads of States, or Catholic princes as they were called in the Curia, were not invited. Which heads of States could be considered Catholics and which not? Could the Emperor of Austria be invited, when with his constitutional laws he had broken the Concordat of 1855? Or Victor Emmanuel of Savoy who had annexed from the Pope the 'Legations' of Romagna and had incurred excommunication? Or Napoleon III who had not allowed the Syllabus to be published in France? Which of these and other monarchs could be considered as his own master, and did not depend on parliaments with anti-clerical majorities, opposed to the policy of the Papacy? To omit to invite them was a prudent act in view of actual conditions, and it was timely in accentuating the autonomy of the Catholic Church from the civil power, at a moment when the prevailing political doctrines denied her any original personality of her own, whether moral, legal, or supernational. This did not mean a separation of the Church from the States; it was the sign that the modern States, in their laic character, had themselves separated from the Church, in spite of the formal relations they maintained with the Roman Curia.

The various Cabinets of Europe were displeased by the calling of the Council. Prince Hohenlohe, the Bavarian Foreign Minister, proposed to the other governments to make diplomatic representations to Rome. Vienna, Paris and Berlin held other views, yet indirectly all the capitals were interested in the Council and in the attitude adopted by the episcopate. Attention had been everywhere aroused by the very lively controversies both among Catholics themselves and between Catholics and Protestants, Orthodox, free-thinkers, moderate liberals, who, by a natural phenomenon, brought forward old and new problems, and these for the most part centred round the nature of the Church, her history, her centre in Rome and the Pope as her chief representative.

Three points formed the main object of studies, debates and ardent controversies—the relations between Church and State, the Papal Infallibility, the Temporal Power. The Vatican Council appeared as a protest against the rationalistic world. It gave the idea of a repetition of the challenge of Boniface VIII to the secular authorities, with the aim of inaugurating a more authoritarian theocracy than the old. There were extremists of positivism, puffed up with their science, who mocked at the grand assizes of Rome as at a dead world that only feigned to live, shadows of the past fluttering amid realities with empty gestures and meaningless words. The bitterness of this opposition revealed both hatred of a strong enemy that would have to be overcome if their own systems were to prevail, and concern lest the intransigent party should be reinforced and a new reactionary alliance effected between the Papacy and the absolute sovereigns or those who only recently and reluctantly had granted constitutions. The complete triumph of liberal ideas or socialist movements was for many bound up with a reign of science, considered irreconcilable with faith, with a progress that would find in the Church insuperable obstacles through her obscurantism and dominion over the faithful.

For the Italian Liberals or Radicals there was especial concern over the temporal power. Rome had been proclaimed capital of Italy by the Parliament of Florence in 1861. Garibaldi in 1867 had sought to seize it by armed force, but had been beaten back by the French troops defending it. The secret and semi-official missions between the Italian Government and the Vatican Secretariat of State had failed, Pius IX had pronounced a *non possumus*, proclaiming it his duty to defend the rights of the Papacy to independence, as bound up with the existence of a territorial sovereignty. If the Council were to proclaim the absolute necessity of the Temporal Power, Italy would meet with an obstacle in the opposition of Catholics the world over, who would press their governments to defend the Papal State. Hence resentment, anxiety, bold suggestions, hatred and anger, of which the daily and periodical press became the mouthpiece. For such the fall of the temporal power would mean the final fall of the Papacy. Pius IX would be the last Pope. The Council was a call for reinforcements in order, were it possible, to avert the catastrophe. While the Protestants redoubled their attacks against Rome, recalling the questions which, they held, invalidated the supremacy and authority of the Papacy, the surviving representatives of Gallicanism and Febronianism brought back into circulation the theory of the superiority of Council to Pope, and contested the theory of a papal infallibility without or apart from the Council.

Catholic opposition was divided into two streams. The first contested the definition of papal infallibility on historico-critical grounds, the second considered a conciliar decision to be inopportune. On the other hand, the supporters of the infallibility, who were the most numerous, both among the bishops and clergy and among the faithful, were also divided into two streams—those who attributed to the Pope an infallibility in a broad sense, embracing even non-revealed and rational matters, and those who limited it to Revelation, when the Pope was speaking *ex cathedra* as 'universal doctor'. In Rome there had been no intention of calling a Council in order to bring into dispute a doctrine reputed as dogma by long tradition. Pius IX had exercised his privilege in 1854 when he had defined *ex cathedra* the dogma of the Immaculate Conception, with the assent and applause of the entire Catholic episcopate. But the opposition of the bishops of Germany and of some in France and elsewhere, among the most cultured and notable such as Dupanloup, Darboy, Strossmayer, Maret, Hefele, Ketteler, with that of writers and apologists like Döllinger, Gratry, Newman, and, among laymen, Montalembert, Lord Acton and other influential figures, made the Vatican determine to hasten definition. The Council, after approving the constitution *de fide catholica*, forsook the disciplinary questions and passed to the constitution of the Church. Events were moving fast. Napoleon was withdrawing his troops from Rome, war had broken out between Prussia and France, the Italian Government was invading certain regions of the Papal State and was preparing to seize Rome. The wearisome sessions of the commissions and of the conciliar assembly went on; on 13 July the draft constitution obtained 451 votes of *placet*, 88 of *non placet*, 63 of *placet juxta modum*, while there were 80 abstentions. In its final form the constitution *Pastor Aeternus* was voted on July 18, 1870, by 533 votes to 2. On the eve a group of 55 dissentient bishops had left in order not to take part in the voting.

In this constitution it was declared that the Council was introducing no novelty but was establishing the Catholic tradition in defining that the infallibility of the Pope is bound up with his function of supreme doctor of the Church, never with that of pontiff, judge or legislator; and that in the dogmatic decrees of the popes definitions are articles of faith only when the Pope speaks *ex cathedra* on matters of faith and morals contained in divine revelation.

Exaggerations on the one side and inconsequences and preoccupations on the other among the Catholics, and the attacks of adversaries, had brought a mental perturbation that agitated the Council itself. This took place in an atmosphere of suspicion. The minority was reduced almost to impotence through restrictive procedure, and the unwillingness of the assembly to listen to criticisms and protests. Pius IX exerted a personal influence which seemed excessive. After the Council there were schismatic attempts both in the Latin Church and in that of the Eastern Uniates, but the time for true schisms was past and the so-called Old Catholics little by little lost consistency, and remained a restricted group with Protestant leanings. It was then declared and reiterated that the definition of the papal infallibility would cut short the trend towards Rome, paralyse the action of Catholics, and widen the gulf between the Catholic Church and modern thought. Such prophecies have proved fallacious.

What the opponents of the Papacy in general and even some of the anti-infallibilist Catholics did not fully perceive was from what spiritual depths the movement rose which led up to the Vatican

Council. They saw the surface appearance, they were troubled by the human side to be found in all Councils as in any activity of the Church (religious history is made also of this human side); they were deafened by the polemics and exaggerations of the intransigents, exaggerations to which the Council itself, not intentionally but objectively, gave short shrift, when in defining the supernatural character and limits of the papal infallibility, it let drop the whole of the worldly scope they had sought to attribute to it.

In order to understand the bearings of the Council (and it is easier to do so now than then) we must bear in mind the trend towards Rome that began in France with the Revolution, struck the first blow at Gallicanism and gave occasion to the birth of Ultramontism and to the struggles to end the schism. It continued in Germany with philo-Catholic Romanticism, in Ireland with the vindication of Catholic rights, in England with the Oxford movement and the conversion of a real *élite*, the most notable being Newman and Manning who became Cardinals. At the same time the so-called Catholic Liberalism in Italy, France, Belgium, Switzerland, Germany and Spain produced men of the first order, champions above all of religious freedom. The names of Manzoni, Montalembert, Lacordaire, O'Connell, Rosmini, Ventura, Ketteler, Balmes and many others cannot be dissociated from the Catholic revival and from the idealisation of the Papacy in the minds and hearts of Catholics of the last century. Montalembert complained in the last years of his life of the exaggerations of a section of the press and of the French clergy, writing that 'of all the mysteries which the history of the Church presents in so great numbers, I know of none that equals or surpasses this so prompt and complete transformation of Catholic France into the back-yard of the ante-chamber of the Vatican' (November, 1869). He saw the excess, losing sight of the substance of the movement of liberation of the Church (especially in France) to which he himself had so potently contributed. If the French clergy went to extremes, it was because it had always done so, either on the side of monarchic authority or on that of papal authority.

With the re-establishment nearly everywhere of the Company of Jesus, the creation of new religious Orders and the renovation of the old ones, with the concordats, the reorganisation of the hierarchy, the mission impulse, this period saw the beginnings of a true spiritual Catholic renaissance in every field. In that of education, the greatest figure is Don Bosco, and close to him, Rosmini. In that of charitable works there was the marvellous achievement of Gottolengo of Turin; under other aspects, Ozanam in Paris, and a little later Father Ludovico da Casoria in Naples. In that of culture there were the Oratorian Fathers Gratry and Capecelatro (the latter would become Cardinal); in the missions Cardinal Lavigerie, founder of the White Fathers and the White Sisters, and many others, in every domain and in every country, whom it would be superfluous to mention. At the same time there was a swarm of new feminine Orders, serving all the spiritual and material needs of mankind with a truly extraordinary spontaneousness, vigour and goodness.

This is the period of the rise of Catholic associations for the Christian training of the laity, the care of the adolescent, education, preparation for civil life, workers' assistance, the defence of dogma, of Christian morals and of the rights of the Church. This movement utilised the margins of freedom left to Catholics in the new régime, which often treated them as citizens of a lower order, or as adversaries of modern society. But this modicum of freedom, which the absolute governments had never granted, and which was enjoyed under even hostile liberal governments, was enough to create a public opinion turned towards Rome as it had never been before.

The death of Pius VI in exile, the struggle of Pius VII against Napoleon, had aroused feelings of admiration and filial piety. The popes who followed, bound as they were to the policy of the Restoration and of Vienna, were not particularly popular, but the trend towards Rome surrounded them with an aureole such as had never been the lot of the popes of the preceding century. Pius IX was the people's pope. His early liberalism aroused delirious enthusiasm. In spite of his change of route and the hatred of the revolutionaries, he remained the popular pope, the pope of pilgrimages, of great religious demonstrations, of the dogma of the Immaculate Conception. If there were excesses, on the part of Rome in acts of authority as on the part of clergies and laity in a cult of the Papacy that was denounced as 'papolatry', this was in a measure due to the personal magnetism of Pius IX and the exceptional circumstances of his pontificate; but more than anything else it was a reaction against the anti-papal campaign of disparagement, which found in the Syllabus, the Infallibility and the Temporal Power so many motives for a violent anti-Catholic struggle.

The fall of the Temporal Power, which followed the Council (already actually suspended through political events, and then adjourned by a bull of October 20), seemed to mark the collapse of the policy of Pius IX, humiliation on the heels of triumph. For the intransigent Catholics it struck a mortal blow at the authoritarian system of which they were the last paladins; for the French, whether Catholic or no, it was a wound to their pride; for Austria, it was a fresh anxiety; for the faithful the world over, a grief. In the presynodal schema of the Vatican Council a declaration on the Temporal Power had been introduced, but the Council had not time or opportunity to pronounce upon it. Apart from variations of form, the declaration reflected the thesis maintained by the popes from the day that such power had come under discussion: '*Ut autem romanus pontifex primatus sibi divinitus collati munus, uti par est, adimpleret, iis indigebat praesidiis quae temporum conditioni et necessitati congruerent.*'[1]

This principle then served to defend the existence of the Papal State as it was in 1870. The same principle would underly the creation of the Vatican City by the Lateran Treaty of 1929, for what formed the kernel of the declaration was the end, to which the temporal power served as means according to the varying historical conditions, i.e., '*quo romanus Pontifex . . . nulli principi subjectus, supremam . . . potestatem . . . per universum orbem plenissima libertate exercere . . . posset.*'[2]

It was natural that Pius IX, after refusing any negotiation that would imply a spontaneous cession of Rome, after refusing to accept the Law of Guarantees, should shut himself up in the Vatican as a voluntary prisoner, and should send his protest to the governments of Europe. These however, one by one, recognised the *fait accompli* while main-

[1]In order that the Roman Pontiff should be able fittingly to fulfil the office divinely entrusted to him, he had need of those safeguards that might correspond to the condition and necessity of the times.

[2]So that the Roman Pontiff . . . subject to no prince . . . may be able . . . to exercise the supreme power . . . in full liberty throughout the world.

taining diplomatic representatives at the Vatican as well as at the Quirinal, whither the King of Italy had transferred himself. The Roman people, summoned to plebiscite, voted for the union of Rome to the Italian State. The value of such acts apart, this was a legal formality, to which the general elections for the new Chamber formed a sequel. The Vatican replied by advising Catholics to abstain from presenting themselves as candidates or from voting, acts which would imply a recognition of the occupation of Rome and of the infringement of the papal rights. Thus the *non expedit*, understood and intended as a prohibition, for half a century would keep the Catholics of Italy remote from political life.

During this period, among certain sections of Catholics there had come to be an atmosphere of mysterious expectancy, as though they awaited a miracle that would restore Rome to the Pope. They counted on the structural weakness of the new kingdom, on party dissensions, on the intervention of Austria or of France, on the unforeseen, as a proof of the divine will. On the opposing side there was a cry that the Papacy was done for, that Pius IX was the last of the series, and that he died cursing modern society. Fortunately the visionaries received a solemn setback from the fact that on the death of Pius IX the conclave could freely assemble and another pope be elected, who, though remaining a prisoner in the Vatican and continuing to lay claim to the temporal power, would enjoy one of the longest and most tranquil pontificates, one of the most celebrated and, humanly speaking, one of the most glorious.

What collapsed in 1870 was not the Papacy, but a particular means of guaranteeing the independence of the Papacy, and one which was no longer suited to the 'condition and necessity of the times'—to use the terms of the presynodal declaration. The recognition of this fact could not be effected at once, nor by the men who had defended the Temporal Power against violation as a sacred right (a violation that in the minds of not a few had been desired out of hatred for the name of Catholic, and as such was celebrated in the sectarian demonstrations that ensued), nor by those others who realised the true position and had said as much before and after 1870, for not even they had been immune from the passions and prejudices of the epoch.

In a free and constitutional Europe it would have been impossible for Rome to remain absolutist like the St. Petersburg of the Czars and the Constantinople of the Sultans, also religious and political heads, constrained by their system to adopt bloody repressions and tyrannical methods. Rome from 1814 to 1870 had followed the policy of repression that had done so much harm to the Papacy. For the Pope to grant a new constitution more or less copied from that of 1848 would have been to expose himself to fresh difficulties, and probably to the necessity of withdrawing it within a short space, with what loss of prestige may be imagined. Nor could the constitution have been such as to meet the wishes of the Roman liberals, who had gained the upper hand. Moreover, the attraction of Rome towards the Italian State and of the Italian State towards Rome was undeniable. Once Venice had been regained in 1866, Rome had become the objective for most Italians. What happened in 1870, through the favourable conjuncture of the Franco-Prussian War, would have happened at the first possible moment on some other occasion. Nor could the Pope have long remained under the protection of the French army, or France have long kept up a hostile attitude towards Italy.

What seemed, and was then, a defeat little by little became a new motive for a greater sympathy towards the Papacy on the part of the Catholic world and of men of good faith in the non-Catholic world. Once the weight of the earthly principality was taken away it seemed to many as if the papal power had become, even in appearances, more spiritual. Certainly it was less concerned with affairs of State, which had rendered the Curia always circumspect and bound to the policy of the Powers and to the interests of the dominant classes. In reality, indeed, the diplomatic and political preoccupations of the Vatican have never ceased, whether they were directed to a restoration of the Temporal Power, or to the quest for terms of a conciliation, or towards ensuring, by a waiting and reserved attitude that was not all passive, that the future should not be prejudiced.

At the same time, it was to the interest of the Church to find a friendly *modus vivendi* with the new kingdom of Italy. As early as 1867 there had been a verbal and semi-official agreement prejudicial to neither party, over the appointment of the bishops who, through previous concordats with the various States of Italy, were mostly of royal patronage. The religious Orders had been suppressed, their vows were no longer legally recognised, their goods sold. In order to regularise the position of purchasers who as such had incurred excommunication, without giving public recognition to the laws involved, the Sacra Penitenzeria made use of wide faculties for 'settlements of conscience' made case by case with the individuals concerned. A few years later the religious Orders were reconstituted without any real opposition from the government (and in some cases with its visible encouragement) as *de facto* societies, and with better chosen and surer members than not a few of the monks and friars who had been dispersed with the suppression of the religious houses. The Government created a Public Worship Fund for poor churches and supplemented the stipends of the parish priests, it may be in order to win the friendship of the lower clergy, whereas the upper clergy was for the most part hostile to the new order, save for a few such as Mgr. Calabiana, Archbishop of Milan, and the celebrated Mgr. Bonomelli, Bishop of Cremona.

There were indeed open collisions between the Italian Government and the Vatican, and anti-Catholic and anti-papal demonstrations in Rome itself, among the most notorious the attempt to desecrate the corpse of Pius IX when it was carried by night from the Vatican to S. Lorenzo outside the walls—or the other, marking the solemn inauguration of the monument to Giordano Bruno, the friar-philosopher who in 1600 had been burned as a heretic. All this notwithstanding, the new and original fact—the co-existence of two sovereigns, two courts, two diplomatic corps, in the same capital, under the aspect of an usurper and a rightful ruler, or better, of a national king and the Catholic, that is, universal pope—could last for over half a century, without causing an acute conflict, indeed with gradual adjustments so that the period of the World War could pass with only certain minor incidents. These were certainly inferior in importance to the incidents that befell the Pope during the wars of the past, whether the Napoleonic wars or the wars of the Austrian and Spanish Succession.

In compensation, freedom of association, of speech and of the press was widely used by Catholics, even with such limitations as were imposed on them through partisan politics, which do not respect the equality of adversaries before the law. On the plane of liberty they were able little by little to regain the positions they had lost, accused as they were of being temporalists and anti-nationalists. The charge of anti-nationalism for long weighed heavy upon Italian Catholics and paralysed their work, the more so since because of the *non expedit* they could not assert themselves on the electoral and parliamentary plane, and passed as citizens of a lower order.

§ 53.—The end of the temporal power of the popes, while it meant the completion of the unity of Italy (save for the unredeemed frontier provinces), coincided with the collapse in France of the Second Empire and the advent of the Third Republic (which opened with the Commune of 1871) and with the proclamation of the German Empire. Austria, which had been the centre of the anti-liberal reaction and was reputed the bulwark of Catholicism, had been doubly stricken, with the loss of the German Confederation from her sphere of influence and with the loss of the provinces of Lombardy and Venetia and of an influence once preponderant in Italy from the Alps to Sicily.

About the same period the constitutional system was becoming general and establishing itself in Europe as in the whole of the American continent, with a progressive advance towards democracy and universal suffrage. (Disraeli's Reform Bill widening the franchise was in 1867; in Switzerland the referendum was introduced in 1866). From the Scandinavian countries to Spain the parliaments were in high honour, while the Irish were demanding Home Rule, the Poles were again in insurrection, Croats, Bohemians and Hungarians sought to vindicate their national personality within the Austrian Empire, and the Balkan countries were claiming their autonomy against Turkey.

Contemporary with the triumph of constitutional liberalism and national and democratic consolidation was the growing vigour of the working-class parties, usually calling themselves Socialist or Communist. They form two currents—the one legalistic or practical, the other revolutionary or messianic. For a certain period the extremist elements got out of control and terrorised the various countries of Europe. In the meantime there was a multiplication of practical enterprises such as trade-unions and co-operatives, which were already flourishing on the margins of the liberal State, while the State was beginning to embark on a policy of social intervention.

From the religious standpoint, the laicisation of the States goes on relentlessly in many directions, in spite of the fact that in most States the official Church, Catholic, Protestant or Orthodox, is still recognised by law. In France it is the moment of Gambetta's slogan: '*Le cléricalisme, voilà l'ennemi!*' For the intransigent Catholics the Republic cannot be anything but anti-religious, and the Monarchy will save France. The decisive victory of the republican party is bound up with the famous *Seize Mai* (May 16, 1877), and the fall of Marshal MacMahon (January 3, 1879). As a result there is the beginning of the secularising education bills, and the laws against the religious congregations. The same phenomenon occurs in Italy, where in 1876 the historical Left, closely connected with Freemasonry, comes into power and accentuates the anti-clerical policy in order to strike at the 'temporalism' of the clergy and faithful. In Spain the Carlism of the Catholics is fought with more or less the same weapons. Austria, after the Vatican Council, had denounced the Concordat, which had already in practice been allowed to lapse, its place being later taken by the laws of 1874, which regulated Church matters in a liberal sense; moreover, she had recognised the kingdom of Italy, an act that had aroused much ill humour among Catholics. In Belgium the Liberals were engaged in a relentless struggle against Catholics on the education question. The Latin Republics of America were alternating religious persecutions and anti-clerical struggles with favours to the Church and clergy, according to which party was in power. The prevalence of anti-clericalism came from the influence of Freemasonry.

In the Protestant countries where there were Established Churches, their relations with the State remained formally unaltered, but their importance was decreasing as gradually the working classes turned away from religion, as the State gained control of the school and secularised it, as anti-Christian propaganda invaded the family, bringing a deterioration of morals, and as culture became pagan and historical and biblical criticism tended to demolish the premises of Christianity. The Protestant churches not only put up but a feeble resistance but were themselves invaded by a rationalistic liberalism that affected even their religious culture and weakened their structure through the continual formation of distinct sects and groups. As a diversion, they sought a fictitious stability in the struggle against Catholicism, and after the proclamation of the Papal Infallibility and the petty local schisms, like that of the Old Catholics, they found a fresh motive for polemics. In England even Gladstone indulged in an attack on the Infallibility (it is the moment when the word papism acquires an exceptional virulence), and Newman replied by a decisive confutation.

In England, the undenominational character of the State schools introduced by the Education Act of 1870 was the result of pressure from the Nonconformists, whose influence had increased with each widening of the franchise. But though the denominational schools, including those of the Wesleyans and Catholics, continued to receive State aid, they would find themselves hard put to it to meet increasing official demands, and undenominationalism would eventually turn to secularism with the decay of religious belief. In the meantime, the Catholic schools were holding their own and developing, notably through the work of Cardinal Manning, whose influence on the Primary Education Commission of 1885 would be generally recognised. His personality and his readiness to co-operate in any work for social betterment, from the Agricultural Labourers' Union to the settlement of the great dockers' strike of 1902, won him a standing in the country that of itself advanced the Catholic cause.

But while in England the restoration of the Hierarchy (in 1850) made it possible for Catholics to advance rapidly and vigorously, under the aegis of civil and political liberties, and even in Holland Catholics were able to breathe, in Germany Bismarck, victorious over France, launched an attack on the part of Protestant Germanism against Catholic Romanism, calling it a fight for culture, *Kulturkampf*. He counted on the division among Catholics caused by the definition of the Papal Infallibility and on the patriotic fanaticism aroused by the proclamation of the Empire. Instead he found himself confronted by the resistance of the episcopate and clergy, who faced persecution and imprisonment with courage and self-sacrifice, and he had also to reckon with the *Centre* and its leader Windthorst, whose generalship was such that in the end Bismarck met his defeat. Henceforth the Catholic parties which had begun timidly, hampered on every side, and on which Rome had looked with mistrust—especially in the case of Belgium, partly because they appeared as an inconvenient third in the diplomatic relations between the Holy See and the governments and Courts of the various countries—would assert themselves as a new lay apostolate, on a platform of common liberties and the representative system. Besides the parties in Germany and Belgium, we find the Irish Party in the British Parliament, and the first attempts at parties formed by Catholics for purposes of religious defence in Austria, Holland and Switzerland, and later in France.

In the United States, after the War of Independence and the proclamation of freedom of worship by the Philadelphia Convention of 1787, the first Catholic bishop was inducted at Baltimore in 1790, and in 1808 four other bishoprics were created. The French emigrant priests gave a notable impulse to the development of Catholicism. Soon an American clergy and hierarchy were constituted, in order to avoid the hostile propaganda of Protestants on a pretext of American patriotism, then justly mistrustful of Europe. The United States represented the type of State in which there was no established church and all religions were equal. But the atmosphere was so charged with Protestant, puritan and Methodist tradition, that this was reflected in the government, characterising its spirit and legislation. This notwithstanding, the other churches were able to develop, with varying degrees of opposition, especially when in 1847 Ireland, after the famine, began her transatlantic emigration and brought to America and British Canada a true spirit of conquest. French Canada was already Catholic. It had been ceded to England by the Treaty of Paris of 1763 and the Quebec Act of the following year granted the inhabitants freedom to profess 'the religion of the Church of Rome'. In 1812 the Catholic hierarchy was recognised. In 1840 the two provinces of Canada were united and received a Parliament.

The phase to which we have so briefly referred, of the trend of civilised States and their respective positions in regard to the various churches, coincided with the development and adaptation to practical life of the prevailing philosophical conceptions, Comte's Positivism,

Hegel's Idealism, Marx's Socialism. We do not mean by this that all those who carried out political plans asked the guidance of the philosophers, but these philosophies at the same time both inspired orientations and interpreted spiritual and social positions, while departures from such philosophies marked the limits that practical life sets to theories.

Positivism, as Auguste Comte conceived it, is not only a philosophy of science but a philosophy of society. In this three factors are emphasised—the deterministic predominance of the social environment over the individual, the superiority of scientific experiment to metaphysical values and mystical intuitions, and of humanitarianism to dogmatic religion. At bottom Positivism was transforming religious dogmatism into scientific dogmatism, the determinism of grace and predestination on the Calvinist model into a sociological determinism, religious sentimentalism of the methodistic type into humanitarianism, and Catholic discipline into secular hierarchism.

The order and hierarchy of the sciences as established by Comte met with immediate criticism from the scientific standpoint and was soon outgrown from that of sociology. He made of sociology a special branch of biology, treating social phenomena as natural history, robbing the individual will of its true value, liberty of any real meaning, human history of any rational and original character. He thus presented the evolution of society as the continual biological action and reaction of the environment on the individual and of the individual on his environment, establishing its laws and framing them in the mechanism of three stages of evolution, theological, metaphysical, positive. Comte is naturally the prophet of the past, in the sense that the whole past is explained in function of his 'positive' science; the whole past is a deterministic movement towards this term, which by this very fact should be final, definitive, a completion. Therefore he could not look forward to a stage beyond the *positive*; if he had done so, he would have had to orient his science towards that term. It would be impossible to do otherwise for one who saw a necessity of development in which there was no room left for free individual initiative. According to Comte, only on the attainment of the positive stage, that is, with the elimination of all theological and metaphysical abstractionism, would humanity have made true progress in the preponderance of truly human factors. The conception of the State that comes from Positivism depreciated individualism and liberty, so much extolled from the Revolution onwards, and gave entire importance to the formation of social environments, to the reinforcement of authority, to State interventionism. Comte admired Catholicism not for its dogmatism, which he believed had debased the intellect, but for its discipline, which he conceived in Jesuit fashion, so that Huxley could define Positivism as 'Catholicism minus Christianity'. It was necessary to replace the idea of God by that of Humanity. This, in Comte's mind, was the Great Being, of which we are but the transient phenomena, for in his system the world is not made up of a host of individuals each with his own free will, but is an ordered organism ruled by necessary laws.

The organisation of a ritual cult of Humanity, as envisaged by Comte, was soon laughed out of court, but the positivist idea of humanity survived, though confused with the rationalist idea of humanity which found its prophet in Victor Hugo, and with the idea of Nation, which likewise assumed the figure of a living entity, the Great Being to which human wills and endeavours must be offered in holocaust. The two streams, the humanitarian and the nationalist, were the two channels of post-Comtian Positivism, and gave their colour to the laic and national States of the second half of the XIX century. Humanity and the Nation, now one, now the other, now both together, assume the aspect of self-subsistent entities above and beyond the individual. For not a few they are a substitute for any other-worldly religious idea, and take its place in secular education. In the name of freedom of conscience religious teaching is banished from the schools, but positivist philosophy and pedagogy is put in its stead.

To the French bourgeoisie, economically flourishing, politically divided, rationalistic and laic as it was, Comte gave a conception of society and of life that could satisfy its practical aspirations and a certain need for general ideas. It was not the same for Germany, which after wavering between Kantian liberalism and Prussian statalism, had already achieved national unity and was in full tide of Germanism. Hegel was the prophet and interpreter of the new order, all the more in that Hegelian philosophy had little by little moulded German thought and culture and was spreading in England, Italy and elsewhere as the philosophy that brought emancipation from vulgar materialism and pedestrian Positivism, then everywhere triumphant under the guise of a concrete and irrefutable scientism.

The Hegelian State is 'ethicity' itself which, becoming self-conscious, asserts itself as the supreme subject of every right and the goal of every liberty. For Hegel the Ethical is the living custom of a people when it finds historical concretion, or better, it is the mode in which a people freely and consciously expresses its national substance. The Ethical is organic; the family is the seat of the inward *ethos*, civil society of the outward *ethos* in the co-operation of Orders and Classes. Only when the Ethical becomes aware of itself does it express itself in the State, which is the ethical foundation of every other institution. The State appears last in the process of the Spirit, but it is first because it is the Spirit itself realising itself and expressing itself in its fullness.

In order to understand such a conception we must remember above all that for Hegel the Absolute Spirit is the universal subject which realises itself by dialectical process, epitomizing and carrying forward earlier realisations and manifesting itself as their principle. In a like process the inward volitive plane of the individual and the manifest and collective plane of a people are one, for in the Ethical the end of the individual concords with the end of all, and the law expresses this will. Hence the distinction between the idea of civil society and that of the State. Civil society is an element interposed between the individual and the State, a kind of fermenting material moved by an *ethos* of its own historically experienced; while the State is its ascensional culmination, sifting out what is corrupt and incongruous in society, in an ideal purification towards the absolute finalistic substance that expresses itself in the State. In such a conception, parliaments and popular assemblies are not organs of the State but organs of society, that is means for the working of brute forces, incoherent and partial wills, which the State must transform, synthesize and actualise. The Hegelian State is therefore not a contractual resultant, as in Pufendorf's jusnaturalism, nor a means for guaranteeing individual rights as in Kant's liberalism; it is the most perfect realisation of the Spirit, the term of its process of liberation; it is immanence and totality. For according to Hegel, abstract or external law, such as contract or property, is the first grade of freedom; the second is morality as the interiorisation of law; the third is the Ethical as the free, collective, self-conscious will of the State.

What place does the Church occupy in this conception? Hegel sought to ensure the subsistence of the State-cum-Church as derived from the Lutheran conception. He declared that the spiritual content of the Church and that of the State are identical, the former in an emotional form, the latter in a rational form. State-cum-Church thus form a unity in distinction, with the prevalence of reason over sentiment. In the case of a conflict, the right of the State, that is reason, must prevail over the Church.

This philosophical, political trend, which in Hegel's mind corresponded to the position of the Prussian State, was then giving its colour to German happenings. The Empire was identified with the German idea, the term of the enterprise of unification of the *Reich*. The authoritarian system was combined with parliamentary representation and universal suffrage. The Lutheran church remained subject, as it had always been, while Catholicism was first persecuted, then tolerated. But the whole environment was more or less impregnated with the nationalist German idea. The interpreter of the more extreme current was Heinrich von Treitschke, with his *History of Germany in the XIX century*. His basic ideas are imperial centralisation, with the abolition of all the petty German States and all the remnants of the old municipalities, free cities and feudal traditions; the enforced assimilation of the Poles of Pomerania, Silesia and Danzig; legislation against the Jews, Catholics and Socialists, since these by their religious, racial and political divergencies break up and disintegrate the Reich and spoil its perfect homogeneity.

A third stream had in the meantime come to the fore and given its imprint to the greater part of the workers' movement in Europe—the Marxist stream. Socialism had had other fathers besides Marx; it had assumed various guises and various names according to period and country, from the French Revolution onwards. But Marxism was the endeavour to turn it into theory, framing it in a philosophy of history, giving it an impulse towards the future, impelled by a prophetism that seized the masses. The historical materialism on which Karl Marx's theory rests reduces all the other social factors to a reflection of the economic factor. This alone creates the social structure. Religion, morality, culture, politics, are superstructures shaped by economic conditions. The individual is absorbed into the social, the social into the economic. Since there are individuals who exploit and others who are exploited, the class war rouses the energies of the proletariat for the conquest of economic resources; when this conquest is complete, economic equality assured, all individuals will share equally in the social undertaking and be equally subject to it. The triumph of collective economy will transform into itself the other values, which before reflected economic disparity, such as politics, to-day centred round the bourgeois State, and religion in the shape of a privileged caste, bound up with the dominion of the wealthy classes.

Three principal elements dominate the Marxist conception—a collective determinism of a materialistic character, which makes a pendant to positivist determinism of the humanitarian type; an historical conception of a dialectic type, tending towards a resolving synthesis, which is connected—while travestying it—with the Hegelian dialectic, with the difference that instead of the Spirit we find Matter; finally, the concept of equality which, from the legal and political plane to which it had been confined by liberalism, is carried to the economic plane. Hence a denial of property which is at the source of social inequalities; a denial of the class which, basing itself on property, seizes power for itself; a denial of the political power as distinct from the economic society; a denial of the Church as organism and spiritual authority, since it creates a dualism within the economico-social unity.

Positivist democracy on the lines of Comte led to the omnipotent bourgeois State; Idealist nationalism on the lines of Hegel to the omnipotent State-Nation; Socialism on the lines of Karl Marx to the omnipotent Class-State. In all three there is the stuff of the totalitarian monistic State, such as would arise after the Great War—that is, an immanent idea, into which all others are resolved, whether it be the humanitarian idea of the laic State, or the mystical idea of the Nation or the economic idea of the Class. All lead to a social levelling covering all ranks, an accumulation of power in the hands of the heads, the elimination of the human individual from every corner of social life.

In practice events come about not through the application of theories but through experiments; the theories serve either as guiding lines or as explanations; they are never applicable in their entirety and are always challenged by other theories and other experiences. Yet the moment may come for their partial realisation, when their convinced exponents are able to impose their will on the rest and to attempt to put their programmes into practice. These will be more or less imbued with the theories to which they appeal, and in the face of the opinion of others, will express their sense and spirit. Thus it could be said that the States of the second half of the last century were either liberal or democratic or nationalistic according to the point of view from which they were considered, and it could well be said that the prevailing currents were the positivist, the idealist, and the socialist, with the variations and alternations presented by the various countries of Europe and America.

The environment was liberal because everywhere parliamentary institutions had been established and the political liberties, of conscience, worship, the Press, meeting and speech, were recognised in the constitutions. This system formed a propitious environment for the co-existence and development of the different political, economic and social currents; what was liberal was not so much the régime as the method. The prevailing parties imbued the liberal State with their ideologies, so that in different countries it was becoming either democratic, or nationalist, or imperialist or semi-socialist. Where (as in England) these currents accepted the free interplay of the parties, that is, the liberal method applied to the electoral and parliamentary contest, supporting the basic institutions, the liberal features of the State remained entire, the real transformations were slower and parliamentary oscillations from one party to another more marked. England thus passed from a narrow economic liberalism to a fair amount of State intervention of an economico-social nature; from a restricted electorate to universal suffrage, which would end by including women; while she has combined democracy at home with colonial and expansionist imperialism. The continental theories of the State have had small immediate influence on the English mentality, which is more practical and slow to concern itself with general ideas. The political class has been formed by a long tradition and selection. Consciousness of personal individuality prevails over that of the group. Tradition wins over innovations, and formality is an aid to correct behaviour. Yet even in England the positivist, idealist and Marxist theories crept in, bringing something of a new content to the parties and weakening the aristocratic and conservative survivals, especially in the legal and economic sphere. In spite of this, given the diffusion of the liberal spirit among all classes, England better than any other country has withstood the idea that the State was to be conceived as a social totality, and the historical logic of the positivist, Hegelian or Marxist theories.

The same came about, more or less, in the United States of America, where the lack of traditions, customs and ancient and feudal characteristics was supplied by the elaboration of a tradition of their own, made up of political isolation from Europe and the knitting together of American interests, of pride in an autonomous thought and of the necessity of giving their own imprint to what reached them from across the Ocean.

The new Italy did not escape the positivist and Hegelian influence or the importation of Marxism, the less so in that she had not created any political systems of her own since the Renaissance and had been indebted to the foreigner for modern political thought. The Risorgimento had an originality through the combination of French liberalism, British parliamentarism, German Romanticism, with Italian nationalism. Its most complete expression was Count Cavour, but he remained a personality apart. The historical Right was not equal to its task; the endeavour to complete the unity of the nation exhausted its political strength. A petty bourgeois liberalism prevailed in politics and economy, with a method of government serving the dominion of this particular class and its practical aims. This explains why Italy did not have universal suffrage till 1913 (and then almost by surprise), why social legislation was delayed till after the violent workers' disturbances of 1893 and 1898, why she kept strictly to the State monopoly of education and intensified it, avoided a desirable decentralisation and intensified administrative centralisation, and, in spite of Cavour's theory of a 'free Church in a free State', perpetuated the outworn and vexatious jurisdictionalism of the kings of Sardinia and Naples or the Grand-Duke of Tuscany, coloured by an unseasonable anti-clericalism.

In substance, nearly everywhere the idea of the State was coming to overshadow that of liberty. The latter had served to supplant the absolute monarchies—first those by divine right, then the legitimist—or while preserving them had reduced them to a constitutional type. In its turn the State, positive entity or idealist entity, political or national, was supplanting liberty. The masses who had been delirious with enthusiasm for liberty now believed more in the strength of their trade-unions and party organisations and aspired to an economic and collective State. In all three theories and in the practice guided by them, the State was assuming the character of an absolute. This does not mean that the ideals of liberty, individuality, humanity had been lost. They too lived on, inspiring perorations at election meetings and assemblies, but their vitality was already subordinate to the prevailing idea of the State, and they were darkened by the great shadow that the State cast.

§ 54.—In this environment of ideas in ferment, Leo XIII took up a position, no longer in a negative sense, like his predecessors from Pius VII to Pius IX, but in a positive sense, to establish the terms of Catholic thought and provide a practical guidance. Leo was not abandoning the traditional lines of the Church, but he was shaking off certain superstructures, breaking old fetters and clarifying old ideas by adapting them to the new situations. Above all, he inculcated the return to the study of St. Thomas Aquinas, not only in theology but also in philosophy. The encyclical *Aeterni Patris* of 1879 gave a vigorous impulse to neo-Thomism, which had already made a beginning in Italy with Sanseverino and Liberatore; Balmes had brought it to birth in Spain, and in Belgium and France there were not a few who were setting the course of ecclesiastical studies by Thomism. Neo-Thomism was then known as Scholastic Aristotelianism, and presented itself as David against Goliath, with his shepherd's sling against the giant armed from head to foot. In spite of inadequate resources and medieval phraseology, it sought out the vulnerable points of the adversary, whether in pure metaphysical speculation, or in ethics and politics.

It was not the intention of Leo XIII to deprive the Augustinian currents, Scotist and Bonaventurian, of their right of citizenship, nor did he wish philosophical, historical and scientific progress to be ignored. The return to Thomism was to be a guide, a systematisation, a starting-point of traditional thought in philosophy and theology, for all Catholic schools, in order to create a common opinion and language and thus to influence also the world of secular culture.

From that time forth the philosophical studies of Catholics, mostly ecclesiastics, made a considerable advance, both as an attempt to build up a system of thought and as criticism of adverse thought. It is true that limited as they were to a task of adaptation of a didactic nature they did not produce a thinker who could rise above the common mean and give proof of creative genius, but their work in breadth and preparation, with the teaching in the Catholic Universities and the institutes and academies kept by religious Orders, served to promote a wide revival of scholastic thought which penetrated even into zones alien to Catholicism. The philological and historical study of Scholasticism and the production of accurate editions of medieval works has done far more than the scholastic manuals and the *Summulae* of modern professors, to bring a sense of the spirit and value of the great philosophies of the Schools. To have understood this and to have traced the path, without certain exaggerations that would come after him, was the merit of Leo XIII.

The Leonine encyclicals, which form an important tryptich, are *Immortale Dei*, on the Constitution of States (1885), *Libertas praestantissimum*, on Human Liberty (1888), *Rerum Novarum*, on the Condition of the Workers (1891). The reaffirmation of the traditional teaching of the Church is so made as to give the faithful a positive guidance in modern problems and to prevent the easy excursions of thought and action into regions incompatible with Catholic doctrine.

The fundamental problem in the constitution of States is the origin of authority. The Church teaches that it comes from God. By this she does not deny that the choice of the subject invested with authority (personal or representative, monarchic or republican) may be made by the people, in accordance with the customs and constitutions of the various States. What is condemned is the theory that the authority with which the people's choice is invested has a purely earthly origin, denying or ignoring the reference to God. The intervention of the people designates the subject of authority, but does not transmit that which is communicated by God. To this thesis, as set forth by Leo XIII, some have given the sense of a kind of mystical communication of authority from God—an interpretation which, if pleasing to the supporters of monarchy by divine right, cannot be equally so in the case of the first French republicans, or the Nazis or Bolsheviks to-day. Others, by a more human interpretation, have understood that authority, like liberty, like every other element of human social nature, is derived from God and is therefore the natural faculty and gift of those who are to exercise it. If a City-State, organised by heads of families, has determined that an assembly of these shall decide on peace and war—even though there is a president or king—no one can deny that in doing so the assembly is exercising the authority that, through the people, comes to it from God.

What Leo XIII wanted to avoid was an a-religious (laic) and amoral (utilitarian) conception of authority. It is impossible in the natural order to have a head who represents only himself or the interests of a class or caste; the head must represent all. Therefore—and here is the crucial point—no one can give what he has not got, no one can give authority over another. Leo was right in saying that without the idea of a divine authority explicating itself in a natural moral law above the will of the individuals, there will be no true authority among men, only tyranny.

A further step—the political liberties. Leo XIII is on the lines of Gregory with his *Mirari vos* and Pius IX with his *Quanta Cura*. He quotes them in order to establish the continuity of thought and to prevent his words from being taken as a variant or attenuation. Yet in half a century the historical positions had changed. In speaking of freedom of worship he insinuates the distinction to be drawn between Catholic countries and mixed countries, and mentions the theory of toleration of evil as an exercise of the virtue of prudence on the part of the civil authority. For freedom of speech and of the Press he asks those limits that will prevent their becoming licence; he denies that error should be upheld in the name of freedom of education, and asks the State for safeguarding laws. On the other hand, lamenting that such liberties should be used to the detriment of religion and denied to the Church, he demands for her those liberties that serve the defence of truth and morality.

On the relations between Church and State, he reiterates with his habitual limpid clarity the Gelasian and Thomist theory of the two societies and the two powers. He demands that the subordination of ends, the co-ordination of means, and a concordatory understanding on mixed matters should be maintained. For all his moderation of form Leo XIII, though he does not deal either with the confessional State or with the 'indirect power' of the Church over civil society, not only does not renounce them but here and there he gives hints that allow no doubt on what had become the traditional theory. He knew well that he could not ask the liberals, positivists, freemasons, who were governing the Catholic countries, either for a return to the confessional conception of the State or for a recognition of what had been called the indirect power of the Church in temporal matters. He asked only for concord, co-operation, understandings, which even they accepted as expedients, especially in the fear of anarchist agitation and an increase of socialism. Religion for them was a means of keeping the people subject.

Leo XIII had not failed to inculcate on the masses obedience to the constituted powers and resignation rather than revolt, yet—what had not yet been done by previous popes—he insisted on the justice of certain of the workers' demands and on the necessity for a better economic system. The encyclical *Rerum Novarum* crowned the aspirations of the Social Catholics, among them two Cardinals and a bishop of European fame, Manning, Mermillod and Ketteler. He thus gave theoretical and practical basis to the movement that took the name of Christian Democracy. At the time it seemed an audacity for a pope to speak so strongly in favour of the Christian organisation of labour. His words encountered an enormous resistance from the Catholic conservatives. They were alarmed at the fervour with which the younger clergy and many of the laity flung themselves into organising workers' leagues and trade-unions, demanding just wages and building up a healthy class consciousness. The words Christian Democracy led to equivocal interpretations, both on the part of supporters and on that of opponents. In Italy, where the *non expedit* was still in force, there was fear lest the movement should assume a political character, till Leo XIII intervened with the encyclical *Graves de communi* (1901), declaring that the Church had no political preferences for any determined form of government, and that therefore Christian Democracy should not be understood politically, but socially as action in favour of the people.

Leo XIII, certainly, did not arrest the course of events or modify the character of the modern State. He helped to orient the forces of resistance, not only of thought and propaganda but also of political and social action. He encouraged Catholics to take part in political life (except in Italy), according to the institutions of the various countries, to contribute to improving them and to making good laws, to fight in defence of the integrity of the family, for the freedom of the schools, for the safeguarding of the interests of the working classes, and for good municipal administration.

Not always nor everywhere did Leo's words gain a hearing. The resistance of the traditionalist Catholics exceeded the imprudences of the Social and progressivist Catholics. The best known and most notorious case of resistance was that of the French Catholics, to whom Leo XIII had suggested that they should accept the Republic. The few who were convinced of the necessity of the *Ralliement*, as this policy was called, who wished to carry out the Pope's words in their entirety, found themselves opposed by the greater part of the episcopate and the religious Orders, allied with the country gentry, who maintained their resistance to the Republic, dreaming of a return to the Monarchy through what they called *la politique du pire*—the hope that the greater the excesses of the Government, the more the likelihood of a speedy reaction. On such a policy of excesses the anti-clericals, freemasons and positivists who formed the government majority were frenziedly engaged, with the aim of finishing once for all with monarchic manoeuvres and the influence of bishops and religious Orders in politics.

The Dreyfus Case and the passions it aroused swept the majority of the Catholics on to the side of the General Staff. It was made not a question of justice, as it should have been, but one of the dignity of the army and the security of '*la patrie française*'. *La Croix*, run by the Assumptionist Fathers, led the relentless anti-Dreyfus campaign, presenting it as a religious and patriotic crusade, and the editor, Father Auguste Bailly, went so far as to write that 'free enquiry is not permitted in these sorts of affairs'. On the other side the Dreyfusards accused the Jesuits of the school of *rue de la Poste*, from which many army officers came, of being behind the anti-semitic General Staff, which was refusing justice to an innocent man. Leo XIII did not think fit to intervene to prevent the Catholics of France from carrying on so disastrous a campaign, which was prejudicing his policy and, more than ever, the interests of the Church and religious peace. The *lois laïques;* the laws of republican defence and the denunciation of the Concordat originated in the monarchic opposition of the bishops, in the failure of the *ralliement*, and in the anti-Dreyfus and ultra-patriotic campaign of the majority of the French clergy and Catholic laity.

Pius X (1903–17) found a very serious situation in France; it was the rupture not only of diplomatic but of religious relations, a separation of the State from the Church that was no amicable separation but one of violence and strife. With his religious rectitude he was ready to sacrifice the economic structure which, facilitated by the Napoleonic Concordat, had grown up in little less than a century. He understood that it was better to retain nothing at a price of political interference and legal vexations, and to regain the apostolic freedom of a poor church.

The new Pope in the case of France saw both the failure of a policy through which the clergy, in large measure through its own fault, had been directly compromised, and the accentuation of deep cleavages in the Catholic field. Under other aspects this was happening in Italy between Catholic Conservatives and Christian Democrats. Nor were other countries immune from an increasing disquiet in all the fields of religious thought and activity. Pius feared lest Catholics instead of conquering the world for the Church would be themselves conquered by the world. The current of culture that would be qualified by the conventional and comprehensive term of *modernism* had followed too closely the rationalistic and critical trends in theology, biblical exegesis, apologetics, philosophy and history. In wishing to place themselves on the same platform as their adversaries and in adopting their methods, its exponents ended—though not all of them, by any means—by throwing overboard a good deal of the scholastic construction in theology and philosophy, of traditional exegesis and of dogma.

Leo XIII had given a great impetus to historical, philosophical and biblical studies; this led to a fine crop of productions and to a breadth of criticism hitherto unprecedented. Mgr. Duchesne, Mgr. Battifol, Father Lagrange, O.P., Father Prat, S.J., and others are in the first rank of modern Catholic thought. Not all remained within the limits of traditional orthodoxy. Leo XIII shortly before his death had constituted the Pontifical Commission for Biblical Studies (1902), with the aim of avoiding the snares of rationalistic criticism. Loisy, as editor of the *Revue d'histoire et de littérature religieuse*, was already arousing concern. A few years earlier, Leo had condemned *Americanism*, which then passed as a modernism before its time. In his letter to the American Bishops, of January 22, 1899, Leo XIII summed up the new error. There were those, he said, who held that 'The Church should adapt herself more to the civilisation of a world that has reached the age of manhood and, relaxing her ancient rigour, should show herself favourable to the aspirations and theories of the modern peoples. Now this principle is extended by many not only to discipline but also to the doctrines which constitute the *deposit of faith*. They maintain, in fact, that it is opportune, in order to win the hearts of those astray, to keep silence on certain points of doctrine as being of lesser importance, or to attenuate them till they have no longer the sense to which the Church has always held.'[1]

The term *Americanism* was fashioned in France on the occasion of the French edition of the life of Father Hecker. Certain tendencies which it underlined, and which were wholly American in their spontaneity, with nothing philosophical or theological about them, were given in France, in the controversies that ensued, a heretical tinge. Leo XIII himself is careful in the letter we have quoted to declare that 'it is far from our mind to repudiate all that the modern genius has brought to birth. On the contrary, we applaud all search for truth, all effort towards the good, which may help to increase the patrimony of science and to widen the bounds of public happiness. But all this, under pain of not being of real utility, must exist and develop while taking

[1] *Testem benevolentiae.*

into account the authority and wisdom of the Church.' He goes on to sum up the points of criticism, that is, rejection of external direction of souls, attenuation of the intervention of authority for a greater individual freedom, preference given to the natural virtues, the distinction between passive and active virtues, giving preference to these last, and so on.

The American Bishops were rather surprised at the clamour in Paris and Rome and ended by making an act of homage to the Pope, assenting to his judgment. The celebrated Mgr. Ireland, Archbishop of St. Paul's, Minnesota, who believed he had been envisaged as one of the most ardent Americanists, wrote to the Pope, in his letter of February 22, 1899: 'Never for an instant did my Catholic faith and my understanding of the teachings and practices of Holy Church allow me to open my soul to such extravagances.' The word *Americanism* remained in the chronicle of the Church, but it was soon overshadowed by that of *modernism*, which indicated all the tendencies to modernise the Church in dogmatic, biblical, historical and disciplinary matters. To the modernists were opposed the so-called *integrists*, who were nothing else than the extreme wing of the Catholic reaction, which excluded all the mitigations brought by Leo XIII, and, in the political field, bound up the fortunes of the Church with those of anti-democracy and political and economic reaction that were taking shape at the beginning of the century.

Pius X certainly did not find the Church in the hands of the modernists. These were few, in every country, and formed centres of culture in the universities, seminaries, religious Orders, round scientific or historical reviews, drawing to themselves the sympathy of the younger and providing fuel for ecclesiastical polemics. But Pius X saw the danger of an infiltration of the errors characterised as modernism, and he wished to prevent their diffusion and strike at the roots. The decree *Lamentabili*, of July 3, 1905, against Loisy, the encyclical *Pascendi*, of September 2, 1907, which was dogmatic and disciplinary in character, and the *Motu Proprio* of September 1, 1910, on the anti-modernist oath, were his most significant acts. He used rigorous, even harsh methods. By a generalisation of their scope they fell also upon valuable enterprises and men profoundly devoted to the religious cause. Fear invaded

Catholic scholars, who for a certain time refrained from tackling arduous and controversial themes. It was a brusque rectification, followed by a period of stasis through a kind of law of suspicion that was everywhere diffused—till Benedict XV, as soon as he assumed the Papacy, by the encyclical *Beatissimi* (1914) had to remind scholars to observe the law of charity in their controversies, ordering that no one should arrogate to himself the role of the Church's magistracy by accusing his opponent of modernism.

The problems raised by modernism were of a cultural, critical character, seeking to orient religious thought in modern life. For the most part the modernist writers were specialists, particularly in biblical and historical research. Those who pursue a specialised and technical branch of scholarship often do not perceive all the cultural links with general trends of thought and of human life, but are affected by them, no matter whether consciously or unconsciously. It thus came about that a mixture of critical rationalism, Hegelian idealism, historical pragmatism, had filtered through into theological speculation, biblical exegesis and historical criticism, producing an amalgam with no real philosophical content or sure theological sense.

The condemnation by Pius X rapidly served to eliminate such infiltrations, which in not a few cases were only superficial, and to bring a stronger sense of theological responsibility and of scientific and critical probity. It has so happened that within a few years Catholic scholars, though rigorously controlled by authority, have succeeded in winning surer positions, on more thorough foundations. Even certain audacities to-day no longer arouse concern, although the conservative wing looks on them with suspicion, and many once unhoped-for advances have been made. This has been the case with the biblical studies of a Lagrange or a Prat, and the philosophical work of Blondel, all three once taken for modernists, a suspicion to-day impossible for anyone in good faith. The Holy See itself has made full use of the work of such scholars, as over the *Johannine Comma*, in the declaration of Holy Office of June 2, 1927.[1]

The modernist trend did not remain confined to the sphere of higher studies, as scientific and critical revision; it overflowed as a practical

[1]See *Nouvelle Revue Théologique*, Louvain, Nov., 1838, p. 1103 (note.)

movement, was carried into the contests of real life, into the internal discipline of the Church, into her political, moral, educational action.

Among all the popularising works of the time *Il Santo*, by Antonio Fogazzaro, stood out above the rest. He was already celebrated for his earlier novels, but *Il Santo* was epoch-making. He was Catholic and wished so to remain; therefore, when *Il Santo* was put on the Index, he submitted—to the scandal of the literary and liberal world in Italy and abroad. But his idea was the reform of the Church from within, not from without; a Catholic reform, not a Protestant one. He was criticising the ignorant and political priests, the intolerant clericalism of his Venetian province, the residuum of temporalism and worldliness in certain spheres of the Vatican, the frenzied hatred of modern culture. But the reformism of Fogazzaro and of others like him was too mixed up with motives of theological, biblical and historical criticism, and this created an irremediable misunderstanding and increased the concern in higher spheres.

The same suspicion extended to the movement of Christian Democracy. Don Murri in Rome had given an impression of philosophical and theological modernism by his speeches. When disciplinary measures were taken against him he wavered and ended by revolt. In France *Le Sillon*, Marc Sangnier's movement of democratic apostolate, was repudiated, and he submitted. L'Abbé Naudet, who for many years had edited the Christian Democratic paper, *La Justice Sociale*, was constrained to silence, which he kept till his death.

This transference of anti-modernist concern from the realm of sacred sciences to that of social action had two fundamental motives. The first, wholly disciplinary, came from the conception of Pius X that every Catholic undertaking should be placed under the diocesan authorities. He had therefore dissolved the organisation of Catholic Committees and Congresses (which since 1871 had directed the lay movement of resistance to statal anti-clericalism and of defence of Catholic principles), believing it too independent and secular; Catholic Action was put under the direct control of the bishops, and the debates of the Congresses were transformed into courses of instruction, later known as Social Weeks. The second motive was political. Christian Democracy had seemed in France, in Italy, in Belgium and elsewhere to be too much in favour of the people; it had roused ideas that were qualified as socialist. The employers used to say, 'Better the Reds (the Socialists) than the Whites (the Christian Democrats)!' In France religious defence against the anti-Catholic laws had been taken up by the reactionary Right, by the monarchic, nationalist, anti-republican currents, led by Charles Maurras, then supported by bishops and prelates. Republican and democratic Catholics were cold-shouldered under suspicion of modernism. In Italy it was the same, through the progress Socialism was making among the masses and the electoral victories of the 'Union of Popular Parties', which then constituted a kind of Popular Front, uniting Democrats, Radicals and Socialists. It was then that Pius X, while maintaining the *non expedit* in principle, attenuated it by individual dispensations, to enable Catholics to vote in the parliamentary elections for the candidates favoured by the bishops; some of these were militant Catholics, foremost among them Cameroni, Bonomi, Meda and Micheli. Under the auspices of the Catholic Electoral Union an understanding was reached with Giolitti's government, and the Gentiloni Pact was agreed upon for a concentration of the forces of the Right and Liberal Centre, with the electoral support of the Catholics.

All this corresponded to the guiding idea of Pius X, of an understanding between Catholics and the moderate elements of Liberalism who were not opposed to religion, in order to face the anti-clericals and Socialists and find through practical adaptations a possibility of life in common between the Church and the modern State. To this end Catholics, while pursuing with due prudence a practical action in favour of the working classes, were to avoid exceeding in method and in pretentious demands, and to maintain themselves dependent on the episcopate in everything, even in electoral questions. This parochial idea of political life clashed with the affirmation of the centralising State in every field, arrogating to itself spiritual dominion over the school, over the physical training and sport of the young, keeping immense armies under the colours, developing economic and social monopolies, taking away all that was possible from the private initiative on which the Catholics counted. The latter had almost everywhere been reduced to negligible minorities. Where they were still in a majority, they were weakened by divisions between conservatives and democrats and by the modernist controversies. This robbed them of the possibility of formulating a political thought of their own, which would hold its own against the three prevailing ones—the positivist, the idealist, the Marxist. The term Christian Democracy then became empty of sense and was buried in silence. The Christian Social School, after the works of Cathrein, Pesch, Pottier, Vermeersh, Antoine, Toniolo and others, produced only manuals and pamphlets of no importance. The *Theoretical Essay of Natural Law* by the Jesuit Taparelli d'Azeglio, published about 1898, remained the most authoritative and substantial book, to which men returned in Italy and elsewhere for legal and political guidance.

CHAPTER XIV

FROM THE GREAT WAR TO THE CRISIS OF THE LEAGUE OF NATIONS

§ 55.—For nearly half a century a European war, bringing the catastrophe of civilisation, had been feared; it was foretold at every diplomatic conflict, at every step towards increase in armaments. The Berlin Congress, the Triple Alliance of Germany, Austria, Italy, the Franco-Russian Alliance, the *Entente Cordiale* between Great Britain and France, the Austrian annexation of Bosnia and Herzegovina, the Morocco disputes, the Italo-Turkish War for Libya, the first and second Balkan War, Serajevo and the Austro-Serbian War, the European and World War, with the participation of Japan, China, the United States . . . The whole world (save for a few neutrals) divided into two camps, by land, sea and air . . . Four years and three months of war, the Russian Revolution, the defeat and collapse of the Central Empires and their dynasties, the economic, political and moral upheaval . . . Such is the history through which we have lived.

From the religious standpoint, in all the belligerent countries where there were differences and collisions between State and Church, efforts were made to ensure appeasement and contact, on a platform of united resistance and the moral and religious assistance of the army. This course was not immediately taken in every country. Italy took care to include in the Treaty of London of April, 1915, an article ensuring the exclusion of the Vatican from the peace negotiations, a precautionary measure desired by the Foreign Minister, Sonnino (a small-minded-man), for fear of a resurrection of the Roman Question or a humiliation of the Italian Government. The Roman Question was looked upon by Germany as a useful pawn to play against Italy. There came, however, a timely declaration from Cardinal Gasparri, to the effect that the Holy See wished to resolve it directly with Italy and with the consent of the Italian people.

A very grave problem for the Catholic Church at that moment was the mobilisation of the clergy, both because the parishes were thus impoverished of their younger elements and because priests and friars were incorporated in the fighting forces. The conflict between Church and State over a fact so contrary to Canon Law, and esteemed as of divine law, might have been very serious and in other times would have been so. But in 1914, in the face of the laic States the matter passed off with mild protests, combined with semi-official approaches on the part of the Church and practical adjustments and mitigations on the part of certain States. Priests and friars in large numbers were drafted to the sanitary services, religious assistance to the soldiers was restored by the appointment of army bishops and chaplains, but, to a varying extent according to the country concerned, priests and religious remained as infantrymen, gunners, or airmen.

The Holy See showed a greater indulgence in tolerating that the clergies of each separate nation should take an active part in war propaganda, not only among the army in the field but also in the interior of the country to rouse the spirit of resistance. For the clergy of the Entente the thing did not present itself as morally repugnant, for the invasion of Belgium, in open violation of her neutrality and of the treaties of guarantee, gave the war a moral aspect—to drive out the aggressor and to protect the weak attacked by the strong. France never believed that she had any indirect responsibilities for the outbreak of war, and the watchword of Defence of the Fatherland for her coincided with the defence of justice and of European civilisation; there were even some who saw it as a defence of Catholicism against Lutheranism. The French Catholics and their clergy had thus obvious motives for a vigorous campaign in favour of the war.

It must not be thought that on the other side Catholics and Protestants did not find that their war was justified. Austria had sought only to inflict a just punishment on Serbia. Germany was defending herself against the menace of Russia, who had mobilised and was ready to fall upon her. She was attacking France in order not to be encircled by Russia and her ally, and was passing through a Belgium which, by a pro-French policy, had lost her title to neutrality. Thus here too there was an appeal to morality, and Catholic bishops and Protestant pastors could maintain the rightfulness of the war and call down the blessing of God upon the Austro-German armies.

The Protestant churches, being national or local, have no *a priori* difficulty in merging their activity into that of the nation to which they belong, but the Catholic Church, through her universal character, was shaken by the profound cleavage in the appraisement of the morality of so grave an international public event as a war. The more so in that it might be said that never before in modern times had the problem of justice been openly raised, in a war in which nearly all the States of the world had taken up arms, in such measure that it was not only a war of armies but a war of whole peoples. While on both sides the bishops and clergy were declaring the justice of the war fought by their particular country, the Holy See was urged to pronounce itself and refused. Benedict XV wanted to make of the Vatican not a judge of the morality of the war, but the Good Samaritan binding up the wounds, and reserving for itself, if opportunity arose, the role of peacemaker.

We believe that Benedict's act was a prudent one, the only one possible for a pope in the conditions in which he found himself. When he was elected to the Papacy the war had already started; the factual motives which had led to the war were overwhelmed by the extension it had assumed and the human impossibility of stopping it. The Governments involved would never have accepted a judgment pronounced by the Vatican, just as they did not accept its appeals for peace. The Governments wanted the Vatican to proclaim the justice of their own cause; such a declaration would have served for propaganda, like the collective letters of the bishops of their respective countries.

The problem of the justice of the war, rising from the depths of the human conscience, showed the ripening of an unprecedented moral crisis with insufficient means for resolving it. We have noted how from the time of the French Revolution, with the passing of the right of war from the hands of the king into those of the people, the morality of a war, once reserved for the judgment of the ecclesiastical and legal advisers of the monarchs, passed to the broad daylight of debate in assembly. The wars of the French Revolution, the first Napoleonic wars, the wars for liberty and those for nationality were believed by their promoters to be just wars, for they were confused with the popular feelings that produced them, in the name of rights to be vindicated or to be defended. The Church, through her anti-revolutionary policy, was contrary to such wars, while she favoured those promoted by the Holy Alliance for intervention to suppress revolts and restore order. The wars of 1820 to 1870 were a part of the whole revolutionary *ethos* we have considered: their morality was not brought into discussion.

The case of subsequent wars was different. The Boer War was the first of our times to raise a wave of indignation against the government of the United Kingdom, even among the English themselves, from the point of view of morality. The Spanish-American War gave a like shock to public opinion, though not so widely: the provocation was attributed to Spain—falsely, as would later transpire. This recall of public opinion to the morality of wars was encouraged by the anxiety over the continued increase in armaments, the unstable balance of Europe, the insecurity of the smaller and weaker countries, and the nationalist and imperialist spirit of the great States.

The theory of war as a natural, bio-sociological necessity, a means of conquest for the strongest, had now taken the place of the theory of war for national defence, proclaimed by the French Revolution, or war for liberty and independence, of the period of the Risorgimento. The bland, humanitarian sociology of Positivism was giving place to an evolutionist sociology founded on the struggle for life and the survival of the fittest. Frederick William Nietzsche gave it literary and philosophical expression as a revolt against the established order through the will to power. The Christian virtues, natural goodness, humanitarian aspirations are, he held, inadequate and unworthy of man; only his will to power will make him live as a man, destroying within and without all that will prove inferior in the struggle. Life in the full sense of the word is only for the superman. When this idea was transferred from the individual to the social group, it gave a basis for the theory of the higher race, the chosen people, the ethical quality of violence.

An aristocratic theory of this kind was not adapted for the masses (it would become so after the experience of the Great War). The Socialist masses wanted peace. They thought that peace would come only in a socialist community, when the States were no longer bourgeois States, but States of a single class, that of the workers. Nor was the theory of bio-sociological war acceptable to the Christian majority in Europe, even though it had lost the habit of considering political problems and that of war in particular in Christian terms. But with the approach of the danger, and when the European War fell like a thunderbolt, the idea of morality and justice emerged from the collective conscience. All asked themselves in what measure their cause was just and moral. Defence of the motherland was certainly an instinctive and irrepressible impulse, but was this defence identifiable with that of the policy of the country? The religious authorities were asked not to resolve a doubt, but to confirm the justice of the cause. The answer came, alike for all, all were fighting for justice. Such was the moral crisis of Europe in 1914.

Could it have been otherwise? Could Catholic and Protestant bishops, once war had broken out, tell their faithful that theirs was an unjust war? If they had thought so and wished to say so, what government would have allowed it? Thus churchmen, at the moment of having to give a moral and religious answer, found themselves bound up with the powers that had prepared and launched the war, or had not known how to avert it. Their sacerdotal word could no longer be freely uttered. One of the reasons for this crisis came from the fact that the theologians and canonists of the XIX century had not brought the theory of the right of war up to date. They still considered war as the business of the monarch who, in his conscience and after hearing the advice of jurists and moralists, must judge of the justice of the war. War was still admitted as an appropriate means of defending a right when, in the judgment of the monarch himself, there was no other proportionate and decisive means. They had gone so far as to justify war for both sides if, by an invincible error, both monarchs believed in the justice of their cause.

This theory took no account of the change in the State which, once absolutist, had become constitutional, nor of the possibility of public debates on the motives of a war in parliament and in the press, nor of the active part played by public opinion and the influence that could be exerted on it by Christian morals, upheld by citizens and clergy. Nor was it realised that in modern war, with its scientific means of destruction, with permanent armies and the possibility of mobilising the whole nation, its aspect as a means of guaranteeing a right was submerged in the more obvious and real aspect of a means of affirming power and hegemony. To this lack of intellectual preparation on the part of the Churches was added their structural weakness in the face of the modern State, through which, from the XVII century onwards, their power of resisting the enterprises of the absolute monarchies, and still more those of the popular governments of the laic States, had progressively declined. The resistance of Innocent XI to Louis XIV, and of Pius VII to Napoleon, were simply papal gestures, at a time when the local clergies were siding with Louis and with Napoleon. In the case of the Great War, when it broke out Pius X had reached the end of his life; Benedict XV found it when it had already begun. The Papacy which in the religious domain might have made an effort to impede it, at the time of the dispute between Austria and Serbia, had not the man able to divine the position and take action.[1]

Benedict XV did not fail to seek to play the part of peace-maker. He made a first appeal in 1916, but it fell on deaf ears. After not a few

[1]It is well known that Cardinal Merry del Val, then Secretary of State to Pius X, was accused of having encouraged Austria to back her ultimatum with armed force, in the course of a conversation on July 29, 1914, with the Austrian *chargé d'affaires*, Count Maurice Palffy. The two documents on which this charge is based are a telegram from Palffy to the Foreign Minister in Vienna, and a report telegraphed by Baron von Ritter, Bavarian *chargé d'affaires* at the Vatican. Recently, in the second edition of *Irredentismo senza romanticismo*, Dr. Mario Alberti, Minister Plenipotentiary of Italy, published three extracts from the unpublished Memoirs of the Cardinal, which rectify the diplomatic telegrams. In the declaration of October 22, 1923, there is the following passage, describing the diplomatic activity of the Cardinal Secretary of State: 'It is perfectly true that immediately after the horrible crime of Serajevo, I said repeatedly that Austria must be firm and that she had full right to the most solemn reparations and to safeguard her existence efficaciously. But I certainly did not use the expressions attributed to me in the text of Baron Ritter's telegram, nor did I ever express the hope that Austria would have recourse to arms. This constitutes a gloss and an interpretation that I do not admit in any way.' An identical declaration was written in the Cardinal's name on January 18, 1926, in regard to Count Palffy's document.

difficult diplomatic proceedings, which gave a certain confidence that it would be taken into consideration, on August 1, 1917, he sent a letter to the different governments, proposing the main lines of a peace plan. He wrote: 'The fundamental point must be the substitution of the moral force of Right for the material force of arms, hence a just accord of all for the simultaneous and reciprocal decrease of armaments . . . the institution of arbitration . . . sanctions to be determined against the State that might refuse either to submit international questions to arbitration, or to accept its decisions'.

The proposals of Benedict XV corresponded to what had already ripened in the consciousness of the peoples at war. He expressed them in an authoritative manner and imbued them with the character of Christian equity. The need for a permanent understanding between the peoples and for the reconstruction of a moral unity on a basis of international law, accepted and respected by all, was already felt. We have noted how, from the Reformation onwards, modern international law had been taking shape. The ideal of a permanent organisation among the States had been gaining ground. In 1849 a Peace Congress had been held in Paris, with Cobden as Vice-President and Victor Hugo as President; the latter had coined the phrase: 'The United States of Europe', looking forward to a day when disputes would be settled by international arbitration, through 'a great sovereign Senate', An effort towards an international understanding on a moral and juridical basis was later made by the Czar of Russia, in agreement with the Queen of Holland (and with the support of Leo XIII), culminating in the two Hague Conferences of 1899 and 1907. Their decisions, though timid and incomplete, marked an important beginning.

During the Great War, the idea that this might be the last war between civilised peoples, and that it would be possible with the triumph of justice and democracy to constitute a new international order, appealed to thinkers and priests, political men and leaders of mass parties. With such an idea Woodrow Wilson, President of the United States, had entered the war on the side of the *Entente* in 1917; the weight of this intervention determined the issue. By his Message of January 8, 1918, he fixed the peace-plan in Fourteen Points, completed by the Four Points of the following February. These proclaimed the constitution of an international society and the necessity for disarmament more or less on the same lines as the proposals of Benedict XV, with the principle of the self-determination of peoples and the system of colonial mandates. All this formed the presuppositions of the armistices and peace-treaties, inasmuch as Germany, Austria and their allies had accepted the Fourteen Points in principle.

Unhappily, in the Peace Conference the representatives of the vanquished countries were not admitted. Peace was imposed, not agreed upon. Neither all Wilson's proposals nor the spirit that animated them penetrated into the treaties. Yet, in spite of many errors, the League of Nations was created 'to develop co-operation between the nations and to guarantee them peace and security'. Side by side with the League was constituted the International Labour Office, and, on another plane, the Permanent Court of International Justice at the Hague. A wave of hope and confidence in the new institution passed over the various countries, realising as it did the dreams of two and a half centuries, from the time when William Penn and Charles Irénée Chastel, Abbé de Saint-Pierre, wrote the first projects for international organisation. From the juridico-political standpoint, the constitution of the League of Nations sought to combine the sovereignty of each separate State with self-limitation through a mutual interdependence; the equality of all the States among themselves with the preponderance of the great nations; the law of the victors with a gradual understanding with the vanquished. The first steps of the new institution revealed the immense difficulties offered by so hybrid and contradictory a conception.

In all countries, after the first enthusiasms, two currents took shape in public opinion, for and against Geneva, guided by diverse and contradictory motives according to whether it was a case of the vanquished countries or the victors, of nationalist or pacifist environments. Thus two mysticisms were created, one pro-League, the other anti-League. Catholics, too, were divided for and against. Those against saw in Geneva a counter-altar to the Catholic centre, Rome—Wilson the Protestant set up against Benedict XV. This idea was nourished by resentment that Benedict's peace proposals had not been accepted by the Powers, and that the Pope had not been invited to send a representative to the assemblies of Geneva—whereas in 1899 the Czar and the Queen of Holland, in spite of the opposition of Italy, sent a message to Leo XIII and received a reply which was read in the public assembly. Article 15 of the Treaty of London could not be applied to the League of Nations, which had not been foreseen, but the States of the *Entente* wished to observe it the more meticulously in that they already foresaw they would be unfaithful in respect of other clauses of the same Treaty.

These feelings of resentment died down with time, partly because with the first activities of the League, already forsaken by the United States and not yet completed by the admission of Germany, it was plain that a representative of the Pope would have been out of place in purely political matters, while a way of co-operation with the Papacy could be found through a papal diplomat accredited to the League. Benedict XV, in his encyclical *Pacem Dei* of May 23, 1920, declared: 'To the nations united in a league founded on the Christian law, the Church will faithfully lend her active and eager co-operation in all their undertakings inspired by justice and charity'. There was nothing in the Covenant of the League of Nations that was not inspired by criteria of justice, peace, charity, mutual help, defence of the weak, raising of the non-civilised peoples, yet there was no reference to the Christian law. This lack sprang from the conception of the laic State, which could be considered as established and unchallenged. The League of such States could not be other than laic. This did not mean that it was anti-Christian, for its ethico-juridical content not only was not contrary to the Christian law, but, as natural ethical law, corresponded to it. Therefore Benedict's offer of the active and eager co-operation of the Church is well characterised as applying to all undertakings inspired by justice and charity—both because in all human institutions (even those founded explicitly on the Christian law) there may be undertakings not inspired by justice and charity, and in order to keep the Church extraneous to strictly technical and political questions.

The lack of a religious ideal and of the official invocation of God, the Father of all men, was the original sin of the League of Nations, for it conflicted with a minimum of social religious feeling. Christians sought to make amends for this, promoting services and public prayer on the occasion of the solemn assemblies of the League. Through the initiative of Baron de Montenach, a Swiss, Mgr. Beaupin, a Frenchman, and Marquis Alessandro Corsi, an Italian, and others, with the approval and encouragement of the Pope, the Catholic Union of International Studies was founded in 1919, to help to form a Christian juridical mentality in international problems, and to support the just attempts to bring understanding between the peoples. Other peace associations arose, either earlier or later, either promoted by Catholics, or interdenominational or neutral, on a plane of propaganda, like the League of Nations Union, which is the most widespread and the most authoritative. There have been others of a strictly pacifist character on the principle of non-resistance to evil based on conscientious objection, and yet others, like the more recent International Peace Campaign, as gradually the problems of peace returned to the front of the picture.

§56.—The Russian Revolution of 1917 had brought the triumph of the Bolsheviks and the formation of the government of the Soviets—soldiers and peasants. Till then Russia had been under an absolute and almost always tyrannical government. The attempt at a parliament, represented by the Duma, had failed. Feudal dominion weighed on the peasants. The nihilism of the anarchic, intellectual and popular currents was the counterpart to the terrorism of the government. In 1917 the people were tired of the war, which was animated by no real feeling and was led by military leaders and court dignitaries with a scornful carelessness of the combatant and with a growing indiscipline at the front and in the interior, which was a prelude to the break up. A man of genius, Lenin, profited by the favourable circumstances and the support of the enemy to overthrow the clay-footed colossus, after Kerenski had undermined its foundations. The decisive success of communism in Russia inaugurated a politico-economic experiment unique in history.

It has been summed up in the phrase *dictatorship of the proletariat*; the reality was more complex. The new State was characterised by the expropriation and collectivisation of private property; the unification of all in a single class, that of labour, and the consequent elimination of the other classes; the constitution of a single official party as an organ of reinforcement for the public powers and of mediation between government and people. At the same time, to avoid adverse reaction, came the expulsion or execution on a large scale of the members of the old political, military, aristocratic, ecclesiastical and intellectual *élites*, who had not fled abroad. In order to create a wide basis of favourable public opinion, propaganda, support and revolutionary enterprise, the communist Third International was formed, with headquarters in Moscow, to be in fact and intent a counter-altar to the Socialist Second International of Amsterdam.

With the collapse of the Central Empires, the authoritarian systems and the aristocratic and military orders supporting them collapsed likewise. The ebullition of the masses led to the various communist, spartacist and anarchist revolts, which broke out sporadically, seeking to form provisional governments, till the Socialists and Radicals, with the support of the Catholic Social parties (the Centre in Germany, the Social Christians in Austria and in Hungary) were able to constitute more stable governments and embody in new charters the democratic principles with which they were inspired. The new States that arose from the ruins and the small States that had been enlarged, from the Baltic to the Aegean, gave themselves very broad democratic constitutions, in order to content the working masses and the soldiers returning from the front, who were in great majority socialist and believed that the hour had come to rise.

In the victorious and neutral countries the crisis of the immediate post-war period was less acute, and nearly everywhere the social institutions stood the strain. The period of the big strikes (due to the transition from a war-time economy to post-war economy) was soon left behind, in many cases through good-will on both sides, and after upheavals of varying gravity. While the socialist and ultra-democratic currents were gaining strength, those of the nationalists were acquiring fresh vigour and ex-soldiers' associations were being organised. The need was felt for an economic and political reaction at home, at the same time as men were becoming conscious of the new international trends towards a league of States.

What were known as the Catholic parties, in the countries where they already existed—in Germany, Austria, Hungary and the adjoining nations and Belgium, Holland and Switzerland—were more or less taking up a central position between Socialism and the nationalist and bourgeois Right; in certain cases they collaborated with the Socialists in building up the new States, as in Germany with the Weimar Constitution. Before the war such parties had confined themselves to the defence of religion and morality and of the freedom of the schools, and to supporting and defending protective labour legislation and trade-unions. In the Central Empires, Germany and Austria-Hungary, all parties had had a very limited role, since the Government was extra-parliamentary. In Holland and Switzerland Catholics co-operated with the Protestants in a wise conservative policy, to the Right but socially open-minded. In Belgium for a long time the Catholics had governed alone, after winning the long battle for freedom of the schools, but the prevailing political policy was conservative of a clerical type. After the war it became incumbent on the Catholics of the various continental countries and on those of Southern Ireland to take a wider and more responsible part in public life. A reconsideration of their political conception and of their social positions became therefore imperative. It was then that the Italian Catholics, after having obtained from the Vatican the promise that the *non expedit* should be raised, formed a party with a public manifesto issued on January 18, 1919, taking the name of Italian Popular Party. This was soon followed by the foundation of the Bavarian Popular Party, the Social-Popular Party of Spain, the Czech Popular Party, the Popular-Democratic Parties of Poland and Lithuania and later the Popular-Democratic Party of France. An International Secretariat of Democratic Parties of Christian Inspiration was founded, with headquarters in Paris.

The course taken by the Popular and Christian-Social parties after the war differed from that before the war not so much through their clearer independence of the ecclesiastical hierarchy and their social programme, as through their endeavour to form their own school of political thought on the problem of the State. The Liberal Catholics of the school of Montalembert had accentuated the note of liberty, which was the problem of the day. The Christian Democrats of the school of Decourtins had emphasised social reforms. The Popular Parties put in the foreground the reform of the State. Civil and political liberties had been won and were then questioned by none. Social legislation had already started and the workers' movements were urging it forward. The chief crisis was the institutional and functional crisis of the State, which had its repercussions on political liberties and social reforms.

In the Manifesto of the Italian Popular Party in January, 1919, it was declared: 'For a centralising State, seeking to restrict all organising powers and all civic and individual activities, we would substitute, on constitutional grounds, a State truly popular, recognising the limits of its activity, respectful of the natural centres and organisms—the family, occupational groups, townships—giving way before the rights of human personality and encouraging its initiatives'.[1] The name given to such a conception was Popularism, a name explained as follows: 'The word 'people' in the sense in which it is used in the Latin expression *Senatus Populusque Romanus*, has always been pleasing to Catholics as indicating at once the collective will and the social hierarchy, a principle of order and of classic consent in the positive sense of the word. But the word 'people' served also all the developments of demagogy and was thus rendered rather suspect. In order to indicate the popular régime it was considered preferable to use the Greek word 'democracy' which has remained current, whereas from the Middle Ages men spoke in Italy of a *popular régime*, or of *government of the people*, and other similar expressions'.[2]

Popularism is democratic, but it differs from liberal democracy in that it denies the individualist and centralising system of the State and wishes the State to be organic and decentralised. It is liberal (in the wholesome sense of the word) because it takes its stand on the civil and political liberties, which it upholds as equal for all, without party monopolies and without persecution of religion, races or classes. It is social in the sense of a radical reform of the present capitalist system, but it parts company with Socialism because it admits of private property while insisting on the social function of such property. It proclaims its Christian character because to-day there can be no ethics or civilisation other than Christian. Popularism was the antithesis of the totalitarian State. It was born in the immediate post-war period, for there were signs that the gravest crisis was that of the State, tending as it did towards totalitarian conceptions.

[1]L. Sturzo, *Italy and Fascismo*, Faber & Gwyer, 1926.

[2]L. Sturzo, '*Popularisme*,' in *Politique* (Paris) Aug. 15, 1928.

Several times in the course of the present study, in examining the character of the modern State and of its logical development into the laic State, we have had glimpses of the totalitarian State as its natural outcome. This presents itself as antithetical to the 'State of opinion' or liberal State. Historically a purely liberal State has never existed nor could exist, without a qualification which, by bringing it into the concrete, bounds it or modifies its character. It is the method of liberty that is the touchstone, whereas the data of concrete liberties may vary. Often not even the method of liberty is respected in democratic régimes, while it is abolished completely in those that are authoritarian or semi-authoritarian. Thus the ideal antithesis between the liberal and totalitarian States disappears as soon as the method of liberty ceases to function.

Russian Bolshevism, when it had become the régime of the Soviets, having gained a monopoly of power in the name of the Communist Party, having persecuted, expelled, or exterminated the other classes, parties and hostile armies, subjected the country to an iron discipline. It abolished all liberty save the arbitrary liberty of the heads of the Party, refusing it rigorously to the dissidents in the Party itself. The totalitarian State was born; it was not so called, because it wished to be the ideal Communist State. The word totalitarian applied to the State was born in Italy in 1926, four years after Fascism had come into power with the March on Rome (1922)—after it had made the experiment of a government in apparent collaboration with men of other parties (1922-24); after it had held elections with a system of a majority premium of three-quarters of the seats to the most successful party (which was naturally the Fascist Party) in 1924; when, in order to break down an opposition that was still vigorous, first all freedom of discussion and of the press was restricted (1925), then all the parties, all free and independent associations were abolished, and all non-fascist political enterprises were forbidden (1926). It was then that the principle was proclaimed: 'Nothing outside the State, nothing above the State or against the State; everything in the State and for the State'. Then the State founded on this principle was called by the Fascists and by their leader the Totalitarian State.

The establishment of this State has come about by gradual experiment. It was easy to abolish political liberty, to reduce parliament to a merely decorative and formal body, to transform parliamentary elections into enforced plebiscites on lists imposed from the centre and voted upon with either yes or no, without possibility either of discussion and propaganda or of any contrary affirmation. When there is a party militia and the police includes a permanent and perfected department of political espionage, a totalitarian régime can be imposed on a country with small or no resistance; an elected Parliament may be abolished as in Italy in 1938, and replaced by a Council of Corporations nominated by the Government, and so on.

Yet, the totalitarian State demands not resignation but consent, not a sullen opposition but joyous surrender. Thus all the more interesting expressions of collective and personal life have passed into the hands of the State—youth associations, sport, wireless, the cinema, newspapers and publications of every kind, private and public schools of every grade and type. Nor is this enough. There must be a discipline of mind, will and body—the militarisation of all, from children of six to adults of fifty-six; hence two effects, the one domestic, that of complete subjection to the State, the other concerning foreign relations, through the creation of numerous and well prepared armies.

Economy is a department in which the property-owner should have freedom of initiative, while the worker must be able to vindicate his rights and defend his interests. Bolshevism suppressed the property-owner and surrogated him by the State (save for certain practical compromises). Fascism has voided a great part of economy of its private content and has interposed semi-State enterprises and State capital. Moreover, it has organised the Corporations as bureaucratic departments of the various branches of economy, under the dependence and direction of the State, for economy too is 'within the State and for the State'. The economic crisis has facilitated this subjection of private economy, through the necessity of the financial intervention of the State. The State has become shareholder, company promoter, trader, monopolist. The necessity for foreign currency led to the monopoly of exchange and later also of foreign trade. Italy has thus applied a system of State Socialism, while Russia has applied that of State collectivism or Communism.

The Communist idea has presented itself in Russia under the sign of materialism and atheism. Liberation from the chains of Czardom (of the aristocracy as maintaining the serf system, of the Church as standing for ignorance) found its motives in the two-fold aim of material prosperity and religious revolt.

The Russian Soviets sought at first to form a State Church, producing a cleavage with the Orthodox clergy who had remained in the country. At the same time they laicised the State, broke all the legal ties between the people and the Church, closed monasteries and convents, tore down religious buildings or transformed them for profane uses, and encouraged anti-religious and blasphemous propaganda. On the collapse of the attempt at a bolshevising Church, there was fierce persecution of all the clergy, religious worship was prevented, and the dechristianisation of Russia became a deliberate aim. Periods of strife have been followed by periods of more or less malevolent toleration. From time to time there is talk of freedom of worship, if there can be freedom under the dictatorships. Many prefer the secret Christian communities, which are developing underground in Soviet territories.

Russia, in encouraging the impious fanaticism of the 'Anti-God' leagues, has sought to create a Marxist 'mysticism', deifying labour, science the liberator, equalitarian collectivism, making of Lenin a myth, in the vast mausoleum in which his body lies, to attract the crowds and inspire them with pride. Communism is a motive of separation from the rest of the world, to obtain a homogeneous structure for the immense Russian empire, and to make of it a magnetic centre drawing the masses even of other countries towards the Third International of Moscow, the beacon of a new civilisation. Communist philosophy, culture, education, literature, art (however disputable) are set against those of the past and of the present, as the expression of a new civilisation of peoples. Communist propaganda in every country has served a two-fold purpose, anti-religious and political, among the masses that were becoming imbued with the mysticism of Moscow.

Other attempts at dictatorial governments, after those of Russia and Italy, have been those of Kemal Ataturk in Turkey, of Primo de Rivera in Spain, of Pilsudski in Poland, of Calles in Mexico, of Carmona and

Salazar in Portugal, of King Alexander in Jugoslavia and of Dollfuss in Austria. There were similar enterprises in Greece, Albania, Bulgaria, Lithuania, Finland; the evil spread to South America, with more or less transient phases, lacking in originality. Some of these dictatorships have collapsed, others survive, according to the phases of local politics. But where they have collapsed, giving place to representative governments, the spirit of party domination and the dictatorial tendency remains, or returns to the fore. What has been happening for the last twenty years in such States has not come about through a conception of political philosophy, but has been precisely the overthrow of political and moral values, through the use of forcible methods for the conquest of power by a party or a group or an individual—with contempt for the right of human personality and of dissident minorities; the abrogation of liberties; political, legal, administrative and moral centralisation in the State; the concentration in the hands of one or of a few of all the means capable of influencing public opinion.

The most imposing experiment is that which has taken place in Germany since 1933. The National Socialist system of dictatorship is practically similar to that of Fascism, only more marked and more brutal—a single armed party; complete State centralisation; the whole economy of the country in the hands of the State and serving the ends of the State; a permanent and general militarisation; State direction for State ends of education, culture, press, sport, cinema, theatre; the violent suppression of personal and political liberty; the reduction of every manifestation of the popular will in the form of plebiscites and elections to manipulations by Party and State in complete fusion of organs and ends; an implacable persecution against adversaries of the Party, to the point of their violent suppression (as on the night of June 30, 1934). There is no moral domain left for the individual conscience that has not been requisitioned by the State, with police and espionage corps who reach the pitch of staging crimes that have never been committed.

The differences between Germany and Italy up to the beginning of 1938 lay in the anti-semitic struggle, the racial conception and a certain religious symbolism arising from it. Nazism seeks to be a system of civilisation peculiar to the German people, expressing its essential nature and power. 'Blood and the soil', that is, the race and the land that fosters it, the environment in which its roots are set, are at the source of this superior, unique, dominant people. This marks the intentional separation from the Christian civilisation on which is founded the spiritual unity of the West. It was Germany that promoted the first cleavage through Lutheranism which, despite the separation, preserved the bond of a Christian faith, that albeit- subjective, was founded on the Bible, the holy book for all. The European community, reconstructed after Westphalia on certain ethical and political principles, on interchange of culture and solidarity of interests, received a first blow from Bismarck's policy and a second from the Great War. But then it was hoped that a common platform of democratic and international co-operation had been finally attained; Locarno and Germany's entry into the League of Nations marked a beginning. Now all this is over. Germany in order to affirm herself as such, has promoted a fresh cleavage in every field, taking her stand on a repudiation of religion, ethics and European culture, to enclose herself, by a titanic effort of self-potentialisation, within a conception of life giving her a superior personality and an unchallenged dominion throughout the world.

From this standpoint Nazism upholds a policy of differentiation from other races, the expulsion, segregation, subjection of the community of other races, especially the Jews, who are proclaimed as enemies of the German people, to be ruthlessly crushed. Eugenic systems and compulsory sterilisation are imposed in order to achieve the best selection and the most perfect physical homogeneity of the German people, as well as a characteristic education and training fitted to form a corresponding mentality. All the German peoples who are under other States must enter into a single political system, just as they form a single race and a single German soul. Hence the feverish rearmament at dizzy speed, in order that Germany may impose herself on the world, the spasmodic tension in order to gain time and distance against future enemies, a mystical titanism, like a race to death and deification.

To create such a movement it is well to have a religion interpreting, symbolising and extolling its sentiments. And therefore the symbols of the old Germanic divinities, crude as they are, have found favour among a large band of the young; they interpret the essence of 'Germanity', which is the divinity that must be worshipped. Hence an angry and odious anti-Christian propaganda, which finds the soil prepared for it both among the masses, already moulded to materialism by Socialism and Communism, and among the intellectual *élites*, educated in scientific Positivism or in philosophical Idealism. The Germans who have remained faithful to Christianity are divided into two large bands. There are those who feel the fundamental and irremediable conflict between faith in Christ and the racial theory and, remaining faithful to the first, seek to fight as best they may against the second, or at least hold themselves spiritually aloof and face the scorn of the many and the persecutions of the Party. The others believe that it may be possible by compromises on both sides to obtain a practical reconciliation. These last falsify Christianity and racialism; they have confounded them with the idea of vindication of the rights of the Fatherland, of the greatness and political strength of Germany, of her superiority of race and culture.

Hitler on achieving power sought to break down the opposition of the Christian churches to his theories and his party. He declared that his Government would respect the two Christian Churches of the *Reich*, the Protestant and the Catholic. For the Protestant Church he sought unification by obliging all the particular churches to form the national Reich Church. He met with obstacles in men and policies. Mistrust was increased by the anti-Christian propaganda favoured by the Nazi party and by the suppression of all liberty. It would be superfluous to speak of the long disputes between the churches, the Minister of Religions, and the Reich Bishop, who has never been completely recognised. In actual fact, it cannot be said that up till to-day either a spiritual unification or an organic unification has been achieved, and in certain sections of Protestants an initial favour towards Nazism has turned into sullen religious opposition. Of the two most eminent Protestant pastors, Karl Barth has fled to Switzerland and Niemöller is in a concentration camp.

The Catholic Church had already signed four concordats with the various States of the Germany of Weimar. Hitler wanted to fuse them into one for the whole *Reich*, so as to give an impression of agreement and sympathy between him and the Vatican. The bishops withdrew (the term used was 'suspended') the condemnations they had issued against the Nazi movement, the Centre was hastily disbanded, certain Christian trade-unions announced their support of the social policies of the new Government, the Nuncio encouraged an understanding between the Catholic leaders and the Nazis. Thus a few months later it was possible to draw up the new Concordat (1933). But neither the Protestant nor the Catholic Church has had any respite in the struggle. The denominational schools, the Catholic youth organisations, and the religious Orders have suffered persistent attacks and encroachments, while the religious Press has been either destroyed or brought into subjection. Thus the position of the Christian churches in Germany has been continually deteriorating. The present situation is one of an insidious and constant anti-Christian persecution, through the titanic self-assertion of Nazi Germanism.

§ 57.—Italian Fascism at the beginning did not aspire to universalism like Moscow, nor to racial predominance like Berlin. Italian Fascism assumed a national and political character; it would make of Italy an imperial Power. To this end it had to find a 'mysticism'—the Fascist State, national and imperial, as the end, with every other idea and activity, whatever its nature, as means to this end. And the Catholic religion and the Papacy? Logically, in the proud idealisation of the Fascist State, they too would be means to the end. This would have been no novelty; religion as an instrument of government—*instrumentum regni*—is an ancient idea, revived from age to age. Fascism, having made of the State an ethical totality, (we should say a pantheistic State), sought in every way possible to bring the Church within it, yet without sacrifice of its laic character. This was the unilateral and paradoxical compromise of Fascism. To prevent the Church from opposing and contradicting it, at the bottom of the Fascist mind (and sometimes rising to the surface) lies the tacit and understood threat of a relentless struggle. And since Fascism has little by little succeeded in capturing all the nerve-centres of public and private life and in imposing upon the Italians a discipline made up of fear and subjection among the tepid, of enthusiasm among its adherents, it has worked in the same way upon the clergy, granting them favours to win their allegiance and at the same time setting the Ovra to keep watch on them.

We have qualified this compromise as unilateral, for here there could be no compromise on the part of the Papacy or of the Italian episcopate and the organised faithful, such as those of Catholic Action and the parish or general associations. Hence a subtle duel, wholly Italian, carried on through partial compromises made with reservations, unexpressed *sous-entendus* clear enough to the initiated, general and involved declarations that yet succeeded in hitting the mark, sullen conflicts, periods of truce and apparent friendship, mutual eulogies, generous gifts and grave losses on the part of either side. The Papacy is accustomed both to open strife and to patient construction, to long waiting, and to the gaining of real advantages at the cost of apparent losses. Having withstood nearly two thousand years it is free from any fear of irreparable losses or total disasters. And for this reason its position in regard to Fascism is of extreme interest more in relation to Fascism than in relation to the Papacy.

The problem of greatest concern to the Papacy on the advent of Fascism was the solution of the Roman Question, and the settlement by means of a concordat of the juridical and economic relations between the Church and the Italian State. There was a wish to seize the occasion of an authoritarian and personal government in order to cut short any opposition from Italian public opinion, which had been nourished by anti-Vatican prejudices and reared in the fear of clericalism. At the same time the need was felt for a speedy contractual settlement of the various questions that had come to the fore in half a century, in the face of a totalitarian State without limit or check, which had suppressed every form of civil and political liberty. The Papacy and the Episcopate no longer possessed the means which from 1860 onwards they had used to defend themselves and the rights of the Church and faithful, and to uphold Christian principles openly, whether against private individuals or against Parliament and Government.

The task of Pius XI was facilitated by events, but he brought to it also a resolute will to overcome all obstacles. In his Cardinal Secretary of State he had an ideal collaborator—Cardinal Gasparri had drawn up a plan for a solution of the Roman Question during the war, he had entered into semi-official negotiations with the two Prime Ministers, Orlando and Nitti, immediately after the war, and he was a man of vast legal culture and diplomatic ability. No sooner had the war ended than Benedict XV lifted the ban against receiving in the Vatican the heads of Catholic States (historically so reputed) when they visited the Quirinal. He also abolished the *non expedit*, which had prevented Italian Catholics from taking part in political life. These were significant gestures, but the Liberal-Democratic governments feared to commit themselves, although they believed that the time was ripe for an understanding with the Papacy. Pius XI, on his election (February, 1922), wished to revive the custom, suspended since 1870, of blessing the crowd from the Vatican *loggia*; this had been received with great favour by general opinion. In June, 1921, Benito Mussolini, then a Deputy, in addressing the Chamber had used the following words: 'If the Vatican finally renounces its temporal dreams, profane and laic Italy would furnish the Vatican with the material aids, the material facilities, for schools, churches, hospitals and so forth, that a profane power disposes of. For the development of Catholicism in the world, the increase of the 400 million men who in all parts of the earth look towards Rome, is a matter of interest and pride also for us, who are Italians.' This 'profane' and broad vision could well be contrasted with the jurisdictionalist and petty outlook of the Liberal governments towards the Papacy, of which the last example had been Article 15 of the Treaty of London. Mussolini, who in 1919 had set in his programme the abolition of the State fund for religious worship and other anti-clerical proposals, in 1921 wished to leap the ditch, on condition of a decisive renouncement of 'temporal dreams': Leo XIII had been too taken up with the events of the fall of the Temporal Power to agree to a solution implying such renunciation, but from Pius X onwards 'temporal dreams' had been out of date. Pius XI in his first encyclical of December 23, 1922, protested 'against such a condition of affairs, not through vain and earthly ambition, for which we should blush, but by a pure debt of conscience, for the nature of the Church demands that the Holy See should be and appear independent and free of every human authority or law, even a law proclaiming guarantees'.

For four years, from the March on Rome (October, 1922) to the end of 1926, there was no more talk of the Roman Question. They were the years when the Fascist régime was consolidating itself against the opposition of the Socialists, Populars and a fraction of Liberal-Democrats—the years of the murder of nineteen working men in Turin, believed to be Communists, of the new electoral law, of the establishment of the Fascist Militia as a State force, of the murder of Matteotti, of the Aventine secession, of the suppression of freedom of assembly and of the Press, of the disbanding of all parties and the proclamation of the totalitarian State. The secret negotiations between Mussolini and the Vatican, through jurists of either party, lasted about three years. The secret was kept even from the Cardinals of the Curia, till the result was assured. The Lateran Treaty was signed on February 11, 1929.

The terms of the treaty are well known. The Vatican wished for a territorial zone over which to assert effective sovereignty, for according to the juridical criteria prevailing in the Curia, sovereignty could not be dissociated from territory, nor could the complete freedom and independence of the Holy See be assured without sovereignty. The Vatican zone, cut off from the territory of the kingdom of Italy, was declared an independent City State under the sovereignty of the Pope; a symbolic State rather than a real one and a city *sui generis*, in which the will of the carefully numbered citizens is merged into that of the Pope, at once sovereign and the one true citizen. All the measures of civil, administrative, fiscal and criminal law of such a city are necessarily adapted to the fact that the Vatican is an enclosed space within Rome the capital of Italy, and that its material and civil life depends on the good relations between the Vatican and Italy. The real and visible liberty and independence of the Holy See, vindicated by Pius XI, is substantially juridical, and such is the situation resulting from the treaty. It is not political, for it is not a case of a State in the true sense of the word, in which there is a people asserting its political personality on an adequate and guaranteed territory. Nor is it international, for there is no title to recognition and guarantee on the part of other nations.

Such conditions called for a permanent moral factor to integrate the strictly juridical character of the new position of the Papacy. It was for this reason that Pius XI made it a *sine qua non* condition that a concordat should be signed ensuring Catholic influence in the Kingdom of Italy. The chief provisions of the Concordat concern the matrimonial system (the suppression of civil marriage for Catholics, ecclesiastical jurisdiction in respect of the marriage-bond, prohibition to introduce divorce); religious teaching in the schools; religious assistance in the army, navy and airforce, in the militia and pre-military organisations; freedom of education and recognition of the Catholic institutions including the University of Milan; recognition of Catholic Action; reorganisation of Church endowments and the budget of public worship; abolition of the old jurisdictionalist rights of control, such as the *placet*, the *exequatur*, and the special taxes on benefices; recognition of the religious Orders as corporate bodies and of the civil validity of their vows; abolition of the right of patronage and regulation of the appointment of bishops and parish priests, through agreement between the religious and civil authorities, with the introduction of an oath of loyalty to the State to be taken by the bishops.

The Vatican sought to give the Italian State a Catholic character, in order to guarantee that the Catholic religion should be genuinely and not only nominally the State religion. Yet, while the terms of the Concordat are of a prevalently confessional character, the spirit of the Fascist State remained unaltered, and its leader sought with shrewdness and audacity to disparage the confessionalism celebrated by the Catholic Press throughout the world, which extolled the new Constantine who had given peace to the Church. This he did in his speech to the Chamber of Deputies the following May, when he proclaimed the role of Rome and of the Roman Empire, saying that 'This religion was born in Palestine. In Rome only did it become Catholic. Confined to Palestine, very probably it would have known the fate of so many sects that have blossomed in an incandescent atmosphere, like the Essenes. It would have eclipsed itself without leaving a trace.'

Fascist resentment showed itself openly against the Catholic Youth organisation, which was assuming an exceptional development and was attracting the sympathy and attention of many. Its public manifestations, processions, pilgrimages, festivals were always thronged, and there was a fear that families might prefer to send their sons to the Catholics rather than to the Fascists. A collision was inevitable. From

March, 1931, onwards there were armed attacks on Catholic clubs, frenzied demands in the Press that these should be closed down, assaults on processions and on the faithful coming out of church, while young men were wounded, priests molested, banners torn to pieces, through the length and breadth of Italy, as though in obedience to a word of command. The solemn and imposing commemoration of the anniversary of the Leonine encyclical *Rerum Novarum*, in which many foreign delegations took part, when Pius XI promulgated his complementary encyclical, *Quadragesimo Anno* (the two together forming the Code of Catholic social teaching), gave the impression to the Fascist leaders that they would have to strike at the roots to prevent a recrudescence of Catholic forces which might be perilous for a totalitarian State. The Catholic clubs were closed, their equipment sequestrated, and it was forbidden to reopen them.

The Pope then wrote his famous encyclical: *Non abbiamo bisogno*, of June 29, 1931. Fearing that its publication in Italy would be prevented and that the Italian police would seize the copies of the *Osservatore Romano* dedicated to it, he sent special messengers abroad carrying translations in various languages, to be published simultaneously with the official Italian text. In this encyclical Pius XI openly condemns the Fascist theory of the State as the end of the individual, deplores the ill-treatment of the Catholic youth organisation and defends it from the charge of seeking to engage in politics; he recognises the distressing position of the faithful forced to take the Fascist oath, and declares authoritatively that such an oath can be tolerated only on condition that each individual in taking it shall do so with the intent of reserving the rights of God and of conscience—a reservation that must be openly expressed if necessity arises, to remove any ambiguity of profession of faith and respect of Catholic morality. The dispute lasted another three months, till through the offices of the Jesuit, Father Tacchi-Venturi, it was possible to establish the terms of an agreement between the Vatican and the Fascist government. Through this the Government undertook to allow the Catholic clubs to be reopened and to hand over the equipment sequestrated, and not to oppose the activity of Catholic Action in general and the youth movement in particular. The Vatican modified the national character of these organisations and accentuated their diocesan character; it consented that they should have no banner save the national flag, and that processions and public demonstrations should be avoided, in order to remove the impression of any wish to compete with the Fascist Youth organisations.

The episode, even though closed, served to mark the dualistic positions of the two powers and to dissipate the illusion, naïvely cultivated by not a few, that Fascism could be made Catholic. Mussolini took good care not to do what he had outlined in his speech of 1921, fearing lest a Catholic Rome might overshadow his dream of greatness. For the Vatican to hold a corner of Rome could be tolerated, but the new Rome was to be the Fascist Rome. He thus continued the tradition of the Third Rome from 1870 onwards, with the difference that the Liberal Rome measured the cost, being bourgeois, while Fascist Rome does not measure the cost, being imperial. In both we may discern the same resolute will to outshine the Vatican, which, whether adverse or amicable, casts a shadow not so much in the outside world by a spectacular and worldly grandeur, as in the antithetical conception that it represents in its permanent Christian affirmation, expressed even in its silence.

History will say whether the solution given to the Roman Question on February 11, 1929, could long withstand the fundamental dualism between the totalitarian State, whatever it be, and the Papacy. When the first conflict broke out Pius XI had to declare that Treaty and Concordat were so interlinked that they would stand or fall together. For the Concordat has to create that moral environment, in the public profession of the Christian faith, that will render the Vatican and the kingdom of Italy morally in harmony, just as they are materially contiguous. The breach of the Concordat would be implicitly and morally, if not legally, a breach of the Treaty.

What, however, would be the consequences if both collapsed, from the standpoint of the Roman Question? Not a return to the *status quo ante*, that is, to the Law of Guarantees, for this was never accepted by the Vatican and had already been unconditionally abrogated by Italy. Nor a return to the positions of the two powers at the moment of the breach of the Porta Pia, for by the Lateran Treaty the Pope definitely and irrevocably declared 'the Roman Question settled and therefore eliminated', and recognised 'the Kingdom of Italy under the dynasty of the House of Savoy with Rome as capital of the Italian State'.

The denunciation of the Concordat by either party would juridically call for revision in view of a fresh agreement, and morally for a reconsideration of all the relations between the Papacy and Italy. Apart from an amicable revision for a fresh general understanding between them, they would have nothing in common. The Vatican, justly, takes its stand on the divine right to pontifical freedom and independence, to which correspond both an historical right to territorial sovereignty and positive international usage. This recognises to the Pope the character of a subject of international public law, not through the Italian laws (Laws of Guarantees or laws ratifying the Lateran Treaty), but by the traditional consent of the nations, which maintain with the Pope, whether he have a real State or no, the diplomatic relations of one sovereign to another, and on occasion draw up treaties, concordats or a *modus vivendi* with him. Italy could not deny this adamantine basis of the papal right, but in transforming it into a treaty she did not wish to give it any other character than that of a bilateral contract, based, for her part, on her national right, to the exclusion of any international recognition or guarantees. Since Italian national right comes from the popular will to constitute a unitary State embracing the whole territory of the peninsula, thus the separation of the Vatican City from State territory had to be approved by laws of the State and ratified by a form of plebiscite. Such was the significance given to the parliamentary elections of March 24, 1929, with the open assent of Catholic Action and of the clergy, who urged the faithful to take part by voting in favour. The plebiscite of March 24, 1929, corrected or completed, according to the various opinions, that of October 2, 1870.

From the sociological point of view, such plebiscites, for the most part un-free or at least not allowing sufficient liberty for an adverse vote, are never the real expression of the collective will, but merely justificatory titles for those régimes that set the origin of their right in the people, or demand recognition of it from the people, though they may have originated from other historical causes. Fascism, which sees the origin of its régime in a revolution still in process, cannot abstain from combining the two principles that go to make up its right to rule, that of the force of its leaders, which imposes itself, and that of the popular will, which consents. The contradiction lies in the fact that the more valid is the force in the hands of a few, the more tenuous and hesitant and ineffectual the will of the people.

The juridical and concordatory settlement of the Roman Question, in spite of theoretical and practical difficulties, may stand the test so long as the European political situation rests on the present unstable equilibrium. Two causes undermine the whole of the European edifice: State totalitarianism and the rupture of international equilibrium. Is it possible for the Catholic Church and the other Christian churches to set a moral and religious dyke against national passions rendered unbridled by totalitarianism, against the armaments race, and above all against the spiritual preparation for a war destructive of our civilisation?

§ 58.—The anxiety lest sooner or later there should come a new European war, graver and more tragic than the last, has increased from the day that Germany became a totalitarian State under the sign of the Crooked Cross. But the spectre of war reappeared with the signing of the Treaty of Versailles and the other peace treaties, for they lacked the spirit of conciliation and compromise needed for a peace that would be not merely the law of the victor, but a real accord between victor and vanquished. It was thought that what was lacking at Versailles, in respect of Germany, had been supplied at Locarno. This was not so, for the successive stages from the evacuation of the Rhineland to the writing off of reparations took seven long years, with laborious discussions and belated decisions, due to the obstinate policy of France which refused to recognise the reality of the situation, and to the uncertain behaviour of England, which rendered agreements and understandings ambiguous.

The crucial point was that of disarmament. Germany demanded parity, France insisted on security; the duel was a mortal one. When in 1932 a *de jure* parity was granted as subordinated to security, not only was there never any definition of in what security consisted, but the disarmament plan maintained the military clauses of the Treaty of Versailles, which refused parity *de jure* and *de facto*. On the other hand, while the debates dragged on without coming to any conclusion, Germany was rearming. During the whole of this period the League of Nations was in the heat of a confident activity, with continual meetings of Assembly and Council, Commissions, congresses, conferences, treaties, protocols, regional and general pacts, technical reports, disarmament plans, plans for European union, projects of mutual assistance against an eventual aggressor. In distant America the Pan-American Union was founded, comprising all the American States, while by the Kellogg-Briand Pact a thin link was established between Geneva and Washington. All this gave a sense of extraordinary euphory, with a confidence that the Disarmament Conference (in which both the United States and Russia were taking part, though they were not members of the League) would succeed in fixing the basis of an international balance of forces and of a League law founded on the collaboration of all.

Three facts could not escape the common observer, who perhaps did not give them due importance—that the League of Nations held within it two States which by their structure denied the principles on which it was built, Japan and Fascist Italy; that France, while upholding the principles of Geneva, counted far more on her political and military alliances, for Germany, though admitted to the Council of the League, nourished a spirit of *revanche* that was barely mitigated by the democratic forms of her government; finally, that the British Government, unwishful to commit itself too far, tended to minimise its League obligations and those of the other pacts that were being signed.

The juridical edifice of Geneva had not the moral assent of all the States, or rather, it possessed it where it responded to the interests of each. Sentiments might be sincere, the aims of each separate State legitimate, but faith was weak, and without faith there is not only no moving of mountains but there is even no taking of risks. Was there, in addition, any State in bad faith? Japan kept silence and was preparing her *coup* on Manchuria. At the opportune moment, when European discord is most acute, Japan, forgetting the undertakings to which she has subscribed to respect the territorial integrity of Member States, to renounce war for national ends, and, in the case of safeguarding her own security, to submit to the procedure of the Covenant—sends her armies, and by curious method, without declaring war but as a police measure, occupies Manchuria, makes of it a vassal State, fixes its laws and takes justice into her own hands. Geneva did not fail to intervene, by a long series of meetings and resolutions and messages to the two conflicting States, and by a Commission of Enquiry sent to the spot. But since neither France nor England wanted to take serious action in concert with the United States (which had taken the initiative) to ensure the respect of international agreements, the League of Nations confined itself to deploring Japan's action and losing her as member.

The example was catching. When Hitler reached power, while he sought to make of Germany a totalitarian State (spiritually in contradiction to the internationalism of Geneva), he cut short the protracted discussions on parity *de jure* and *de facto*, repudiated the hypocrisy of the Disarmament Conference, which was becoming a Rearmament Conference, and forsook Geneva. The reaction of the other States and of the League itself was weak and negligible. It was believed that Hitler could be brought back by a policy of indulgence and manoeuvre. France and England were never in full agreement. Thus nothing was done to impede the rearmament of Germany, nothing to clarify the moral and juridical positions of the two parties. The persecution of the Jews was tolerated without a single diplomatic step being taken or a protest either from the separate States or from the League. Nothing was done to mitigate the war on the churches and on adverse parties. The moral abyss that was opening between Germany and the civilised peoples was felt by all, but no Government would admit it publicly.

At the same time Russia was drawing closer to Geneva and knocking at the doors of the League of Nations. Not that she had any great faith in the international principles that for so many years she had been discrediting through her propaganda at home and abroad, but because, placed between Germany and Japan, both prepared to make war for their totalitarian policy, she thought it well to have recourse to European alliances with the support of the League of Nations and under its ægis. And the League, in admitting the Soviets, asked nothing that could have formed a common ethical platform with the other States—neither religious and civil liberty, nor renouncement of methods of violence, nor any attenuation of Russian totalitarianism and propaganda for the class war.

How indeed could the League of Nations have done so, when it had tolerated Fascist Italy, which, from the first dispute (that of Corfu, in 1923) had ruled out its intervention, and often, in official speeches, had disparaged its ideals, derided the efforts towards disarmament, sung the praises of 'cannon', 'bayonets', 'muskets', and was pursuing a policy of spiritual militarisation of the young? The Fascist Government had the right to pursue a policy of its own and the duty of safeguarding Italian interests, the more so in that France and Great Britain were always acting in their own interests and took no account of Italy save when they needed her support. But Italy was not loyal to Geneva, pursuing as she did a policy of sabotage of international ideals while remaining within the League.

Her turn came. The Wal-Wal incident of December 4, 1934, opened the way to the Abyssinian dispute, which had been preparing for some years. Through the Rome Agreement of January 7, 1935, France gave Italy a free hand in Abyssinia, and the Fascist Government acquired in Laval a clever and unscrupulous wirepuller at Geneva.

The first phase—the appeal of the Negus to the League of Nations is met only by dilatory measures to avert the application of the Covenant. He gets no support for the arbitration he asks and to which he has a right by the Italo-Abyssinian Treaty of 1928. There is an unjust limitation both of the matter for arbitration and of the competence of the arbitrators enquiring into the territorial sovereignty over Wal-Wal. An arms embargo is applied, with unilateral effect, leaving Abyssinia disarmed just when the League of Nations has failed to induce Italy to suspend the sending of troops and munitions to Eritrea and Somaliland. It was during this phase that Hitler struck another violent blow at the Peace Treaty system, officially announcing the rearmament of Germany in violation of the military clauses of the Treaty of Versailles. France, Great Britain and Italy, having met at Stresa, each with her own axe to grind, resolve to invite the League of Nations to deplore the German action and to declare formally that no further violation of the treaties will be tolerated, under threat of repressive measures. Strange to say, not one of the three Powers was clean of violation or non-observance of the treaties (especially the clauses on disarmament), and Italy was already breaking several treaties in preparing a war that was visibly becoming inevitable.

In the second phase, the action passes to London, thus giving the impression that the British Government, while declaring its wish to defend the Covenant, is merely safeguarding its own interests, which might be compromised by the Italian venture. Mr. Eden's journey to Rome, the resentment of the British Press, the three-cornered conversations in Paris which seemed a revival of the Three Power agreement, the sending of the British fleet to the Mediterranean, brought tension between London and Rome to a head; as a result the moral and juridical principles of the Covenant, and the protection of the State about to become a victim of aggression, passed into the background.

Finally, the epilogue. The Fascist Government would never define the aims of its diplomatic and military action against Abyssinia. It refused all the proposals made in the name of London and Paris or of the League of Nations. In order to justify itself it presented a memorial against Abyssinia. Granted as proven the various heads of accusation (among them that of slavery and slave-traffic), a distinction must be drawn between the cases that occurred or originated before 1922, when Italy (in agreement with France) supported Abyssinia's request to become a member of the League—since by that act such cases were obviously condoned or recognised as condonable—from those that occurred between then and 1928, when Italy signed a fresh treaty of friendship with Abyssinia and undertook that any differences that might subsequently arise should be settled by arbitration. Only these last could have led to a legitimate war, after they had been established by arbitration, and only in the event of an Abyssinian refusal to carry out its decisions, and after the procedure laid down in the Covenant had been followed. Italy, on the contrary, cut matters short and without either ultimatum or declaration of war sent her troops to invade Abyssinian territory, and carried on the war with the most rapid and modern methods, including the use of poison gas and the aerial bombardment of the unarmed populations.

The Assembly of the League of Nations, as soon as the war had broken out, declared Italy to have violated the Covenant, and, while deciding to apply economic and financial sanctions, continued the negotiations that led to the Laval-Hoare Plan. This was rejected by Abyssinia, rejected by Italy (who had privately solicited it), and withdrawn morally (if not legally) by the Council of the League. The League continued the equivocal system of seeking to treat and at the same time threatening an intensification of sanctions, constantly proclaimed and as constantly deferred. Hitler's moment had come. Seizing the occasion, he made his master-stroke, occupying the demilitarised zone of the Rhineland, in breach of the Treaty of Locarno (March 7, 1936). The protests of the French Government against such breach of treaty found London as lukewarm for action as France had been lukewarm for action against Italy. The fear of a European war drove the Abyssinian War into the background. This was hastening to its end, with the defeat of the Negus, his flight, and the capture of Addis-Ababa. After which the Assembly of the League registered the inadequacy of collective action to prevent war and to guarantee the territorial integrity of a Member State. It lifted the sanctions a few months after the Fascist Government had proclaimed the annexation of Abyssinia and proclaimed the King of Italy Emperor.

This epilogue marked a grave defeat for the idea of collective security based on morality and international law. It definitely stripped the League of Nations of that character of universality with which it was born and to which it aspired. It gave a new impulse in every country, including the most pacifist, like Great Britain, Belgium, Switzerland, to a speedy and complete rearmament, obliging them to an unambiguous return to the pre-war system of military alliances, neutrality or isolation, as the case might be. Hence a denial of the aspiration of the peoples to an international solidarity, to the limitation of armaments, and to the outlawry of war, of all war. Italy demanded the recognition of the new Empire and the exclusion of the Negus from the Assembly of the League of Nations. Failing to get satisfaction, after much wavering she decided to withdraw from Geneva. The international crisis had reached a fresh phase, even graver than before.

Events after the Great War had thrown a particular light on the relations between the Church and the international community, between the Church and the several States, in regard both to the moral and juridical edifice of the peace and to cases of war. A new problem had been set: if and up to what point can and should the Church accept and morally support the international order as an order of lawful right? The Church considers the State as a natural and necessary institution and commands that its authority and the legal order should be respected. Thus the oft-quoted reply of Christ: 'Render unto Caesar the things that are Caesar's.' Does an international society, established on a basis of natural ethics, partake of the authority of the State and of its character of guardian of order? The problem is a new one, not in that it was not raised and solved in the past—Christendom of the Middle Ages with the diarchy of Pope-Emperor was an international society—but because the international society of the past was based on a Christian conception, while the League of Nations has a secular character. The one was strictly bound to the Papacy, from which it originated; the other is outside all Church interference. This is the case not only of the League but also of the Pan-American Union, which has the same ethical and legal character. These societies of nations are contractual, positive, and, through political uncertainties, may be considered as more or less temporary. The Church can and should take them into account as means for creating an international law and rendering it effectual; as such they are contractual organs, possessing authority in so far as through them and in them an international interdependence is created which is a mutual limitation of sovereignty. Inasmuch as through such societies and unions of States legal bonds are created, useful undertakings are promoted, and wars are prevented by means of compulsory procedures, arbitration and authoritative decisions, the Church cannot fail to regard them as exercising in common that authority with which the States are invested. So long as they do not offend against justice and morality, they deserve the support that the Church gives to each separate State for the common good, its specific end.

In making this statement we do not at all mean that the Church should mix herself up in international politics, just as she does not mix herself up in national politics; but only that in the same way as in each State she defends religion, morality and law, and supports their undertakings to this end, she works, in so far as is possible to her, in the vaster and co-ordinated field of unions and societies of States. Never has the Catholic Church abandoned her lofty social and civilising function in this regard, not even under the pretext that the modern States are laic (a pretext that certain ill-advised Catholics have put forward in regard to the laic character of the League), for where morality can be defended and right consolidated, it is the office and duty of the Catholic Church to have her say. This has been the policy of the popes from Leo XIII onwards, whether in favour of understandings and unions between the States, or of the formation and consolidation of international law, or in support of the efforts towards disarmament. The other churches have openly and unrestrictedly supported the new international enterprises.

Where the work of the Church corresponds most closely to the spirit of the Gospel and to the needs of the present world is in promoting and contributing to moral disarmament, to attenuating the causes of war, supporting efforts for peace and taking the initiative if need arises, causing moral values to be appreciated above the egotistic interests of the peoples. And since the case of war is the central point of the present international constructions (League of Nations and Pan-American Union), so the Church, without being bound to their particular policies, cannot fail to uphold the principles apt to avert war—the keeping of treaties, the necessity for arbitration, the equity of timely treaty revision, the elimination of war-motives, the condemnation of those who take justice into their own hands, dragging the peoples into the horrors of war.

In this respect the case of the Italo-Abyssinian War was graver for the Catholic Church than that of the Great War. The other churches, Protestant and Orthodox, were not directly concerned, save the Coptic-Egyptian-Ethiopian Church, which naturally upheld the justice of the defence of Abyssinia. The Protestant churches were against the war promoted by Italy, and hence for the defence of the people attacked and of international law, except those of Germany, Hungary and France, which made no public declarations.

Pius XI found himself in a very delicate position and was accused by the Protestant bishops of favouring the Fascist Government. He was bound by Article 24 of the Lateran Treaty, by which 'The Holy See, in regard to sovereignty even in the international field, declares that it wishes to remain and will remain extraneous to the temporal competition between the other States and to the international conferences summoned for such an object, unless the contending parties agree to appeal to its mission of peace, while reserving to itself in any case the right to make its moral and spiritual protest heard'. Through this last reservation the Pope, in his address of August 27, 1935, expressed his mind on the conflict that was about to lead to war. If this, as was believed abroad, were a war of conquest, an offensive war, it would be 'truly an unjust war'. He added. 'We do not believe, we will not believe in an unjust war.' In Italy there was talk of a war of defence and of a need for expansion, he continued, but 'if the need for expansion is a fact that must be taken into account, the right of defence has its limits and moderation that must not be overstepped if the defence is not to be culpable'. A subsequent official *mise au point* in the *Osservatore Romano* made it clear that 'the need of expansion is not a right in itself; it is a fact that must be taken into account but which is not identified with lawful right'. The Pope ended by recommending to the men responsible not to do anything 'that might aggravate the situation and irritate hearts', not to lose 'precious time', and to carry out a 'work of pacification'. Thus indirectly he defined the positions of Italy, of the States concerned and of the League of Nations.

In this address there was no mention of the moral obligation of keeping treaties and of the pledge of arbitration which bound Italy to Abyssinia. Yet this moral and juridical position had been undermined by the Council of the League of Nations, which had limited the scope of arbitration and had promoted the three-party meeting (London, Paris, Rome), with the exclusion of the interested party, Abyssinia, who was treated as less than a minor. The care taken to exclude any moral implication and any recall to the treaties, in order to place the Italo-Abyssinian conflict on the political plane as the business of the three Great Powers interested, was the initial error, at once moral and psychological, to which the Secretariat of the League of Nations lent itself, with the representatives of the other States, great and small.

In antithesis to this equivocal and utilitarian position a conflict of conscience arose in public opinion on the nature of the war, even before the Assembly of the League had declared Italy a violator of the Covenant, and hence an aggressor. It was too obvious, to the unbiassed eyes of those unperturbed by immediate passions or particular interests, that the Fascist Government intended a conquest, for which the Wal-Wal incident (closed by an arbitral decision declaring both parties free from blame) gave no adequate pretext. Therefore there were many who urged that the League should act promptly and effectively to prevent war, even by sanctions which in this case were considered legitimate not only from the formal standpoint, since it was a case of a clear and intentional breach of the Covenant, but also from the moral standpoint, since it was indisputably a war of aggression and conquest. That it had been prepared and intended ever since 1932 is confessed by General De Bono himself in his book *The Conquest of an Empire*.

This notwithstanding, most of the bishops, clergy and Catholic press of Italy took up a clear position in favour of the war and against sanctions. From abundant documentation it may be noted that the ethical problem raised by the war was considered from three standpoints: (1) That the government of a country was sole judge of the justice of its own cause and that the people was obliged to obey; (2) that the African war was a war for Christian civilisation; (3) that sanctions were immoral as seeking to impede Italy in the exercise of a right. Since no contrary voice could make itself heard in Italy, we have the right to suppose that not all the clergy nor all Catholics held these opinions, although it was very difficult, even for them, to form an independent opinion, in view of the Fascist propaganda, carried on by every means, and the absolute lack of contrary voices and possible control of information.

In the other countries, Catholics were in majority against the war, judging it as immoral, and were distressed at the behaviour of the clergy and Catholic press in Italy.[1] The address of Cardinal Verdier, Archbishop of Paris, on the theory of the just war was a *mise au point* without specific reference to the conflict in course, but such as to embrace it. The Catholic press was divided pro and contra, according

[1]The most authoritative reviews, such as *Les Etudes*, of the Jesuits of Paris, *La Vie Intellectuelle* of the French Dominicans (then at Juvisy), *Blackfriars*, of the Dominicans of Oxford, *The Catholic World* and the *Commonweal* of New York, the groups of Catholic writers of France and Spain (to mention only the most notable expressions of opinion) frankly discussed the Italo-Abyssinian case and concluded for the injustice of the war.

to whether their tendencies were nationalist or democratic, philo-Fascist or anti-Fascist. The fact that the Italian Government, even during such a war, was in good relations with the Holy See and that the papal diplomacy (as far as could be known) favoured a solution of compromise, and still more the fact that in the various countries the parties of the Left were the principal leaders of the campaign against Italy, held back not a few foreign Catholics from uniting their voices with what they called the chorus of 'Freemasons and Bolshevists'. For such as these the moral problem thus passed to the background, as in France at the time of the Dreyfus Case.

The use of hyperite and poison gas not only against the combatants but also against the Red Cross hospitals and the unarmed populations (who were without any means of technical defence) aroused a chorus of indignation in every section of public opinion, as contrary to natural morality and forbidden by international agreements. No diplomatic protest was made to Rome by the several governments, nor by the Council of the League of Nations, perhaps because it is notorious that great and small States are manufacturing the worst kinds of gas in readiness for the next war. But on the part of the clergy and faithful this would have been a timely opportunity for raising their voices against a terrible means of destruction of human lives, without possible discrimination between belligerents and the civilian population.

The episode of the Italian war in Abyssinia revealed the beginning of an unprecedented moral crisis. Doubtless it is to be connected with the moral, psychological and political crisis left by the Great War, but this new phase is characterised by the formation of the totalitarian States. These, in spite of their diversities in programme and attitude, are giving an imprint to an epoch, with the suppression of all liberty, the monopoly of all means of public opinion, the subjugation of the souls of the young, the dominance of all intellectual activity, of all personal or associated initiative in every field, even those remote from politics; a dominance extending to economy and its ends, to domestic life and religious life, with the militarisation of the whole people and a continual rearmament knowing no limits. They are thus creating an iron structure for the whole of society.

Small wonder if the frail edifice of an international society has been shaken, not so much because it was unable to prevent a war of aggression as because it had not the strength for a timely and integral defence of the ethico-juridical principles on which it was founded. The men responsible considered the problems of the Italo-Abyssinian War in political terms rather than in moral terms. In their spiritual poverty they did not know how to appraise the political effects that spring from public morality. On the other hand, the Churches in present-day politics have not such a voice as to gain a hearing, and often priests and faithful are carried away by the political passions seething in the world.

§ 59.—The period of the Abyssinian War had not closed when the revolt of the Generals broke out in Spain, transforming itself immediately into a civil war and soon after into a camouflaged international war with sidelights of a religious war and of a war of ideas, expanding throughout the world. What the connection, through politics and intrigues, between the war in Spain and the Abyssinian War is not easy to determine and has no importance for our study. Future historians will be able to solve or attempt to solve this problem in the light of documents or revelations which we do not possess. What can to-day be stated with certainty is that the Italian Government at the end of the Abyssinian War found itself with a debt of gratitude towards Berlin and with a violent resentment towards London and Paris. The understandings between Rome and Berlin led to a marked modification of Italian policy in Central Europe. On July 11, 1936, Hitler received the Austrian Chancellor Schuschnigg at Berchtesgaden, to draw up the first agreement. By this the foreign policy of Austria was made subordinate to that of Berlin, while the Government in Vienna was reconciled with the Nazi régime.

The Mediterranean repercussions of the new policy, which would be later described as the Rome-Berlin Axis, might already be divined from the military reinforcement of Libya, of the islands of the Dodecanese, of the island of Pantellaria linked up to Sicily, and later of Sardinia. A circumstance which escaped public attention was the following: the Assembly of the League of Nations decided the withdrawal of sanctions against Italy and at the same time refused to recognise the annexation of Abyssinia on July 4; the Austro-German Agreement of Berchtesgaden was on July 11; the date of the order given to the airplanes of the Italian air-force to proceed to Spanish Morocco was four days later, July 15; it was these airplanes that enabled the troops in Morocco to be transported to Spain.[1] Finally, it was on July 17 that General Franco made his military *pronunciamento* in Morocco, and on July 18 came the military rising in Madrid and the Spanish provinces. It was said that the revolt was decided upon as a sequel to the murder of Calvo Sotelo, on July 14, (a reprisal on the part of police agents who were friends of the sub-lieutenant of the police Guards, Castillo, murdered a few days earlier by the Spanish Fascists). But by now it can no longer be doubted that the revolt had been arranged some time before and that it was merely anticipated by a few weeks owing to the speeding up of events.

Even if the political connection between the happenings in Spain and the situation created by the Abyssinian War were less close than we believe, this would not affect the facts of how the new crisis arose. Above all, there was the spread of the war atmosphere in Europe; the dread of a general war becomes more tangible, the conflict of ideologies passes from the plane of theoretical discussions, electoral contests and economic preoccupations to the bloody plane of war. Russians, Germans and Italians try out in Spain the newest make of weapons, aeroplanes and tanks; the effects of war inventions are measured in European civilised countries, prepared for long drawn out wars. The bombers fly over famous and beloved cities, populous and filled with works of art—Madrid, Toledo, San Sebastian, Granada, Seville, Bilbao, Oviedo, Valencia, Barcelona. The International Brigades are formed, on the one side spontaneously, without equipment, on the other partly spontaneously, partly by official order, and well equipped. The horrors of a war of this type are increased by the ferocity peculiar to civil war, by the rancour of both sides—of those confronted

[1]This date was ascertained by the French authorities from the documents found on two Italian pilots who landed by mistake in Algeria. The use of the Italian airplanes for the transport of Moroccan troops into Spain was published in the Press and confirmed by books and articles in the Italian reviews. (See Guido Mattioli, *L'Aviazione Legionaria in Spagna.*)

with an unexpected and vigorous resistance and of those surprised at finding themselves betrayed and forsaken by men they believed sure and trustworthy.

The revolt of the generals against the government of the Republic in the first few months had three characteristic features. The first was the rapid disorganisation of the forces of the State through the fact that practically the whole army, part of the police, many civil servants and diplomats, the clergy, the rich landowners and many young men of the middle classes went over *en masse* to the side of the rebels. The second was the fierce resistance of the working masses, without military organisation, without sufficient arms, in an atmosphere of anarchism in which the formation of mobile, violent groups, prepared for anything, took the place of authority, which found itself unable to control the forces of resistance. And finally, there was the religious persecution, the frenzied assaults on churches, presbyteries, religious houses, the burnings and massacres—an explosion, it seemed, of long-smouldering fanaticism, with a vengeful delight only possible when all legal restraints have collapsed, as they had through the two-fold revolution. In this atmosphere the impunity of crime, of any crime, was a feature of the resistance.

These initial aspects of the revolt give their colour to the civil war and create the impassioned atmosphere in which the whole world has followed, commented and spiritually shared in it. For the partisans of the Government all the bishops were rebels who were conspiring with the generals; the priests were shooting from their church-towers on the crowds; the religious houses held deposits of arms and munitions. For the partisans of Franco all the Republicans were Communists, urged and helped by Moscow to plot against the whole of Spain, to suppress private property, to kill priests and religious, to forbid religious worship and bolshevise the nation; Franco's counter-revolt came just in time; if it degenerated into a civil war lasting over two and a half years, that was the fault of Russia and of France, who helped the Government of the Republic and obliged Franco to seek aid of Italy and Germany. Against this last assertion the supporters of the Government replied that the intervention of Italy was assured well before the revolt, and at the same time the benevolent support of Hitler had been obtained; moreover, that Franco had had at least twenty times more military help from the foreigner than the Republicans.

The international press for over two years was full of these mutual accusations, which formed the material of an intensive propaganda, serving to procure for both sides help in money, men, arms and munitions, and, from the humanitarian standpoint, medical aid, food and clothing. Thus from 1936 till to-day the Spanish war has been the most popular and passion-creating war that has ever been fought for an ideal cause, and at the same time the most ferocious and inhuman war that has ever ensanguined the soil of Europe. To find a historic comparison we have to recall the Spanish revolt of 1820 for the restoration of the Constitution, the armed intervention of France in the name of the Holy Alliance, Great Britain's refusal to intervene, the anti-liberal reaction in the name of Catholicism and the horrors of the Carlist war and of the ensuing repression. To-day in place of France (then jealous of Great Britain) there is Italy (now jealous of France), sending troops, Fascist militia and volunteers; in place of the anti-liberalism of a century ago there is the anti-communism of to-day. Then there were the atrocities of the anti-liberal reaction just as to-day there are those of the anti-fascist reaction, but the fanatical mobs of those days were far more on the side of reaction, whereas to-day they have been far more on the republican side. The terrible moments of the first six months of the civil war, with recrudescences in 1937, may find a term of comparison in the French Revolution. A century ago Europe and America were divided for and against the liberals of Spain, for and against the authoritarian governments of the Holy Alliance; the liberal ferments had spread throughout the world and the Spanish episode aroused on either side hopes and fears, political trends and religious crises. Then, as to-day, the ecclesiastics of Spain were in majority on the side of the Holy Alliance and took an active part in the Civil War, bringing upon the Church the consequences of such an attitude.

This time the sudden and violent persecution of the clergy, the massacres of priests and religious, the burning of churches while the authorities looked on, powerless or passive or conniving, gave an immediate motive for the clergy to range themselves on the other side. The Holy See protested to Madrid, but received no reply. Pius XI, in receiving bishops, priests, religious and laymen who had fled from Spain, on September 14, 1936, set forth in an interesting address the characteristics of the resistance of the Church: *martyrdom*, where this bore witness to the persecuted faith; *resistance*, where this could be carried on without excesses; *prayer*, even for the blinded adversary. In regard to defence, it is well to quote the text of the papal declaration: 'A task, we have said, both difficult and dangerous, for it is only too easy for the very ardour and difficulty of defence to go to an excess, which is not wholly warranted; and further, intentions less pure, selfish interests and mere party feeling may easily enter in to cloud and change the morality and responsibility of what is being done. Our fatherly heart can never forget, and in this moment more than ever it must recall, with the most sincere and fatherly gratitude, all those who, with purity of intentions and unselfish motives, have sought to intervene in the name of humanity. And our gratitude is undiminished even though we have had to realise the failure of their noble efforts.' He continued with words of affection for those sons that had gone astray, for the persecutors of the Church, which many would do well to re-read to regain a sense of Christian charity.

The *Osservatore Romano* of September 18, 1936, distinguished three facts: (1) The military *pronunciamento* and the civil war for political ends; (2) the loosing of the revolutionary masses against the churches, religious houses and faithful; (3) the legitimate defence of these. In regard to legitimate defence, the *Osservatore Romano*, after reproducing the words of Pius XI in his address of September 14, added: 'Thus the *reason* and the *limits* of the action of Catholics in defence of their faith are established. The *right of defence*, as the Holy Father said on another occasion, *has limits and demands a moderation that must be observed if the defence is to remain blameless*. The same principle is to-day confirmed in blessing those who have shed and are ready to shed their blood for the faith. And not only these, but even those who, by a miserable blindness, hate the faith . . .'

The reiteration of the words pronounced by the Pope in August, 1935, in regard to Italy's war on Abyssinia, was not without intention.

The hypothesis of legitimate defence if applied to Italy could not imply the conquest of the opposing Empire; just as the legitimate defence of the Catholics assaulted and killed for their faith and of the churches burned could not imply a civil war of extermination lasting over two years and a half. But these positions were soon outdistanced by Catholics who maintained the entire legitimacy of the military revolt. This thesis was in itself very disputable. Not long after, in March, 1937, Pius XI in writing to the Bishops of Mexico one of his greatest encyclicals (*Nos es muy*), had occasion to lay down the guiding principles of the right of revolt, its character and its limits. It was the first time in the annals of the Church, from the days when the medieval popes released citizens from their oath of allegiance to their government, that a Pope had tackled this difficult question, giving the most equable solution possible both for authority and for the citizens, and purposely drawing a distinction between these and the clergy and Catholic Action.[1]

That the norms traced by Pius XI for the case of revolt were those followed by the Catholics supporting the Spanish generals in the case of the revolt in Spain, would be hard to say—especially since this had been long prepared, rather to overthrow the republic than to check the government that resulted from the elections of February, 1936. But this phase soon merged into the second, that of the armed resistance of Catholics attacked by the mob in their churches and monasteries, the suspension of religious worship, the murder of the priests. According to the *Osservatore Romano* the Catholics merely put up a legitimate defence. Now this could be said, and was the truth, in individual cases when the actual assault of the mob was met, where possible, by an armed defence that did not exceed the limits of an *inculpatae tutelae*. But it was not the case of Spain in the second half of July 1936; isolated acts of defence against the mob were almost impossible; often only flight could avail. The murder of thousands of ecclesiastics and faithful, or of persons reputed inimical to the people, came like a hurricane. There was no real resistance to the excesses of the mob. There was a rapid decision to take sides for this party or that,

[1]For this see my study in *Politics and Morality* (Burns, Oates and Washbourne) pp. 206–12.

forming war fronts, provinces against provinces, towns divided, villages conquered by force. In a few days the revolt became civil war.

The third phase, that of the war, came so swiftly, in view of the resolute will of the republican and working-class population to defend itself, at any cost, and in view of the will of the rebel leaders to win at any cost, that no one had time to measure the responsibilities he was assuming, not even the men of the Church, and particularly the bishops, those who had left their dioceses to take refuge in the rebel camp or abroad, fleeing either certain death or terrible imprisonment. Thus the greater part of the Spanish Hierarchy (with a few exceptions, among them the Cardinal of Tarragona, the most authoritative and the best known) opted for what was known as the national cause and gave it their support. It was then that in Spain and abroad among Catholics and their clergy the theory of the 'holy war' came into existence. Father P. J. Mendendez-Reigada, a Dominican, in an article in *Ciencia Tomista* of Salamanca (later reprinted as a pamphlet) declared: 'The Spanish national war is a holy war, the most holy war registered by history;'[1] while another Catholic philosopher, far better known in the world of culture, M. Jacques Maritain, maintained the opposite view in a study published by the *Nouvelle Revue Française*, and reprinted as preface to Professor Mendizábal's book *The Martyrdom of Spain*.

Needless to say, the thesis of the holy war, whether applied to the civil war in Spain or to any other war past or future, is untenable in Christian doctrine. The idea of the holy war is entirely Mohammedan; it means the armed conquest for the faith, the temporal and military society assuming the task of religious propaganda, of the establishment of the kingdom of God in the world, with the physical destruction of every other faith. There are those who confound the crusade with the holy war. It is a mistake. The Crusades were wars proclaimed by the popes, with spiritual privileges for the combatants in order to gather together armies and impel them to the defence of Christendom. Such wars did not fall outside the fundamental principles of the just war or war of defence. The religious motive could not overrule the criterion of justice. If the infidel State had had a just cause for promoting a war against a Christian State, the latter would have been

[1] *La guerra nacional española ante la moral y al derecho* (Salamanca, 1937).

bound to do justice and to avoid the war. If among the motives of war there had been a religious question (as in the time of the wars of religion between Catholics and Protestants), the first duty would have been to eliminate the religious factor from the war-motives, never to turn it into the main motive, arousing in the name of religion the worst instincts of slaughter and extermination.

What happened in Spain was that the religious factor, originally subsidiary or concomitant, became for many the predominant motive, or was identified or associated with the politico-social motive of overthrowing the republican government of the Left and installing an authoritarian government of the Right. The religious motive impelled many to support the generals and their followers, and sustained them in the civil war which they soon realised would be long and bitter. But the differentiation between the two camps was intrinsically political and social. Republicans and autonomists, Basques and Catalans on the one side; monarchists, Carlists, Phalangists on the other; the working masses, Socialist, Communist, Anarchist on the one side, capitalists and land-owners on the other; anti-clericals and free thinkers on the one side, clericals and churchmen on the other. The lines of demarcation are not absolute. Many people found themselves on the one side because on territory where the Government might be holding its own; others found themselves on the other side because the rebels by swift moves seized important positions. Thus each man had a personal case to resolve in the light of his own conscience or his own interests. While the bulk of the clergy, except the Basque priests, and some of Catalonia or Madrid, were with Franco, not a few Catholics believed that they could not refuse armed defence of the legitimate government, even though public worship had been violently suppressed by the mob. Others fled to enrol on the side of Franco, who both by conviction and by interest has not ceased to protect the Church at the same time as he has made use of her.

In view of the uncertainty of Catholic opinion abroad on what was happening in Spain, the Spanish bishops were asked by the Government of Burgos to write a collective letter to the bishops of the Catholic world, explaining their attitude and defending the thesis of the national cause. All save the Cardinal of Tarragona and the Bishop of Vittoria assented. Fortunately, in the letter which appeared on July 1, 1937, they did not adopt the theory of the holy war, but took their stand on the thesis that the triumph of Franco's party would be for the national and religious good of Spain. They defended themselves against the charge of having fomented the revolt against the constituted power of the Republic (to which the Spanish bishops had given their assent as to the legitimate government) and of having wanted the war, whereas their aspiration had been one of peace. 'When the war broke out, we lamented more than any one the painful fact, because it is always a grave evil which often enough is not compensated by problematical advantages, and because our mission is one of reconciliation and of peace.'[1] (p. 4). Further on: 'The Church has neither wished for this war nor provoked it, and we do not think it necessary to vindicate her from the charge of belligerency with which the Spanish Church has been censured in foreign newspapers. It is true that thousands of her sons, obeying the promptings of their conscience and of their patriotism and under their own responsibility, revolted in arms in order to safeguard the principles of religion and Christian justice which had for ages informed the nation's life; but whoever accuses her of having provoked this war or of having conspired for it and even of not having done all that in her lay to avoid it, does not know or falsifies the reality.'

The bishops, on the other hand, examining the events prior to July, 1936, believed that they could justify the revolt and the ensuing civil war, both as a measure for preventing a communist plot to bolshevise Spain, which, they held, had been prepared between Moscow and Madrid, and as a means of surrogating a government that had no longer any authority and could no longer be considered legitimate. Leaving aside the polemical part of the letter and of the analysis of the facts, which on various points would find it hard to withstand objective criticism, we may note that what concerned the bishops was to bring out that the 'national' movement was wholly corresponding to Catholic principles; therefore they defended it from charges of injustice and atrocities. As for the future: 'We trust in the prudence

[1] Joint Letter of the Spanish Bishops to the Bishops of the whole world concerning the war in Spain. (Catholic Truth Society, London.)

of statesmen that they will not accept foreign models for the structure of the future of the Spanish State, but that they will consider the requirements of the national life from within, and the course marked by past centuries.' The allusion to Fascism and Nazism is plain.[1]

What distressed many Catholics abroad in this letter was the reference to the Basques. The bishops wrote: 'All our admiration for the civic and religious virtues of our Basque brothers. All our charity for the great misfortune that afflicts them and which we consider ours because it is that of the mother-country.' (p. 27). But the bishops accused the Basque leaders of blindness, declaring that they had taken the side of Communism against Catholicism. Now the thesis that on the one side there is nothing but evil ('Communism') and on the other nothing but good (Catholicism and patriotism) and that 'the war of Spain is the result of the struggle between two irreconcilable ideologies', is, to our mind, an oratorical and not an historical thesis. As for the Basques, no account was taken of the obstinate refusal of the nationalist leaders and of the Spanish Right parties, even before the revolt and on the eve of the revolt, to recognise the historic rights of that people. Of such rights the bishops make no mention, as legitimate elements of a future of appeasement, while Franco and his government have always refused

[1]Cardinal Goma, in November, 1938, in his appeal on the occasion of the 'Crusader's Day', wrote as follows: 'And neither shall we be able to be free if we do not preserve the specific physiognomy given us by our character and our history, shaking off every yoke of a spiritual or social order that would seek to subject us to dogmas, customs and orientations in contradiction to the Christian spirit which has made us what we have been.' Not long after, Father Merklen, the editor of *La Croix* of Paris, speaking of General Franco, wrote: 'The spirit of revenge and hatred, carried to an extreme development, will make it difficult for him to restore a moral union . . . The Hitlerian influence, for its part, is gaining ground daily in the entourage of the Generalissimo. If the condemnations of racialism by the Sovereign Pontiff have passed almost unnoted in Spain, the writings of Hitler, Rosenberg, Streicher are translated into Spanish and widely circulated. Señor Serrano Suner, Franco's father-in-law and Minister of the Interior in the Franco government, does not conceal from his visitors his sympathy for German National-Socialism and the Cardinal Archbishop of Toledo has been obliged to bring the reminder that in order to be a true Catholic, it is not enough to call oneself a Spanish Catholic, one must be a Roman Catholic. Between two false mysticisms, two unilateral and erroneous conceptions of society and of life, we have no choice to make. We are Catholics; we have but to remain ourselves.' (*La Croix*, December 15, 1938.)

to recognise them, just as they have arranged to suppress the rights of the Catalans.

The bishops of all countries replied to their Spanish confreres with personal and collective letters, by nation or region, assenting to their standpoint. This episcopal plebiscite was registered case by case by the *Osservatore Romano*, which never, either then or later, published the Letter of July 1, 1937. It was natural that the Catholic press in the dependence of the bishops or of Catholic Action should take its tone from the policy outlined by the Spanish Episcopate. There were indeed reservations, comments, criticisms even from the Catholic side, especially in France, where writers and thinkers like MM. Jacques Maritain, François Mauriac, Edouard Mounier, and the Spaniard Alfredo Mendizábal, took up a very clear and courageous position against the identification of the Church and her supreme spiritual cause with Spanish nationalism, and against the religious and political justification of the civil war—an impression often given by unskilful defenders of the position of the Spanish bishops. Such apologists often went so far as to defend the aerial bombardments of civilian populations, and believed the executions of prisoners of war and of civilians to be justified (especially of the Basques, against whom the hatred of Nationalists has been and is implacable); they even opposed any proposal of mediation, truce or armistice, not seeing any salvation for the Church and for Spain otherwise than in the complete and total victory of Franco and the total crushing of the republicans, for them 'Reds' or 'Communists'.

The endeavour to promote a peace by conciliation goes back to the beginning of 1937, when a group of Spaniards abroad (nearly all Catholics) led by Professor Mendizábal constituted in Paris the Committee for Civil Peace in Spain. They spoke of 'civil peace' as opposed to 'civil war'. Soon after, a group of Frenchmen (in majority Catholic) formed a committee of their own, calling it the *French Committee for Civil and Religious Peace* in Spain, in the wish to emphasise that civil peace would be impossible without religious peace, and with the intention of helping the efforts of those Catholics who, on the side of the Government, sought to restore public worship in Government territory. A similar Committee was formed in London, yet another in Geneva, and the movement has supporters in various countries.[1]

May be in the last period of the resistance of Catalonia the Government might have been ready to treat for an honourable peace; President Negrin's appeal of May 1, 1938, may have been a sign. But differences and hatred were too great. Moreover, by then General Franco felt too sure of ultimate victory, given the open and decided support of Italy and Germany, not to have rejected any proposal of mediation. This notwithstanding, the idea of a peace of conciliation had so profound a moral and religious basis (for there can be no true peace unless there is conciliation), that the effort to achieve it remained valid even after General Franco's victory, as a necessity that will have to be met if Spain is to come to any true unity and appeasement.[2]

[1]The Chairman of the French Committee is M. Jacques Maritain, and among its members are the Academician, M. Louis Gillet; MM. Louis le Fur and Georges Scelles, both professors of International Law at the Sorbonne; and Mgr. E. Beaupin. The British Committee has as Chairman Mr. Wickham Steed and its members include Viscount Cecil of Chelwood, the Hon. Harold Nicolson, M.P., Mrs. V. M. Crawford, Mrs. Corbett Ashby, Professor Gilbert Murray, Mr. Richard R. Stokes, M.P. It consists of Catholics and non-Catholics in about equal numbers.

[2]Cardinal Goma, in the appeal already quoted, in November, 1938, declared that 'Spain will not become One without a reconciliation of all Spaniards. To this end, rather than the rout of the adversary, let us call for their reincorporation in the true spirit of the nation, while awaiting, with open arms, the day when as Spaniards all we shall give each other the kiss of holy brotherhood, as sons of the same God and of the same Fatherland.'

In January, 1939, an article appeared in the *Osservatore Romano* over the initials M.C. (Father Mariano Cordovani, Master of the Sacred Palaces), blaming *La Croix* for having printed, without reservation, a resolution framed by Professor Mendizábal, in which he declared that 'faced with the Spanish tragedy Catholics, as such, remain free to manifest their preferences and to grant their sympathies to either side'. *La Croix* cleared up the misunderstanding and hastened to accept the view of M.C. that 'the only and true attitude of justice and charity that Catholics must adopt is that of which the Holy Father himself (Pius XI) has given us the example, in his memorable Allocution at Castelgandolfo to the Spanish refugees (September, 1936), which constitutes the charter of Christian and papal thought in this matter'. *La Croix* on January 26 published a *mise au point* by Professor Mendizábal on the exact bearings of his resolution, drawn up, as he said, in haste, but implying neither acceptance of Communism nor approval or tolerance of the crimes of the mob (as it had appeared to M.C.). What he had in mind, on the contrary, were the words of the Archbishop of Paris, Cardinal Verdier, who, in August, 1938, in regard to 'the divergences

§ 60.—The Spanish Civil War and foreign intervention created a new political case which could not fail to be laid before the assizes of Geneva. But the League of Nations had emerged so weakened from the Italo-Abyssinian adventure that a fresh effort to put it back in the saddle could come only from the united resolution of Great Britain and France. France was passing through a phase of conflict between the capitalist world and that of the working classes, which had become acute through the electoral victory of the Popular Front and the advent of the Blum government. Hence flight of capital, strikes, occupations of factories, complicated by a kind of conspiracy of adventurers of the Right with contacts abroad—the *Cagoulards*. In Great Britain the death of King George, the accession of Edward VIII and the question of his marriage were absorbing the attention of the Baldwin Cabinet. Moreover, the Spanish business was never considered in its full significance; it was believed to be one of the many risings that would end in two or three months. To avert international complications, early in August France had hastened to propose a non-intervention agreement to Great Britain. To the proposals of France and Great Britain, Germany, Italy, Russia, and Portugal assented, with varying degrees of sincerity and with tacit reservations; Czechoslovakia, Sweden and Belgium followed the Anglo-French policy. These Powers formed the Non-Intervention Committee in London, notifying the League of Nations. But the meddling of foreign powers in Spain was evident from the first months. The attempts of the Spanish Government to get the matter taken up in Geneva (in the Assembly of September-October, 1936), with the intention of preventing any foreign help to the insurgent side, had no practical effect. The fear of a bolshevisation of Spain was conclusive for many governments, in view of the political—rather than military—intervention of Moscow. While the fear of a fascistisation on the other side carried far less weight. Many thought that Spain, like Portugal, in the hands of the bourgeoise

separating French Catholics on the Spanish question' had declared that 'the Hierarchy does not pronounce itself in this domain'. The *Osservatore Romano* took note of the declaration of *La Croix*, and in a subsequent article had occasion to blame those journals that had taken the opportunity of attacking the French organ. In this controversy the 'peace by conciliation' upheld by Professor Mendizábal and the Committees was never called in question, as some had believed.

would soon become once more economically and politically bound to England.

Soon after, the occupation of Majorca by Italian forces that had come to the help of General Franco gravely perturbed Great Britain, who extracted repeated assurances from the Italian Government that it had no territorial aims in Spain. On January 2, 1937, what was known as the 'Gentleman's Agreement' was signed, to the effect that the Mediterranean *status quo* should remain unaltered and collaboration between Great Britain and Italy be restored. But that very day 4,000 Italians disembarked at Cadiz, after 6,000 had disembarked on December 22. The political fiction of Non-Intervention, with all its phases of weakness, cunning, indulgence, resistance, continued to throw into relief the understanding between Rome and Berlin, now called the Rome-Berlin Axis. The Anti-Communist Pact signed between Berlin and Tokyo became a Three Power Pact with the intervention of Rome. It was then that submarines began to appear in the Mediterranean, hunting down the ships carrying food and supplies to Republican Spain. At the same time Japan started on another and vaster military occupation of China. Another war of aggression in the Far East, undermining the positions of the Great Powers (which entered into the plan of the Axis) and subjecting China to a long and terrible trial of blood and fire! China, like Abyssinia knocks at the doors of Geneva for moral help, and Geneva recognises that China is a victim of unjust aggression, but the declarations of September, 1937, are worth less than those of five years before over Manchuria. The signatory Powers of the Pacific Pact meet at Brussels, but they are able to do nothing practical to prevent the war, or to limit it, or to guarantee the balance of power in the Pacific. They leave Japan to continue her march into China, her inhuman bombardments of unarmed populations, the exodus of helpless peoples. The crisis of an international morality, so loudly proclaimed, has extended from the West to the East.

Meanwhile Great Britain and France were coping with the Mediterranean piracy. All knew to whom the unknown submarines belonged and no one had the courage to say it. The interested Powers rapidly arranged a conference at Nyon in Switzerland. Agreements were entered upon for forcible repression of the submarine offensive. This stopped as by magic. The swift success of such a move impelled the Cabinets of Paris and London to ask Rome for a three-Power meeting, to solve the problem of the withdrawal of foreign volunteers, which had proved a stumbling block for the Non-Intervention Committee. The initiative came from Mr. Eden, then Foreign Secretary, who wished to place Mussolini in the dilemma of a decisive choice. But the latter, too clever for him, on the one hand replied that on the Spanish question the decision must come from the Non-Intervention Committee and on the other showed himself prepared to negotiate an agreement with Great Britain over the Mediterranean and Red Sea.

It was Hitler's hour. All the anti-Semitic campaign in Germany, the reinforcement of the Berlin-Rome Axis, the support for Tokyo, the intervention in Spain, had been a preparation for his design of subjugating Austria. Mr. Eden's resignation from the Chamberlain Cabinet through his refusal to accept Mussolini's 'now or never' for negotiating the new agreement, Mr. Chamberlain's orientation in favour of an understanding with Germany, cost what it might, even though it meant washing his hands of Central Europe, precipitated events. Hitler on February 17, 1938 summoned Schuschnigg to Berchtesgaden to intimate to him that he must take Seyss-Inquart as Minister of the Interior and of the Police, a Nazi Catholic who would serve as Trojan Horse. The unfortunate Austrian Chancellor gave way under Hitler's threats. Then, repenting, he calls a plebiscite, but Hitler has the way clear for armed invasion. On March 11th everything collapses, Government and President leave their posts, some are arrested, some flee. Hitler annexes Austria to the Reich, making it a province under the name of the Ostmark. The Cabinets of Europe and America make no protest, note the *fait accompli*, withdraw their diplomats from Vienna. The Holy See withdraws the Nuncio, the League of Nations keeps silence. It has nothing more to say, after Manchuria, Abyssinia, Spain, China; it is merely constrained to register the fact that Austria, a Member of the League, no longer exists.

The moves of the political game become accelerated. The Anglo-Italian Agreement is signed on April 15. The Non-Intervention Committee on July 16 fixes the lines of an agreement for the withdrawal of the foreign troops from Spain. The Nazi Party of the Sudeten agitates for autonomy in Czechoslovakia. The British Government sends out a peacemaker, Lord Runciman, while Hitler mobilises over a million men for the summer manoeuvres. We are now in September. The Sudeten leaders refuse any agreement on autonomy and demand annexation to the Reich. Hitler threatens to occupy Czechoslovakia by armed force. Then comes Mr. Chamberlain's journey to Berchtesgaden, the agreement between London and Paris, bidding Prague give way. Mr. Chamberlain goes to Godesberg. It seems as if war is inevitable, with mobilisation in Czechoslovakia, partial mobilisation in France, precautionary measures in Great Britain. At the meeting of the four at Munich, Germany, Great Britain, France, Italy, agree to impose on the government of Prague the cession of the zones of the German Sudeten, giving an unworkable guarantee for the new frontiers. But Poland and Hungary demand their territories. There are armed threats and partial invasions. Czechoslovakia is dismembered and six months later is to be occupied by German troops. Slovakia becomes an autonomous State though nominally bound to Prague. Hosts of refugees leave the country; populations are forced to submit to new governments against their will. Germany dominates as master, in march towards the East. France and Great Britain are kept at a distance and look on, impotent and perturbed at the collapse of the whole post-war system of Central Europe. And while first Great Britain and then France exchange with Germany declarations of friendship and pacts of non-aggression, and seek to propitiate Italy by recognising the Italian Empire in letters accrediting their ambassadors to the King-Emperor (all this in November, 1938), the armaments race grows more and more intense, Great Britain is even prepared to introduce conscription if voluntary service fails, and the threat of a general war with the Italian pretensions to Tunis, Jibuti, Corsica, Nice and Savoy, and Germany's manoeuvres weigh again upon a disoriented, agitated and blood-stained Europe.

These grave events, of which we have traced the historic outline, would not concern us if they were not part of a profound moral crisis, which affects both the temporal order (the State and the society of States) and the spiritual order (the Church and churches). That is, our whole civilisation. Anyone who thinks that in the events narrated there is nothing but a political connection, or indeed an episodic and incidental conjuncture, is deluding himself on the true reality of what is happening, which reaches to the very roots of our civilisation. Compare the American and French Revolutions, which, from the political standpoint, marked the end of the ancient régime in Europe and the colonies, and for this might be detested or extolled, while, considered in their profounder and ethical significance, they reaffirmed not a few Christian principles, though under a naturalistic aspect and even presented as opposed to Christianity. This is what happened after the Great War. The values of international co-operation (League of Nations), of inter-State justice (the Hague Court), of international co-operation of labour and capital (the I.L.O.), the system of colonial mandates for the raising of the native peoples and their progressive autonomy, the ideal of universal peace were principles established in the common conscience, though presented together with the peace treaties which contained injustices and were the law of the victor. The experience of the last twenty years, brief as it has been, has destroyed the League system. This fact in politics must lead to the formation of another system, either that of the hegemony of a Power or group of Powers, or one of equilibrium, or some other, for it is impossible for the world to be without an international system. But what is of import for civilisation is that this system should be founded on moral principles, and as such Christian, for there is no human morality that is not implicitly Christian, there is no immorality that can be upheld in the name of Christianity.

And here is the tragedy of our time. Nations like Germany and Italy, not to mention Japan, are more and more consolidating themselves on anti-Christian principles. For them, to destroy the system of Geneva was practical politics. But how could it be destroyed without a repudiation of its fundamental ethical principles? To say that Geneva was the hypocritical guardian of the injustices of the victory of the Entente, created in the name of justice and morality, and that therefore it had to be destroyed, might hold good if the principles in the name of which Geneva was repudiated were those of justice and morality. But the principles put forward have been those of aggression, as in the case of Manchuria and Abyssinia and China, those of revolt, of armed intervention and civil war as in Spain, those of invasion and violent annexation as in Austria, those of the breach of treaties of alliance and of the violent dismemberment by armed force of a State, as in the case of Czechoslovakia.

At bottom there is the substitution of force for law, the permanent threat of recourse to war to induce the threatened Powers to give way and to oblige the small and weak to submit to the law of the stronger. There is the exaltation of the race and of the nation as the ultimate principle of morality, to which individuals and collectivities are made subject. This principle justifies the racial war on the Jews, the religious war on the Christians, the political war against dissidents, even against political nonconformists. This struggle brings the suppression of every liberty, of liberty itself, and the unconditional and divinised dominion of a person or of a party. Totalitarianism is as such immoral, for it admits the subordination to an irresponsible power of everything, body and soul, moral and material goods, national and international interests.

From the day of Hitler's advent to power and the proclamation of the race principle, the hurricane of anti-semitic persecution has swept through Germany. This has been the sign of a crisis of civilisation, for a principle of discrimination has been created that will go to the roots. In fact the persecution has extended to Christians, Protestants and Catholics, who uphold the principle of human brotherhood before men and before God. The anti-semitic persecution has spread as step by step the power and influence of Nazi Germany have increased—to the Saar, Austria, Danzig, Poland, Hungary, Roumania. When Austria was annexed, the anti-semitic laws and those against the Catholics were imposed with their full fury. It seemed as if anti-semitism and racialism would not cross the Alps. But no, Mussolini too is seized with a frenzy of anti-semitic laws and racial principles, and rages even against the pity shown by Italians towards the unfortunate victims. Now Czechoslovakia has been brought into line and persecutes the Jews. Even countries like France and Great Britain have been reached by the wave of anti-semitism, which has laid hold of a certain germanophile press and certain political philo-fascist sections, giving the impression of a contagion the more dangerous the more it is unconscious, especially among the Catholics.

The German pogrom against the Jews came exactly a month after the surrender *à discretion* of the democratic Powers over the question of Czechoslovakia and in the height of the campaign for the return of the German colonies. The civilised voice of protest against such new barbarities has not failed to make itself heard. Not only the labour and socialist parties, not only the Christian democratic parties and the press of the Catholics of France, Belgium, Holland and Switzerland, but the whole of civilised opinion (with a few exceptions) has been roused. President Roosevelt in recalling the United States Ambassadors, first from Berlin, then from Rome, significantly expressed the reprobation of a barbaric anti-semitism raised to a method of government. The civilised nations that can still be accounted such, on the initiative of Holland, entered into an agreement to receive and assist the refugees from the anti-semitic persecution. This only rendered the dictators more recalcitrant and more ferocious in their proposals of extermination. The Hitler organ *Schwarze Korps* reached the point of writing in November, 1938, the following cynical lines: 'The Jews must be relegated to special streets, they must be distinguished by special signs and deprived of the right to possess land or a house.' This is the first step; excluded from every remunerative occupation, the Jews will be forced to turn criminal. 'When they have reached this point, we shall find ourselves in the necessity of exterminating the Jewish world with the methods that we always use in the struggle against criminals, that is, with the *sword and with fire*. The result will be the complete end of the Jews in Germany, their total destruction.'

All the Christian churches have risen up against such a monstrous attitude. But above all Pius XI adopted an eminent position with authority, continuity and inflexibility. It is sufficient to recall the circular of the Congregation of Seminaries and Universities, defining eight propositions of racialism and State totalitarianism as to be confuted in ecclesiastical teaching, both from the scientific and theological standpoints. When he learned that racialism had been introduced into Italy, the Pope, in an address on July 15, 1938, sought to define the Catholic standpoint. 'The universality of the Catholic Church', he said, 'certainly does not exclude the idea of race, of descent, of nation, of nationality, but the human race, the whole human race, is but a single and universal race of man. There is no room for special races. We may therefore ask ourselves why Italy should have felt a need to imitate Germany.' Against anti-semitism, he spoke even more strongly. This in its modern form has been condemned by Holy Office in a Decree of March 25, 1928.[1] The Pope wished to claim a semitic affiliation for Christians as did St. Paul: all are children of Abraham. Pius XI in an important talk to the Belgian pilgrims on September 6, 1938, gave lofty expression to this glorious descent and ended, moved to tears, with the phrase: 'Anti-semitism is inadmissible. We are spiritually semites'.[2]

To quote the addresses of Pius XI during 1938 on this question would take many pages; he combined the condemnation of racialism, anti-semitism and the nationalism that he qualified as exaggerated, and he emphasised all the peril they imply for our Christian civilisation. In the report of the address of July 15 in the *Osservatore Romano* we may note this significant passage: 'The Supreme Pontiff added that he had never thought of these matters with such precision, with such absoluteness, one would almost say with such intransigence of formula. And since God gave him the grace of such a clarity, he wanted to make his sons sharers in it, since all had a particular need of it in these times when such ideas raised so much tumult and did so great a harm.' A few days later, receiving the students of the College of the *Propaganda fide*, in regard to the nationalism that was reaching even the mission countries, he expressed himself thus: 'The nations exist and so does nationalism, but the nations were made by God. There is therefore room for a just,

[1]On the occasion of the suppression of the Association of the Friends of Israel, the decree of the Holy Office contained the following passage: '*Qua caritate permota Apostolica Sedes eundem populum contra injustas vexationes protexit, et quemadmodum omnes invidias ac simultates inter populos reprobat, ita vel maxime damnat odium adversus populum, olim a Deo electum, odium nempe illud quod vulgo "antisemitism" nomine nunc significari solet.*' 'Moved by this charity the Holy See has always protected this people against unjust vexations, and just as its reprobates all rancour and conflicts between peoples, it particularly condemns hatred against the people once chosen of God, the hatred that commonly goes by the name of anti-semitism.'

[2]*Cité Nouvelle*, Brussels, September 15, 1938.

moderate nationalism, associated with all the virtues, but beware of exaggerated nationalism as of a real curse. It seems to us unhappily that events justify us when we say "a real curse", for it is the cause of continual divisions and very frequently of war'.

This is the moral crisis of to-day in the relations between peoples, nations and races, the crisis of the denial of the permanent values of Christian civilisation, which still survive in the modern laic States and in the League of Nations, and which form the wholesome ferment of the religious currents in the various Christian countries, and above all are proclaimed by the supreme authority of Catholicism—values which the totalitarian countries deny for a policy of demands and pre-dominion, and the countries known as democratic often betray through dissension, weakness, self-interest, and cowardice.

CHAPTER XV

THE PRESENT SITUATION

§ 61.—In order to determine the nature of the relations between Church and State to-day we must gauge the main factors of interaction and antagonism between them from the point of view of historical sociology. The laic State from its beginnings (which we placed, as a point of reference, at the Revolutions of the end of the XVIII century) brought no small change to the character and value of such relations and created fresh motives of antagonism. The present experience impels us to emphasise the fact that the laic State, in order to win complete autonomy from any factor conducive to dualism of power, has tended more and more towards a kind of 'confessionalism' of its own, for which the Church serves either as a term of opposition or as a constructive element. It is for this reason that the stages traversed by the laic State, seen as a whole, to-day appear as historically logical, with a rigorous rational connection, whereas, taken separately, period by period, or else in the states of mind of those who determined them or in their underlying theories, they appear inconsistent, here and there contradictory, and practically discontinuous.

The historical significance of the conquest of freedom of conscience, worship, assembly, speech and the press, paled when the laic State rid itself of the remains of absolutism and confessionalism, which had reappeared with the Restoration. It was not long before the positions were reversed; in all the varied and chaotic experiences of the new State a kind of 'laic confessionalism' was making its appearance, in as much as the State, in order to defend itself against its adversaries, old and new, denied them the liberties on which itself was founded. We use the term 'laic confessionalism' instead of the more usual one of 'State conformism,' for the laic State sought to obtain from its citizens not merely formal and outward assent (which would suffice for a certain conformism) but a convinced and entire support, which is best expressed by the word 'confessionalism'. Instead of a confession of faith in God and in the Church, there was a kind of confession of faith in the laic State. As little by little this was extending its sway over individual activities, with control and monopoly in culture and education, and subsequently in economic and political life, liberties were restricted or falsified or suppressed. This reversal of the positions has reached its climax to-day with what are known as the totalitarian States.

The Church, which, towards the end of the XVIII century and the beginning of the XIX, had been against the introduction of political liberties, in the following period of veiled or open separation and strife was compelled by events to demand these liberties for herself, in place of the old privileges that had been abolished, if she would carry on her religious activity. But liberties are coherent or they cannot exist; if they were denied to the Church as the adversary of the State, they would soon be denied to all who were considered as adversaries of the State (whatever might be its prevailing character), till they became the monopoly of the Government and its faction. If on the other hand the Church demands them for herself, she admits or supposes that such liberties are general for all. The tendency to refuse liberties to the adversaries of power, especially to the Church, so considered through her historical position, sprang precisely from the conception of the State as having its own ethical content, autonomous and all-embracing. This was inherent in the laic State of the XIX century, but there was no real consciousness of it.

This fact has characterised present relations between Church and State; the resulting situation has no parallel in the history of Christendom. In the earliest period, the Church represented the preaching of an exotic minority that was insinuating itself into the Roman Empire, and was persecuted as an element of disturbance and impiety. Although the Roman Empire was authoritarian, often tyrannical, and compelled its peoples to worship the Emperor and the Goddess Rome, it was in no wise either a laic or a totalitarian State as this is conceived of to-day. From Constantine to the Reformation, the Christian basis of the State was a progressive achievement. Originally outside the Church, the secular power became co-operant and often dominant within the Church, working for religious ends, whether those understood by the various currents outside union with Rome, or those of Catholic orthodoxy. In the Reformed States, notwithstanding the mutual antagonism of Catholics and Protestants, the Christian and religious basis of the political power was never questioned. Indeed the union of the temporal with the spiritual was so close that the spiritual suffered; protection, control and mutual superposition ended by confounding the characters and ends of the two powers in a politico-religious confessionalism. Reaction to this led first to toleration, then to laicism, with or without the formal separation of State from Church. But the modern State, born with the Renaissance and reaching maturity with the Reformation, remembered its original titles, and, while at bottom not wishful for separation, proclaimed its *autonomy* in the name of natural law. This would turn to *separation* in the name of liberty, *opposition* in the name of democracy, *laicism* in the name of bourgeois and working-class radicalism, *totality* in the name of nationalisms and racialisms of every species. Each of these principles was a denial of Christianity under particular aspects—jusnaturalism as natural law cut off from the supernatural; liberty as the autonomy of human reason; democracy as establishing the origin of authority in the Sovereign People (ignoring God or denying Him); radicalism as the vindication of human and social rights that were not recognised by the political and religious powers of the time, then in union; nationalism and racialism as forming a social totality in which the individuals were confounded and submerged, with all their values, including those spiritual and supernatural.

This process, like every historical process, has neither followed a straight line, nor lacked opposition and moments of recoil. Without such conflicts it would not have been a process, and they have not checked its course. The elements brought into it by the resistance and penetration of the Church have added particular features, which it would be vain to ignore or to minimise, or to take as dross to be purged out in the melting pot of history.

The laic State carried with it a notable ethical element, imbued with Christian values. It is true that the theoretical premises and ends of this ethic were prevalently naturalistic, but the principles of the respect of human personality, of individual liberty, of legal equality, of justice in private relations without distinction of class, of abolition of slavery and legal serfdom, were impregnated with Christianity. The failure to recognise this was the mistake made by many, who sought to defend as it stood the historical position to which the Church was then bound.

It was not long before the social rights of the working classes were put forward to counterbalance the errors of economic liberalism, which had created the army of proletarians. Marxist theory and the anarchist movements that accompanied and incited the vindication of the workers' demands should not have blinded men to the Christian elements these contained, as justice and charity. Of this enlightened men were aware, such as Lacordaire, Montalembert, Ketteler, Windthorst, Manning, Balmes, Mermillod, La Tour du Pin, Volgesang, Winterer, Decourtins, Harmel, Toniolo, and others, even before Leo XIII took up the workers' cause. The time that elapsed between the Communist Manifesto and *Rerum Novarum*, nearly half a century later, shows its effects even to-day in the dechristianisation of the working masses.

Finally, international peace and the comity of peoples were Christian ideas that the French Revolution took as its own and the Holy Alliance revived for the benefit of political reaction. Later they assumed a colour of humanitarian pacifism, and thus because of the naturalism underlying them they were opposed by Catholic writers, till with the outbreak of the Great War the catastrophe brought them back as realities of Christian thought, and Benedict XV expressed them in undying words in his letter of August 1, 1917.

These and other Christian elements that had found their way into the laic State under naturalistic guise, are to-day denied by the totalitarian State, not only through failure to recognise the moral values they imply, but principally because these are subordinated to the supreme values of the State. This process was a partial one in the earlier forms of the laic State, but it went forward steadily, with the absorption of every autonomous value into the single value of the whole. All the efforts of the Church to give a religious content to the ethical, social and international advances of modern times, have broken against the antagonistic will of the State to absorb and reduce everything into itself.

The struggle between Church and State during the Reformation was waged chiefly over a particular confession, accepted and upheld as the State religion. In the period of the Revolution it was, fundamentally, the defence of the historic rights of the Church against a veiled or open separation. To-day it is carried on in the moral field, in the fundamental conflict between the morality of Christianity and that of the State. It would be inexact to speak of 'state morality'; at bottom it is a case of Hegel's 'Ethical State'. Few really know the Hegelian theory of the State and not all understand it in the same way, but whatever its metaphysical premises, the currents of thought, the practical trend of the prevailing governments and parties, the formation of public opinion, all tend to identify the political ends of the State with the ethical conception of life. This implies the 'Ethical State', origin and fount of liberty, morality and right, norm and end of individuals who in the State find unity and sublimation.

Christianity is menaced by a powerful antagonist which without being either a religion or a divinity assumes the character of both, to cancel them, were it possible in itself, and certainly to absorb or dominate them. Christianity, studied from the sociological standpoint, as we have seen, is a personal, universal, autonomous religion. The State, as the end of all activity, to-day claims human personality for itself and suppresses all liberty in order to transfer the course of liberty to the group that it represents. It leaves, it is true, freedom of worship (even in Russia nominally, in Germany with restrictions, in Italy effectively), but it seeks to render it barren by separating morality from worship and emancipating State morality from any heteronomous bond, the source of which would be other than the State itself.

Individual morality was the first to be proclaimed autonomous. How could the State stand without a common morality as basis of social life? What authority could be attributed to codes and laws? Through the inadequacy of the individual will and the difficulties of reconciling its autonomy with its subordination for social ends to the will of the majority, the State came to be conceived as a vital and perennial totality of these very individuals. This was the title of the State to the name of 'ethical'; the State alone therefore would be truly free, for no one could lay down rules for it and no one could bind it either inwardly or outwardly. Being free the State itself would be morality because it was the State.

The morality of the Church either coincides with that of the State or should be eliminated. The State not only takes no account of it in its laws, which may include anti-Christian measures such as divorce, legalised abortion, eugenic sterilisation, compulsory laic education, Nazi, Fascist or Communist, but it sets its authority above the Church, forcing the Churches to give public support to the acts of the political power, even when these are immoral, such as breach of treaties, unjust war, civil war, hate-propaganda, persecution of religious, political or racial minorities. The exaltation of similar misdeeds to-day is such, and so grave is the fanaticism aroused in the masses, that the idea of social group (State, nation, class, race) makes it hard to conceive of a personal religion bringing the obligation to repudiate the law of the group and to seek purification for the crimes and misdeeds it may have committed. Hence the character of a personal religion, possessed by Christianity ever since it first appeared, is stricken at the roots.

The universality of Christianity may be contested by the political power either as hierarchy or as dogma or as morality. The confessional States always sought to undermine the universality of the Church in her hierarchy, and, by rebound, in her dogma, leading to heresies and schisms; only indirectly was Christian morality affected, in the cases of royal divorces, simony in the investiture of benefices, or the concubinage of priests. But in these cases no one pretended to create a new morality, nor were divorce, concubinage or simony proclaimed as acts of a higher and therefore heroic morality, springing from a higher ethical conception than the Christian.

The laic State, in proclaiming a morality of its own, created an irremediable dualism with Christian morality, but so long as the State left the individual citizens free to profess, propagate and defend their moral and political ideals, there was no danger of an ethical schism between the faithful of a particular State and the Church. When, however, the laic State claimed to impose its own morality on all, in the name either of the will of the people (as in the radical democracies) or the will of the nation, or of the class or race (as in the totalitarian States), then apostasy, initially confined to the central power, became the apostasy of the masses.

In consequence autonomy, which is the third sociological feature of Christianity as a personal and universal religion, (that is, above the social groups—family, nation, State, comity of nations), suffers an exceptionally far-reaching limitation in the ethical field. Each particular State seeks to impose its own morality, which consists in the divinisation of the new whole it would incarnate. 'The man who in every nation prays to the God of peace does not make a god of his own nation', wrote Pius XI in his letter *Caritate Christi compulsi*. To-day the totalitarian States train the masses to make a god of their own nation. Christianity is thus stricken in its three characteristic features, as a personal, universal and autonomous religion.

§ 62.—The empire of the State over the soul is in continuous progress both where evolution towards the totalitarian State is reaching fulfilment and where the State, while not totalitarian, seeks to give its own imprint to the educational and cultural formation of the country. It is the task of all the Christian churches to resist. The more they can counterpose a truly modern Christian formation, the better will they be able to face the new peril. It has been easy for them to organise in the sphere of modern culture and education in countries where all enterprises are free, and where the State does not interfere to direct education, as in the United States, and, apart from certain differences, in Great Britain, as in Holand and Switzerland too, when the last resistance of Protestantism had been overcome, and finally in the Scandinavian countries with the fall of the last barriers raised by the Reformation against free cultural movements. Belgium was noted for the long fight of the Catholics for freedom of the school. France, in spite of her positivist laicism, has up till now been able to save the confessional schools and to open various Catholic Universities, which have had no small influence in checking the dechristianisation of studious youth.[1]

[1]In Italy under the liberal régime educational freedom was never won, Catholics stood outside political life, and the Roman Question preoccupied the governments. This notwithstanding, private Catholic schools arose and several obtained parity with

One of the most notable enterprises of the Catholic Church to-day has been the formation of intellectual *élites* and the spread of Catholic Action, even in the mission countries. We noted the birth of a Catholic lay movement in the middle of the last century, with the character it then assumed, of an anti-liberal reaction yet taking up the political position rendered possible by the régime of liberty, and later a social position in the Labour or Christian Democratic field. It was Benedict XV who in 1915 unified the Italian movement under the name of Catholic Action (which had already been used by Pius X), and dissociated it from electoral organisation. Pius XI confirmed its character as a lay apostolate in dependence on the hierarchy, and promoted its formation in all countries, making it a matter for concordats. Those who see in the dechristianisation of modern society a return to paganism and in Catholic Action a co-operation in the priesthood, often recall the example of the early Church, when the laity, men and women, co-operated in the labours of the apostles and in the propagation of the Gospel.

It cannot be doubted that for the last century the Catholic laity has given many remarkable examples of spiritual elevation, self-sacrifice, courage and militancy. There have been flowers of sanctity, as in Italy Giuseppe Toniolo, the theorist of Christian Democracy and for half a century the champion of Catholic Action, Vico Necchi and Giorgio Luigi Frassati, both of Catholic Action and of the Popular Party (the informatory causes for their eventual beatification are now in course), and in France Marie-Pauline Jéricot, Léon Harmel and Marius Gonin, not to mention the great figures of the past, most notable of all O'Connell, Montalembert, Windthorst. The recent movements of Catholic working-class youth, like that of the Jocists[1] and others similar, are

the State schools. On the foundation of the Popular Party, its most vigorous battle was for the State examination, which would have done away with the scholastic monopoly. At the same time, through private initiative, the Catholic University of Milan was founded, and was inaugurated in 1921 by a Popular minister. It was the Fascist Government that recognised it as a public institution and convalidated its degrees.

[1]Founded in Belgium, and diffused in other countries. The name Jocists comes from the initials J. O. C. (*Jeunesse Ouvrière Catholique*). The English equivalent is known as the Young Christian Workers.

developing with an enthusiasm that exceeds that of Christian Democracy forty years ago, and recalls in certain respects the medieval movements of the Franciscan Third Order.

The Protestant churches have no precisely similar movements. Some of them, congregationally organised, have always maintained a co-operation between clergy and faithful. On the margins of the churches, however, there are certain movements of a special character. The Salvation Army has over sixty years of indefatigable labour behind it. For a time there was much talk about the 'Oxford' Group Movement. Its aim was to restore the men of to-day, deafened by external life, to an inward spirituality founded on purity, love, honesty and unselfishness. From the Christian point of view a movement of this kind, not being a church, could exert only an individual influence within the various denominations into which Anglo-Saxon religion is divided up.

Catholic Action has no political character and does not seek to substitute itself for the political parties formed by Catholics where these still exist (as in Belgium, Holland, Switzerland), nor to take their place where they exist no longer (as in Germany, Italy, Austria, Czechoslovakia). To understand the impulse behind Catholic Action we must realise the idea of a Christian apostolate within a modern State, whether democratic or totalitarian, where politics affect the whole of life. A lay apostolate in the Church has never been wanting, both in the Catholic and in the dissident churches, according to the needs of the time and the phase of culture. The basic idea of Catholic Action is the Christian formation of all, of every class and age, beginning with the children, so that all may co-operate in the priestly ministry and share in its very mission. It is natural that Catholic Action should concern itself with the formation of the Christian as a citizen, to give him a clear conception of national and international, political and social problems, so long as this does not only not conflict with Christian principles, but responds to the very spirit of Christianity, which is one of truth and love.

It is inconceivable for a man of Catholic Action to accept the ethico-political conceptions of naturalism, rationalism, positivism, Hegelianism, in the same way as he cannot accept the practical expressions of liberalism, Communism, Socialism, Fascism and Nazism, inasmuch as they contain erroneous or anti-Christian theories. The Christian has his own conception of earthly life and of supernatural life, which he must assert in his life as a citizen and in his apostolate in Catholic Action. Is this politics? Indeed, the charge repeated in Germany and Austria against the Catholic organisations is the same as that which in Italy in 1898 led the Conservative Government to dissolve them all by decree, in spite of the protests of Leo XIII. Mussolini's Italy did the same in 1927 with all the sports associations and, in a violent manner, in 1931, with the Clubs for Catholic Youth. In the summer of 1938 he threatened rigorous measures against Catholic Action itself, because of its opposition to the racial theories adopted by the government of Rome.[1]

At the bottom, there is an irremediable confusion of terms. The modern State aspires to be a *Weltanschauung*, a conception of the world and of life, in substance, a religion. Christianity too is a *Weltanschauung*, besides being a supernatural religion. Between Christianity and the modern State conceived as a *Weltanschauung* conflict is inherent and inevitable. It may be carried on in a civilised fashion in countries where the State loyally observes the method of liberty, but it becomes open

[1]Pius XI in his Allocution to the College of Cardinals on December 24, 1938, speaking of the tenth anniversary of the Lateran Treaty and Concordat with Italy, felt himself obliged to say—'as a debt of apostolic sincerity and truth, and for the edification which, also because of our age, we owe to all . . .'—that this anniversary had brought him 'real and grave anxieties and bitter sorrows. Bitter sorrows indeed', he went on, 'when it is a case of real and multiple vexations—we do not say that they are precisely general but certainly very numerous and occurring in several places—against Catholic Action, which is well-known to be the apple of our eye. Catholic Action—a fact that has had to be recognised and confessed as resulting from the seizure of various of its headquarters and archives—neither engages in politics nor brings an undesired rivalry, but solely seeks to make good Christians living their Christianity, and by that very fact elements of the first order for the public good, especially in a Catholic country like Italy, and as the facts have proved.

'Noting the zeal among inferior strata, it seems too clear that although Catholic Action was distinctly envisaged in our Pact of Conciliation, there must be wide—or rather secret—gestures of permission and encouragement from the top, so that these vexations are incessant in different places from end to end of the Peninsula. And not only in small or unimportant places. Yesterday we were told of Venice, Turin, Bergamo. To-day it is Milan, and precisely in the person of its Cardinal Archbishop, guilty of an address and a teaching that falls precisely within his pastoral duties, and which we cannot but approve.'

strife where the State denies liberties to the Church, and when, worse still, liberty is suppressed for all and State interference covers the whole of human life. Then the Church is persecuted, for even in the catacombs she arouses fear (as to-day in Russia); deprived of all human resources and able only to pray she arouses fear (as to-day in Germany and in Austria); if she merely protests against an erroneous theory or against a moral violation, she arouses fear (as to-day in Italy). The Church is always the spiritual antagonist of a State that seeks to become the *Whole*.

The Holy See has sought to avoid religious conflicts with the totalitarian States, giving way wherever this has been possible, to remove the motives or pretexts for persecutions. To-day concordatory methods are preferred, in order to define the positions involved and to carry disputes that might arise on to a legal plane. Since the Napoleonic Concordat this method has been widely used to ward off the blows of the authoritarian States and to systematise positions compromised by modern laicism combined with the remains of the old jurisdictionalism. Since the Great War two types of concordats have been employed. The one is a *modus vivendi* to establish the position of the Church in respect of her hierarchy and Catholic culture and education, either with a laic State or with a non-Catholic State in which there are Catholic provinces. Such were the Concordats with the three States of what was once the Little Entente and with some of the States of what was once the Weimar *Reich*. The other type has a wider scope, implying over and above the sections concerned with canonical questions a kind of co-operation of the Church for the ends of the dictatorial State—such the Concordat with Italy in 1929 and that with Nazi Germany in 1933, of which we have already spoken. By this we do not mean to disparage what good may result from such concordats; we wish merely to underline the fact that the States exacting such a co-operation do so through their intrinsic totalitarian character, and for their part cannot but subordinate their acceptance and execution of the Concordat to the ends of the State. The Canonists of the Curia once, in the face of the Regalists, maintained that concordats were not contracts implying the parity of the contracting parties, but gracious concessions made by the Holy See, through which it voluntarily bound itself to the States. To-day the theorists of the totalitarian States reverse the positions; it is the State that graciously binds itself to the Holy See so long as this falls in with its totalitarian policy. Germany acts on this theory, violating the concordat (which served the purpose of moral recognition of Hitler's dominion) openly and without scruple, and preparing to denounce it. Italy has nearly always observed the Concordat, save recently by the anti-semitic marriage laws, but on condition that the Church should not disturb her enterprises. The state of affairs that could arise between them was indeed apparent in the spring of 1931 over Catholic Youth. If by chance a certain number of bishops had raised obstacles to the military training of infancy (one of the worst measures of the régime) or had merely expressed reservations on the justice of the African war, then, in spite of the Concordat, they would have felt the thunderbolts of Fascism.

In March, 1937, Pius XI published three Encyclicals, one a week, which form an imposing and characteristic summary of the present situation of Christianity in the face of the totalitarian States. The first, *Divini Redemptoris*, is not only a reiterated and more mature condemnation of atheistic Communism (as seen in the experience of the Bolshevist régime and its propaganda in the working class world), but an urge to a reconstruction of the labour world on Christian and humane foundations—an enterprise that meets with its chief obstacle in the powerful tentacles of Capitalism, which has infected the propertied classes with its materialistic spirit. The second, *Mit brennender Sorge*, is in defence of persecuted Catholicism in Germany, and in condemnation of the Nazi and racial theories in the name of which persecution has been launched. Without naming them, but describing them, the Fascist theories divinising State and Nation are condemned, as they had been in the Encyclical *Non abbiamo Bisogno* of June 1931, against the Fascist persecutions in Italy. The third encyclical, *Nos es muy*, is addressed to the Bishops of Mexico, on resistance to the dechristianisation of life in their country, on the rights of Christians as citizens, on the character and limits of resistance to the constituted powers, on Catholic Action and its office.

In all three encyclicals two fundamental themes prevail. The one is the integral supernatural conception of life in all its phases, private and public, economic and political, in the name of which materialism, atheism and pantheism, to-day predominant in the theories and activities of the States, must be fought and overcome. The other is that of the action of Catholics who, like the early Christians, by their apostolate and sacrifice must save classes, States, society, all their brethren who are carried away by error and iniquity.

From March 1937 to the end of his life, Pius XI took up an ever clearer and more resolute attitude in the ideological conflict raging in the world. To the Social Week of the Catholics of France in July, 1937, which dealt with the theme of human personality, to-day imperilled, he sent a letter through his Secretary of State, Cardinal Pacelli, extolling the human and Christian value of the person, who is the end of the State and of every other society, never a means to the State's end. The Social Week the following year dealt with Liberty, and the Pope's letter, sent through the same channel, is one of the most illuminating documents on the nature of true liberty. We may note this significant passage: 'It is not surprising that the Church has remained the sole and greatest defender of true liberty'.

The experience of Bolshevik totalitarianism created a belief that the remedy for working class agitation inspired by Communism would lie in the totalitarian régimes of the Right. Hence the favour with which Fascism and Nazism were greeted by industrial and agrarian capitalists (who were profuse in economic help when these movements started), and also among the bourgeoisie and among those Catholic sections that feel the influence of the propertied classes. We have seen how the German bishops, with a few exceptions, were hostile to the Nazis. Those of Italy were not favourable to the Fascists, but once these had reached power, it was believed possible to try a new union of 'Throne and Altar', that is, of the dictatorship and the Church. The experience of German Nazism has given a negative result. Catholic Bavaria has lost all its confessional schools; Catholic Austria in a few months has been spiritually laid waste, through the Bishops' trust in Hitler and the lack of moral resistance among the Catholics. A characteristic fact in Austria has been the apostasy of hundreds and hundreds from the Catholic faith, for a Nazism conceived of as a spiritual totality. In Italy motives for grave anxiety had not been lacking. The experience of such forms of totalitarianism has given the hierarchies of the Church a new appreciation of free régimes; as a result we have had the collective declarations of the bishops of France, Switzerland, Holland and Belgium in favour of the régimes of their respective countries, which are democratic, where men may still freely manifest their ideas and convictions and are free to organise. Cardinal Dougherty of Philadelphia, in his pastoral letter of November, 1938, hoped that the United States would become 'the fortress of democracy at the turning point of world-history, and that they would fight energetically against those who even in America mock, attack and endanger these principles. Freedom must be preserved and those subversive doctrines fought which threaten to destroy all that is just and noble in the land of liberty which is America.'

This movement of opinion among the Catholic hierarchy in free countries in no wise means that the Church, and through her the Holy See, has changed the traditional system of treating with all governments and continuing relations even with governments that attack her, as to-day in Germany and Mexico. It was not through the Holy See that in Republican Spain public worship and the hierarchy were not re-established. A first cautious hint at the reorganisation of public worship was made towards the end of 1938. Even with Russia the Holy See would re-establish contacts. When the Russian Delegation of the Soviets intervened in the Genoa Conference, in May, 1922, Pius XI spontaneously sent a representative, Cardinal Pizzardo (then a Monsignore in the Secretariat of State) to confer with Chicherin, then Foreign Minister. But the Church needs liberty, it is her right to demand it, and to-day liberty is her only safeguard against the totalitarian tendency that threatens the world.

The Protestant churches in the totalitarian countries, since unlike the Catholic Church they had no single organisation of doctrine and discipline extending throughout the world, found themselves isolated in the face of the political powers. Some churches gave their complete adherence to the political régimes of the country, in order to preserve their own personality (thus they did in Italy), or to gain momentary advantages, as recently in Austria, or where clergy and faithful were divided between those who favoured the régime and those who were against it, as in Germany. Those who fight with courage and perseverance have the sympathy and solidarity of the Protestant Churches abroad, especially the Anglo-Saxon ones on both sides of the Atlantic, and through these they can affirm the principles of liberty, morality and autonomy of the religious conscience as against the political power and the totalitarian and racial conceptions on which it rests.

A place apart must be reserved for the position of the Church of England. Through the instinct of conservation and tradition peculiar to this country, the Church of England finds itself, in its formal positions, what it was in the past, with no modifications other than an adjustment of its relations with the Crown and Parliament. Yet the substance has been changing as little by little the régime of toleration gave place to a régime of liberty for all religions, including Roman Catholicism, and gradually the State took such civil measures as those concerning divorce, the undenominational school, freedom of education, the impunity of offences against religion and recently of blasphemy, which completed (without saying so) its secularisation or laic character. This notwithstanding, the Church of England has remained the official church, legally and in its administration. The King receives religious consecration (like the Orthodox kings), and takes an oath of loyalty to his church. The bishops are appointed by his government, Parliament decides on the proposals of the Church Assembly in questions of doctrine, formularies and ecclesiastical justice.

A considerable stir was caused by the Prayer Book controversy, which provided a motive for reconsidering the relations between Church and State. The Church assemblies had proposed modifications corresponding to the demands and currents among clergy and laity, especially over Holy Communion and the reservation of the Eucharist. Parliament, exercising a kind of guardianship in the name of the common feeling, rather than a dogmatic and liturgical control, for which it could hardly claim competence, had the right of accepting or rejecting the new version as it stood. A majority voted against the innovations to the 1662 text, among the members who voted being some who did not belong to the Church of England. The resentment of the clergy in favour of the new Prayer Book was such that they adopted its use in their own churches. The bishops in order to get out of the difficulty subsequently authorised the use of the new book pending a fresh attempt at legislation when the time was ripe; this decision was criticised as unlawful. Discussion, which had arisen on other occasions, was then revived on the question whether the relations of the Church of England with the State should not be altered and whether it would not be better to reach disestablishment. Many oppose the idea of separation and consider it necessary to maintain the Established Church, because of the privileges it so enjoys over all the others, and for fear of an increase of influence of the Roman Church,[1] or in order to maintain the Christian character of the Crown of the United Kingdom and of the British Empire itself.

It is not surprising if, in the midst of such variations and upheavals, the Church of England continues to hold its old positions. From the internal standpoint, it cannot be said to have a fixed and common creed; the rationalistic current of theology (known as liberal, or even modernist) is very strong and sets an axe to the roots of dogmatism; the other current, that of the Anglo-Catholics, seeks to revive the pre-Reformation ritual and accepts from Rome many devotional practices (including the cult of the Sacred Heart). Where an inward unity is lacking its place is taken by an external and formal unification in the State and in the hierarchy dependent on it. All this corresponds to the rather indefinite religious spirit and the pronounced individualism of the Anglo-Saxon countries, so that neither Church nor State represents a complete collective unification, but only a centre of an administrative, organic and legal character. Here each individual is his own State and his own Church.

It is not the same in Scotland, where the Church is independent of Crown and Parliament, though its existence and its rights are recognised. The congregationalist and puritan spirit has been preserved against all the encroachments of the kings of the XVII and XVIII centuries, and in spite of the introduction of the régime of liberty. Recently the Established Church and the United Free Church of Scotland have joined together, but their sense of autonomy is enough to guarantee the personality of each. The schools are State schools, but

[1] 'The Church of Rome would gain much ground and claim more.' (*Church and State*, by the Bishop of Norwich. 1936, p. 11.)

all the churches (including the Catholic Church) appoint boards of education by a system of proportional representation.

With the formation of the Irish Free State (now Eire) and the resurrection of Poland, there were Catholics who thought it possible to return to the confessional State, known euphemistically as the Christian State or Catholic State. These had none too clear ideas on the nature of a Catholic State, but in both cases Catholicism became bound up with a typical nationalism founded on the Catholic tradition of the country. In reality, neither one nor the other could be inscribed on a past of historical struggles, political and confessional, to-day left behind. Ireland installed democratic forms of government and inter-confessional toleration. There was indeed a certain attempt to introduce something of ecclesiastical control into public life, but it came to nothing since it was exploited by both parties, which, apart from their different conceptions, are both catholico-national. Poland passed rapidly from ultra-democratic to dictatorial forms. Traditional Catholicism was exploited by the nationalistic spirit in the struggle against the Ukrainians of Galicia. Anti-semitism, the influence of German Nazism and anti-Ukrainian nationalism have made the position of the Church in Poland an extremely difficult one.

After the Lateran agreements a section of the foreign press, from ingenuousness or ignorance, spoke of the Catholic State of Fascist Italy. The illusion was short-lived, save among those who still take their vain wishes for realities. The idea of the Catholic State was revived with the none too happy experiences of the Austria of Dollfuss and Schuschnigg. These, good Catholics but poor statesmen, had the illusion that their anti-socialist, authoritarian and philo-Fascist policy would enable them to realise their dream of a Catholic Social State, based on the encyclicals *Rerum Novarum* and *Quadragesimo Anno*, and there were those abroad who believed in it and wrote of it with enthusiasm. They did not realise the fundamental contradiction of a minority government of Catholics, representing not more than a third of the people and in disagreement among themselves, seeking to impose on the other two-thirds (Socialists, Pan-germanists and Nazis) a type of State that had no traditions of its own, as if it had dropped from heaven. They did not understand that the support of Fascist Italy was conditional on the introduction of an anti-democratic and authoritarian system, on the crushing of the Socialists (hence the bloody revolts of February, 1934), and that Nazism was undermining Austrian independence. In such a climate the attempt to revive Austrian and Catholic patriotism (with a dubious Hapsburg tinge) and a corporatism imposed by authority even though clothed in papal phrases, was merely a pious illusion. Dollfuss fell a victim to assassination, Schuschnigg lost Austria, at the cost to himself of unmerited sufferings as Hitler's political vengeance.

Those who still seek for a Catholic and corporative State in the present day go to Portugal to study Salazar's experiment. Salazar, an excellent administrator and almost a silent dictator, has the merit of having placed the finances of his country on a sound basis. His corporations show the effects of the climate of State authoritarianism in which they were born, and of which they are emanations. The Church of Portugal has been able to take up an active and autonomous position from the time that, following the lines laid down by Benedict XV, it accepted the republican State without dynastic *sous-entendus* and without attachments to the *ancien régime*, and from the time that the Republic abandoned the anti-clericalism from which it had arisen with the overthrow of the monarchy. It is to be hoped that the Salazar experiment will not lead to a new wave of anti-clericalism. For Portugal is half-way between Europe and Latin America. And in those countries the passage is easy from concordatarism to fanatical anti-clericalism, just as it is easy from democratic forms to pseudo-dictatorships and vice versa.

Spain remains. The very people who deluded themselves over the Catholic State of Austria or Portugal, were ready to believe in a new Catholic State in Spain, under a Franco victorious over the Reds, who would install a Christian corporatism in close union with the Church. All General Franco's acts have been imbued with the ideal of a national and Catholic Spain. The shadow of Phalangism, which arose in imitation of Fascism and then came to set its course more and more by Nazism, was not unmarked by the hierarchy. But the necessities of war for long led to a minimising of the dangers of totalitarianism.

In this illusion of the Catholic State (or Christian State), there is at bottom an inexact vision of history. History is not reversible; the historical process, in spite of its involutions, goes steadily forward. One experience is followed by another, and each is that particular experience, with its own character. The Christian State of the XX century could be neither the corporative State of the Middle Ages nor the confessional State of the Reformation and Counter-Reformation, nor the Union of Throne and Altar of the Restoration on the Continent. To-day we have the totalitarian dictatorship, or the democracies of a liberal type, or the intermediate and ambiguous forms which end by becoming unstable and arbitrary governments or transitory and anarchic demagogies. The Church has not to choose between them, for it is not her task to choose the political type of the State, but she cannot identify herself with the totalitarian State merely because its governance is in Catholic hands (as in the case of Franco or Salazar, or of Dollfuss or Schuschnigg), without assuming responsibilities for the oppression of the dissentient population not only in the name of a totalitarian government, but in the name of the religion which that government has made its own. This danger is to-day all the greater in that there is a wider zone of the population practising no religion, apart from those belonging to other churches. But that is not all. Every totalitarianism bases itself on certain mystical elements (race, class, empire, nationality and the like); there could be nothing more dangerous than a totalitarianism basing itself on Catholicism, or uniting Catholicism with its own profane mythus.

Just as the Church remained above the liberalism, democratism and socialism of the XIX century, so she must remain above the totalitarianism of the XX century. She cannot but treat with the laic States, whatever their nature, on a basis of religious morality and respect of human personality, which are at the basis of Christianity. And while for the Church it is necessary to concede to the State, or better, to the temporal society, all that is not repugnant to the essence of Christianity, yet since that society is to-day fundamentally laic, she cannot but maintain her own personality and an ever more visible and stronger autonomy.

The same criterion is adopted by the Church in the mission countries which have their own civilisation and their own political organism, so as to create real relations between State and Church. The national public rites in China, India and Japan and among other peoples of old civilisation, have always had a religious character, so that Christians could not take part in them. This prohibition gave conversion to Christianity the aspect of a denationalisation, of a repudiation of the caste, race, country, of a separation from the society taken as a whole. Hence an insuperable obstacle (and not the only one) to the spread of the Gospel. The attempts at a compromise made by the Jesuit missionaries in China, which created so much stir in the XVIII century, was completely abandoned as a result of a Roman decision. The situation has to-day changed, both through the fall of the Chinese Empire, and through the recent public declaration of the State authorities of Japan and Manchukuo, that the national ceremonies 'have no religious character whatever'. A letter from the Vicar Apostolic of Manchukuo in March, 1935, to the Cardinal Prefect of the *Propaganda Fide*, reported the opinion of the bishops on the conduct to be followed by Catholics in these circumstances; the measures they had adopted received the approval of Rome.[1]

The *Osservatore Romano* in publishing this interesting document on July 2, 1936, noted: 'Even in recent times certain civil ceremonies appeared too bound up with superstitions and therefore they were believed forbidden to Catholics. But in this last period there has been a profound evolution in the thought and customs of the Far East. The atmosphere which in past centuries was, as it were, impregnated with superstitious sense, has been rarefied and transformed by the laic thought and by the religious liberty imported from the West'. It is evident, indeed, that laic thought has been an influence in the achievement of religious liberty even where, as in the Eastern empires, the religious conception is closely bound up with the divine or quasi-divine character of the dynasty. From the disengaging of the civil from the religious, Christianity has everything to gain—it indeed may be

[1]Catholics are authorised to tolerate: (1) that the image of Confucius shall have a place in their schools, even in a niche if this were ordered, so long as it is declared that the honours paid to it are civil honours, and no altars are set up before it; (2) that civil and military officials may go as a body into the pagodas in the suite of the authorities, so long as they do not take part in the religious songs but only in the civil and patriotic songs, and so long as they do not partake of the sacrificial victims, etc.

noted to-day, now that the relations of Catholicism with such States are on a plane of freedom and friendly understanding.

Another difficulty, which is still a grave one, for missionary preaching in territories occupied by European States, comes from the exploitation of the coloured races, or else from the political and *policier* methods employed to keep in subjection peoples already ripe for independence. The missionaries themselves have not been wholly free from an imprudent nationalism and an inopportune attachment to their own flag, and this has prejudiced an apostolate that should cut itself off from any tie with its country of origin. Therefore the Catholic Church lays stress on the formation of native clergies and has reached the point of appointing coloured bishops, where the centres of faithful are sufficiently prepared to ensure a dogmatic and moral tradition. The formation of missionary *élites* is widely used by the Protestants also.

The position of the Christian missions is exceedingly difficult in the face of economic exploitation of the natives by undertakings authorised by the colonial governments. Forced labour (for it is a case of this) has grave consequences, moral, domestic, social, hygienic. The missionaries, if they speak out, are often looked upon askance by the government representatives. If they do not speak they are false to their duty of defending the oppressed. Religious propaganda is thus compromised. The problem often cannot be solved on political lines, either those of the metropolitan country or of the colony. The intervention of the League of Nations is here more necessary than ever.

Unhappily, the weakening of the League has extended to the colonial field, where to-day little stress is laid on the obligations assumed by the States through the institutions of the mandate. This, applied to the countries taken from Turkey and to the colonies of the old German Empire, should have been a first step in a process of moral, economic and political elevation of the subject peoples, tending towards their autonomy in an international system of law and towards a civil parity between the colonial country and the metropolitan country. The groundwork of this process consisted chiefly in the abolition of slavery, the prohibition of native recruiting on the part of the mandatory countries, a prohibition to establish naval and military bases, and so on. To-day there is discussion of the return of colonies to Germany, unconditionally and without the intervention of Geneva, as though the mandatory powers were the owners of them and could dispose of them at will. No account is taken either of the wishes of the natives, or of the moral character of the rights of the League of Nations, or of observance of the principles laid down in the creation of the mandate.

This backward step is wholly prejudicial to a wider international understanding not only on the problem of native recruiting, but on the other civil and moral problems like compulsory or forced labour, slavery and slave traffic, white colonisation, the open door, and so on. With all this Christianity, as a missionary religion, is deeply concerned, and cannot see without regret the disappearance of an intelligent and honest international action like that of the League, and the increased political power of the totalitarian or imperial countries (even if they are democratic) that are tending to exploit the colonies, and to-day more than ever for military purposes. Here too the crisis of political morality in the international field rebounds on to the most important and characteristic functions of the Church and weakens the structure of Christian civilisation in the world.

§ 63.—In the experiences of the laic State as a whole, whether liberal and democratic or authoritarian and totalitarian, the Church has lost the diarchic position she had won in the Middle Ages in a more or less theocratic form (cesaro-papism or Latin organisation), and then maintained in the Reformation and Counter Reformation with a prevailing aspect of confessionalism in the Protestant 'Church-State' or of jurisdictionalism in the Catholic Church. This notwithstanding, a third kind of diarchy has crept in, which we have called 'individual' when we first encountered it in its Protestant beginnings, and which merits the term still more to-day, for the diarchic power of the Church is to-day mainly expressed as a spiritual power over the faithful as individuals, and no longer in an authoritative and juridical form over States.

We have seen how gradually the politico-legal bonds between State and Church were dissolved first by toleration, then by laicism, and how the point was reached of denying the Church any organic and authoritative share in affairs of the State. Even where concordatory relations have been reknit (for the Catholic Church), or where official and formal relations still persist (for certain Protestant churches and the Church of England), the ethic of the State is outside the orbit of Christianity and of any supernatural religious conception. The cleavage between the two powers is substantial, apart from survivals from the past or external and formal superstructures. If to-day we can rightly continue to speak of a diarchy of Church and State as a duality of powers, it is because the Church maintains her religious power over the faithful, which, expressed in the form of teaching and public precepts, continues to have an influence on society, whether her relations with the governments are good or otherwise. The Church, in spite of the lack of State support (and in certain not infrequent cases, as a result of it), has been able to maintain and increase her religious influence over the consciences of the faithful, so that they adhere to her with such conviction as to be able, if need arises, to resist the hostile propaganda of anti-religious laicism upheld in the name and with the resources of the State. The keener this consciousness, the more effectual the diarchy. If, on the contrary, this consciousness dwindles and goes out, the diarchy loses or collapses, for, from the sociological standpoint, social power is a collective consciousness of possession of such power before it can assume organic form and become a force able to impose itself. The faithful to-day have such a consciousness in communion with the authoritative organs of the Church. If the Church has only her spiritual means of vindicating her potency, yet its moral efficacy remains entire, and no one can doubt that such efficacy has social and political effects.

It is a mental habit to seek to reduce everything to juridical schemas, a habit due in large measure to the medieval tradition when all human relationships (even public and ecclesiastical ones) were seen in a private and contractual guise, and could be fixed only in legal form. With the advent of public law and the idea of sovereignty, this private form disappeared and contractualism turned into jurisdictionalism. It took the experience of laicism to bring out the moral character of the relations between Church and State and to show how sociologically the diarchy Church-State has its roots set at a deeper level than that of a legal co-partnership in society.

The Roman Curia, by its tradition which on this point is linked up with that of Roman Law, sets great store on legal formulation, which is always clear and precise, but in the public domain to-day most of the criteria and provisions of Canon Law would remain unilateral if they were not translated either into friendly compromises with the civil authorities, or into moral and disciplinary instructions to the faithful—apart from those concordatory measures concerned with legal competences, as to-day in Italy over marriage questions. Pius IX by the *non expedit* invited the faithful to take no part in the parliamentary elections of the new Kingdom of Italy. The invitation was interpreted as obligatory (even before the later papal declaration of 1895) and was respected to a varying degree, according to how far the faithful realised its importance, that is, to how far in their consciences the idea of a religious duty prevailed over that of a civil duty. Pius XI condemned the *Action Française* and forbade priests and faithful to belong to it. Under the *ancien régime* this measure would have had to be drawn up as a bull; this would have had to pass the Council of State or the Parlement of Paris, and to be published by royal order; then only would it have become a law of the State. In the absence of these formalities it might lead to a jurisdictionalist controversy. In the two cases we have quoted the efficacy of the papal measures has been no longer on the legal plane but on the spiritual plane, and yet their moral effects ended by modifying (in certain respects) the political situation of the countries concerned.

It is over the family and education that to-day there is sharpest opposition between Church and State, the one armed with laws, economic resources and coercive force, the other with spiritual weapons and spontaneous assents. The Catholic Church has been more efficacious than the others in condemning laicised marriage (known as civil marriage), divorce, contraceptives, and authorised or, worse, enforced sterilisation. She has fought for over a century and will continue to fight in defence of the sacramental institution of marriage, just as she has fought and will continue to fight for the Christian education of the young. If she can come to an understanding with the State, all the better. If not, she appeals to the faithful and lays upon them the gravest responsibility, that of resisting even with personal sacrifice, for here is something touching the roots of Christian morality. Pius XI has returned to the themes already exhaustively treated by his predecessors (especially Leo XIII and Pius X), in order to clarify Catholic doctrine and its application in the present time, in his two encyclicals, *Divini illius Magistri* on the education of the young (December 31, 1929) and *Casti Connubii* on Christian marriage (December 31, 1930).

This antagonistic position of Church and State is connected with a basic sociological principle, that of the limitation of power. There can be no unlimited power; unlimited power would be not only a social tyranny but an ethical absurdity. The problem raised by the modern State turns precisely on this point. It has denied any external limitation by a principle other than its own, or, as the philosophers say, heteronomous, for laic thought has proclaimed the autonomy of the State. In order to limit its powers, appeal was made to the freedom of the people, and since all liberty resolves itself into power, the whole of power was attributed to the people. But the people could not exert its power actually, possessing it only potentially, by original title, while the actual reality passed to the State as legislative and executive power. Mutual limitation between people and State ended by becoming a formal and organic fact, without ethical substance. This was sought, occasion by occasion, and resolved itself into positivist pragmatism.

This process has been arrested by two forces which were believed extraneous to the State and reduced to impotency: the Church and the popular conscience. The first as the perennial voice of a higher morality, often unheard or seemingly unheard, ignored, despised, contradicted, disparaged by adversaries, falsified or weakened by too compromising friends, followed by but a few of the faithful, and yet an insistent and efficacious voice, for it is the perennial voice of the spirit that is never silent. Is the Church heteronomous to the State? From the legal standpoint, as the principle of a juridical diarchy, now that the State is outside and not within the Church, and has a large number of citizens who do not belong to a given church or to any church, the Church may be said to be heteronomous to the State. But as the voice of the conscience of the faithful, who are citizens, working as citizens, she is not extraneous, she enters into the State, shares in its ethical ends, cooperates for the wellbeing of the nation and shares in the intrinsic, inward limitation of the statal powers.

When Christians as citizens vindicate the moral conception of public life, in peace and in war, in the question of education and that of the family, in the protection of labour and of the workers and in the struggle against the excesses of capitalism, and so on, they limit that power which seeks to become unlimited, absorbing, totalitarian. In the Middle Ages the Papacy intervened by authority with kings and peoples; it could abrogate a law, depose a sovereign, release the people from the bond of their oath of allegiance. This was what was known as '*direct power*'. In modern times this power was pared away, disciplined by concordats and rules of jurisdiction; the theologians called it '*indirect power*' in the sense that it touched temporal matters as a consequence of the defence of religious principles. To-day this power is still operative, whether direct or indirect, but it can have no efficacy on the laic State and appeals to the conscience of the faithful. It could now be called '*directive power*'. The form has changed, but the substance is the same. It consists in the individual diarchy which prevails, in the persuasive power of consciences which carries weight, in the efficacy of the Christian citizen who succeeds in bending the power of the State, or else in opposing it in the name of Christian morality, that is, in the name of an ethical principle that touches collective life and which cannot be other than inward and conducive to a State with a Christian civilisation.

The more effectual and extensive is the action of Christian society and of the several faithful in the State, the more the Church, though without either authority or juridical control, co-operates in the formation of public life and to the end of the temporal commonweal. The weaker and the more uncertain such action, the more the course tends to be set by the State, which to-day is assuming the character of a religious myth and an original ethic, supplanting the Christian religion and its morality. The dualism between Church and State that develops in an individual diarchy, is a natural consequence of a two-fold ethical conception upheld in the names of the two opposing principles.

In the Catholic camp as in the Protestant, there have been men of study and action to whom this dualism is so disturbing as to send them perpetually in quest of conciliation, a mutual adjustment. In the liberal period it was maintained that the Church must adapt herself to the progress of the times. To-day, in the height of Fascism, this is repeated, the more insistently the more it is denied that Fascism has a theoretical content and hence an ethic of its own. The same has occurred with Nazism, which could not be accused of lacking a theory, since the easiest thing for Germans is to create one; hence a group of theologians, whose views were echoed by Kuno Brombacher and Emil Ritter in 1936, in their *Message from German Catholics to their compatriots and co-religionists.*[1] In Austria a Community of Work for Religious Peace has been formed. Both enterprises have been disqualified by the bishops, but they have met with support among priests and faithful, who cannot conceive of an ethical conflict save in political terms, and hence would wish to reduce its scope by a passage from ethics to politics. There are, on the contrary, stages of struggle in which all values must be summed up in ethical terms in order to check the tendency of politics to swallow up everything. This is the process of spiritualisation of a social life rendered worldly by passions, interests, power. In this sense now the Church as a religious institution, now the faithful as Catholic Action or even as a political party, have taken their share in struggles on a ground believed to be reserved to politics. Although this may lead to ambiguities, resentments, strife, the Church cannot renounce such action, nor can the faithful fail on occasion to take the initiative in it and accept the responsibilities it implies. Evidently on the historical plane this leads to victories and defeats, to excesses and to weaknesses, and the Church, as an historical organism, suffers the full consequences, as we have seen in the course of nearly two thousand years. But it is this that gives vitality, strength, experience, this that sifts men out, brings to birth new institutions, promotes the development of doctrine, the adjustment of praxis, the outgrowing of outworn positions and the spiritual renewal of militant centres.

It was an idea favoured by certain mystical currents, to keep the respective churches apart from political passions. The liberal idea of the separation of State from Church and the conception of religion as a private affair seemed to make it feasible. On the other hand, confidence in human reason, or rather in rationalism, the assurance of scientific progress, the ideal of liberty carried to the point of the autonomy of

[1] Ascherdorff, Munster in Westphalia, 1936.

the person, led men to look for a civilisation enfranchised from the Church, not anti-Christian but simply human. The prevailing conception was then that of the State as guardian of liberties and executor of the laws with the widest expansion possible of individual life. This vision did not correspond to reality. Progress was soon cut short, science was turned to war power, the great working class agitations supervened, with anarchic propaganda and the overhanging dread of a European conflict. Then the war, the post-war agitations, the Russian Revolution, Communism, Fascism and Nazism, the new wars, the dread of another general war, the anti-semitic barbarities, the violation of every right, the hatred that has invaded the world. The idea of any Church outside politics, that is, separated from life as we live it, with its struggles, its crises, its disappointments, its tragedies, would be neither historically conceivable nor spiritually possible. To-day more than in the past, the States have monopolised almost the whole of social life and a great part of individual life, they have laid hold of the direction of the trends of thought and orientation of their countries, passing from the plane of politics as a technique of government to that of politics as a conception of the life of the world, a *Weltanschauung*. The churches either resign themselves to existing on the margins of society, as the spiritual comfort of a few faithful, undisturbed because they have placed themselves outside all real activity, or else, wishing to remain at the centre of the cultural and moral life of society, they must take part, on the religious plane, in all the enterprises and all the conflicts of the dynamism of the age. And since politics are saturated with all the ethical values, it is to politics (not to the technique of politics, nor to the earthly interests that politics contain, but taken as one of the all-absorbing expressions of social life) that the churches must draw near, facing, at the right moment and with spiritual vision, the titanic struggles before them.

We say 'with spiritual vision' to emphasise the wholly religious character of the ends and means with which the Church is able to establish contact with politics, considered in their ethical and social value. Unfortunately in every age there have been ecclesiastics of varying rank who in the contacts between the Church and politics have sought to make use of the religious power for earthly ends; others have made use of earthly means for religious ends, and, deeming them necessary even if not perfectly moral, have been ensnared by them. Both classes have been wanting in a spiritual vision of ends and means. It is not astonishing; ecclesiastics too are men who may fall to so-called political realism, in good faith or bad, as history shows us in so many happenings. For this reason the Church has been accused of engaging in politics, of being bound by earthly considerations, of wishing to maintain her prestige and the financial resources of her institutions by compromises at the expense of Christian spirituality.

This impression is enhanced by the exploitation of the Church on the part of nationalists and Fascists and their governments, especially by a certain press which, though laic and pagan, poses as the champion of religion. Such as these (and it is a current that is creeping among the conservative and nationalist clergy) would have the Church not only bind herself to the dictatorial governments in order to fight bolshevism and the advanced democratic currents, but form a kind of league, as in the time of the Reformation for the wars of religion or of the Holy Alliance for the union of Throne and Altar and the anti-liberal wars. In the absence, to-day, of a defence of the confessional State or of the principle of legitimacy, the principle of social conservation is put forward. The Church should support the bourgeoisie and militarism so as to bar the way to the proletariat and to suppress civil liberties, where they still exist, in favour of a dictatorship of the Right. The persecution of the Church in Russia, in Mexico, in Spain, are put forward as justifying a benevolent policy towards the anti-bolshevist dictatorships, like that of Hitler, in spite of the paganism of the race principle, in spite of anti-semitism and the anti-Christian propaganda of his most stalwart adherents. The support of a part of the episcopate and of the faithful in Italy for the Abyssinian War, the open participation of the clergy in the civil war in Spain on the side of the insurgents have given practical proof of this trend, creating motives for accusing the Church as though she were bound up with all forms of Fascism, even in the bloody experiences of revolts and wars.

A certain criticism is not unfounded, but it is too general and above all does not take into account that the present historical experience is very brief compared with the other experiences the Church has undergone. But this first period had sufficed for Pius XI—who had lived through the profound crisis from its beginnings—to come to a practical awareness of all its perils. His encyclicals and addresses touched upon all the features of this assault of the modern State on the soul. If not all Catholics, and not all priests, have realised the doctrinal and practical value of such documents, it is due to the fact that the crisis has invaded the whole of society, of which, whether churchmen or laymen, we are all part, breathing its infected air. Fortunately there is the salutary reaction of the mystical streams, the voices of Cardinals such as Faulhaber, Cerejeira, Verdier and Plassa, of generous and combative youth, of men of learning and faith, anxious for the fate of the Church and of society.

Pius XI, in the last year of his life did not cease to insist on the peril of apostasy from the Christian faith through the ultra-nationalist currents. He had summoned the Italian bishops on the occasion of the tenth anniversary of the Lateran Treaty for an address by which he set such store as to beg his doctor if it were possible to prolong his life to that day. He died on the eve, on February 10, and his speech was not made known to the public. It was surmised that it would have been a renewed and wider protest against the marriage laws introduced into Italy, as racial and anti-semitic measures, in open violation of the Concordat annexed to the Lateran Treaty. Perhaps too it was a recall to the spiritual reality of the Italian situation, compromised as it was by the exaggerated nationalism that had come to infect a wide section of Catholics and clergy.

The Conclave elected as his successor, with unusual rapidity, Cardinal Pacelli, the Secretary of State (in defiance of the Roman traditions); it may well have been to emphasise a continuity of government. The same reason (personal homage apart) may have led the new pope to take the name of Pius XII. His first message was a message of peace to the whole world. It came at an opportune moment in a period of upheavals and growing anxieties; the whole world (and not only Catholics) had paid moving homage to the memory of Pius XI, known as the Pope of Peace, and greeted the new Pope with widespread confidence. The mission of peace is intrinsic to the nature of Christianity, and the Papacy cannot fail to bring all the weight of its moral authority to bear, working not only for the inward peace of souls, but also for peace among the peoples, as a work of justice and charity, as the reconstruction of a new order.

Jacques Maritain, the celebrated French Thomist philosopher, having broken away from the *Action Française* after its condemnation, has been turning his thought, with increasing ripeness and profundity, towards the political problems of the present hour in relation to the traditional Catholic conception. He seeks in St. Thomas an adequate comprehension and solution; his effort sometimes seems too closely adherent to scholastic formulas, but beneath this vesture he seeks to shift the emphasis from the juridicial position of the Church to her cultural and spiritual one. He expresses the mind of many who would restore the value of Christian civilisation in its complexity, ecclesiastical and laic, cultural and charitable, mystical and active, in order to influence the various modern currents (called by some by the inappropriate name of 'civilisations') which are nearly all a-Catholic or anti-Catholic, in order that Christianity should penetrate their environment, and take what they hold of constructive value to righten and purify it.

This vision implies two moments: that of penetration, that of purification. Communism, Fascism, Nazism must feel the workings of the Christian yeast. The world cannot be treated as if made up of closed compartments, a co-existence of uncommunicating groups and contradictory foci; it is made up of vital syntheses and active organisms. If we insist on the duality of Church and State, it is not that we overvalue the Church, at a time when the number of her true members has dwindled through the apostasy of the *élites* and of the masses, but because the two stand for permanent and indestructible syntheses. State and Church do not signify merely two powers, each in its own department of competence and jurisdiction; they signify two principles, the monistic and the dualistic, the immanent and the transcendent, the naturalistic and the supernatural, with their mutual influence and mutual strife, not formal but substantial, taking place within our very consciousness.

The Church would not and could not effect a severance between the Christian and the citizen; the State, on the contrary, in most cases—whether governments and parties say as much or not—to-day seeks to bring about the severance and the apostasy of the citizen from the Christian. That is why another French philosopher, Etienne Gilson, has raised his cry of alarm, calling upon Catholics to close their ranks and to create a cultural and educational organisation of their own, capable of making them convinced and combative men, living in the world but able through their truly Christian spirit to overcome the world. It may be that between the two, Maritain and Gilson, there is only a difference of view-point, which may be merely a difference of personal experiences. Indeed, so long as Christians, and especially Catholics, continue to treat political problems with a technical mentality as problems of administration, of finance, of elections, of forms of governments, or else avoid them as something unclean, or worse still, make acts of confidence in men in government, (especially dictators), failing to see the ethical substratum that alters all the values of social life including religious values, then neither penetration nor purification of the modern currents will be possible, nor the conquest for Christianity of present day society.

Maritain in his *True Humanism*[1] presents the vision of a 'new Christendom', not as a repetition of that of the Middle Ages (history being irreversible), but as 'conceivable to-day'. 'It would no longer be', he writes, 'the idea of the *sacred empire* possessed by God over all things, it would rather be the idea of the *holy liberty* of the creature united to God by grace'. Maritain places the new Christendom within a temporal society in which the co-existence of nuclei of various modes of feeling is assured by civil toleration, power maintains its autonomy, the rights and liberties of human personality are recognised, economy is emancipated from the capitalist yoke, so as to render possible the construction of what he calls 'personalist democracy', tending towards the achievement of a 'fraternal community', Co-existence, in the 'temporal city', between believers and unbelievers would be the fruit of this fraternity, into which the believers would bring the moral values proper to Christianity and would utilise and purify those others that, derived from Christian civilisation, are thrown into relief by non-believers in their natural character and for the ends of temporal society.

Maritain's endeavour is two-fold: to lessen the present antinomy

[1]Geoffrey Bles, 1938.

between the political society and the Church, and to determine a course towards an awakened consciousness among believers, tending towards a future in which this dialectic will be superseded by the dialectic of '*liberty-grace*'.

The problem of the political society, from age to age, now in one way, now in another, has appeared to many as irreducible to Christian thought—as we have several times noted. The Fathers saw in power (as in property) a consequence of Original Sin, the privation of a complete good, a duality which could not be unified and which St. Augustine carried on to the mystical plane of the City of God and the Earthly City. After the medieval experience (which was incomplete and disturbed by violence of passion), through which the State, formerly outside the Church, passed within the Church and also, in certain respects, under her guardianship, the old problem was raised anew with the effort to purify the Church from the worldliness in which she had become involved. The State, in the Reformation, held all outward power, even ecclesiastical power, and the Church retained only inward spiritual power. The consequences, even in the Catholic camp that had resisted the protestantising of the Church, worked out as the jusnaturalist conceptions of the State and rationalist conceptions of society. These are at the source of the attempt to separate the natural from the supernatural, in an effort, which has gone on for two hundred years, to reach the absorption—if this were possible—of the supernatural in the natural. The State to-day presents itself once more as irreducible to Christian thought, even more so than in the days of the Fathers or of the Reformation. For the former, the problem was how to reduce power from pagan to Christian; for the latter, it was how to refashion in purity a Church that had become worldly. The Protestant Reformation and the Catholic Counter-Reformation came as the answer. To-day instead the problem is how to impede the absorption of the supernatural in the natural and the Church in the totalitarian State.

Maurice Blondel has built up a philosophy that seeks to bridge the ever more open and irreducible cleavage (in modern thought) between nature and the Christian experience. Unlike many spiritualist philosophers, who in their rational abstractionism combine Aristotle and Descartes, he takes his stand wholly on concrete reality and following all its manifestations brings out from them the presence of Thought, the value of Being and the creativity of Action. Under this three-fold aspect, which is a three-in-one, there is a permanent dualism between reality and its exigencies, which brings the urge to further realisations, a heterogeneity tending towards a synthesis, an incompleteness that calls for its completion—pacification, says Blondel, with a striking image. Every higher stage of thought, of reality, of action, may be considered as a completion of what is below it, but this completion is such only for the stage at which it occurs, and therefore it calls for a further elevation. By these experiences human history has lived and lives. Can we look upon it as only a rational experience without its mystical side? As an immanence that goes on completing itself by itself without transcendency? As the worldly without the divine?

In Blondelian philosophy, Christianity appears under three aspects—as a continuous and indestructible historical experience; as a spiritual integration not of nature in the abstract but of historical man, inasmuch as fallen from initial grace; as an orientation guiding even those who are outside it, through the luminous quality of its doctrine and works. The experience of natural reality in the union of nature with Christianity is transformed into a spiritual experience; this comes about through the communication of the grace that God willed to give to man on his first appearance upon earth, so that we may say that there has never been a strictly natural moment of humanity that has not at the same time been graciously supernatural. There is a link between Blondel and the Leibnizian tradition and, in certain respects, with the thought of Vico. His philosophy might be considered a beneficent Platonism adapted to modern thought and interpreting the anguish of a world stricken by an unnatural and unfecund separatism. To dwell as many do on rational and natural motives, either through speculative abstractionism or in accordance simply with methodological criteria (with the praiseworthy aim of not confusing the two planes, the natural and the supernatural), renders them inapt to see the synthetic values of reality and to fight the original separatism that is at the bottom of the modern crisis.

In the Christian conception, the whole being and activity of man is to be carried on to the plane of the Redemption: 'He that is not for

Me is against Me'. Outside Christ we find not a state of nature but its negation. All men, according to Christian theology, live by the supernatural, under the influence of grace, even those who have not known Christianity. Of these last, to those who fulfil the moral law and listen to the inner voice of conscience, the grace that Christ has obtained for all by His sacrifice will not be wanting. On the contrary, those who do evil, whether they have faith or no, are outside the mystical body of Christ, and by that very fact unworthy of the human character. The visible Church, with the magistracy of Revelation, the communication of sacramental grace and the participation in the Communion of the Saints, promotes and achieves the passage of each man from the dominion of sin to life in the mystical body of Christ. This theological vision embraces not only the faithful (who have greater bonds and duties through the wealth of aids received), but the whole world, which mystically has been won by Christ and potentially lives in Him.

The fundamental error is to conceive of Humanism and Christianity as separate, to keep their values distinct and often to oppose them, and finally to eliminate one of the two from the redeeming synthesis. But whereas the peoples that have not yet received the light of the Gospel do not know the two terms of the synthesis, and their supernatural aspirations are infected with superstitions that mar even their natural thought and feelings, the peoples that have known the Christian experience can no longer separate it from human values, which are bound up with it. Although they may be harassed by terrible crises, shaking the ethico-religious structure, always the small seed of the Gospel sends forth new shoots, and there is a return to the Christian experience. Nature and Grace can no longer be separated. The negation of grace is error, immorality, hatred, injustice, all negative data that no one in sound mind could attribute to nature. The naturalistic crisis of the XVIII century was not based on a sound conception of nature.

Leviathan is not Christian, but neither is Leviathan natural. Is the State necessarily Leviathan? Looking back through history, we might say that from certain points of view the State, by its intrinsic character, tends to become Leviathan, that is, it tends to be monistically conceived, for power by its nature is a unifying force. It is not only the modern State that is monistic (even if it be tolerant or liberal or concordatory), nor only the totalitarian State. That of the *ancien régime*, that of the Middle Ages, the Christian Roman Empire were at bottom monistic, like the old pre-Christian States and Empires. If this appears to us only belatedly, in the light of a more evolved historico-sociological criticism, to give us the key to the history of relations between State and Church, it is none the less exact.

We say that *only under certain aspects* does the State tend to be Leviathan, for the human conscience rises up against a constant encroachment on its rights, the violation of morality, the subjection of religion (points which give the conception of Leviathan its true value), and tends in every social structure to preserve margins of freedom, of resistance and of refuge; it thus creates a sociological dualism, basic and irrepressible. The Christian Church has polarised this dualism, it has made it lasting and permanent and has given it the light of a supernatural truth: 'Render unto Caesar the things that are Caesar's, and unto God the things that are God's'. This conception lies at the basis of the Christian experience. Every attempt to overstep such limits, from either side, has violated the laws of nature and those of Revelation. The duality does not mean dualism, but it may become a dualism; it is not always diarchic, but it becomes a diarchy. Such is the story of two thousand years.

The diarchy admits of a gradation of powers, an unification of tendencies, of realities and of ends. The duality postulates a synthesis; the dualism, instead, is a more or less transient moment of strife. According to the age and according to the historical positions of the various peoples, we find all three experiences in the relations between Church and State; providential experiences, which have rendered possible and effective a constant elevation of society from monistic stasis to dualistic dynamism, from immanent forms to transcendent aspirations, from the worldly spirit to the divine. The antithesis that has so often revealed itself in the struggles between Church and State has given our Christian civilisation, especially that of the West, the motives for the loftiest speculations, the urge towards ever wider aspirations, and the profound crises that serve the cause of human progress. The battle waged by the Church so that she should not be subjugated by the secular power, that she might liberate herself from encroachments when they had occurred, that she should not be confounded with the State, has given the human conscience its grandest moments of elevation and has held firm the values of human personality.

In the titanic struggles between the worldly and spiritual forces, it is no wonder if the Church, becoming rich and potent, should from time to time have taken her stand by the side of the temporal power and herself have represented its interests, till a breath from the mystical currents, that are never wanting, has revived the sacred flame, till the whole of society has been shaken by moral stirrings and by the convulsions of renewal. Such is the period through which we are now passing. The apostasy of the masses and of the *élites* have accentuated the antagonism of State to Church, and rendered their separation the deeper. Through this fact, even natural morality in the political sphere, national and international, suffers a profound crisis, for while of itself it is incapable of resisting in autonomous form, either as personal morality or as collective morality, it is no longer upheld by the Christian faith. This is the field in which the Church reassumes her position of guidance and her restorative and integrating function. Her moral influence and the releasing of the mystical currents will reawaken oppressed consciences, restore its vigour to human personality, subdued as it is by the monstrous weight of the power of the State. A new diarchy will form itself in the collective consciousness, on the ruins of an individualism that has already seen its day and a totalitarianism that must be overthrown.

What form the diarchy of Church and State will assume to-morrow cannot be foreseen to-day, but we may venture to affirm that it will be in the ethico-social sphere. For the working-class masses demand a justice that is their due, the nations yearn for the ending of wars, of armaments, of jealousies, and for a beneficent peace; the intellectual classes feel the emptiness of Positivism, the inadequacy of Idealism, the superficiality of Phenomenalism, the barrenness of Aestheticism. The arrogant concept of a State above everything, the centre of complete unification, the fount of ethics, the expression of the common will, mystical aspiration of the unity of a people, has resulted in the totalitarian monster, Communist, Nazi, Fascist, which to-day holds Europe in a triple strangle-hold. A new breath of mystical spirituality and of pacifying re-organisation must come (and cannot fail to come) from Christianity, in its character as a personal religion, universal and autonomous, profoundly felt and vigorously actuated by the faithful, who are partakers in the mystical body of Christ; then Church and State will find again their rhythm of social duality and spiritual unification.

NIHIL OBSTAT, Georgius Can. Smith, S.Th.D.; Ph.D., censor deputatus.

IMPRIMATUR, Leonellus Can. Evans, *Vic. Gen.*

WESTMONASTERII, *die 24a Martii*, 1939.

CONTEMPORARY BIBLIOGRAPHY

[This bibliography is confined to a selection of the modern books consulted by the author. Sources, reference books, collections and documents are omitted, as well as works referred to in the text.]

ACTON, Lord John Emerich, *The History of Freedom and other Essays*. London, 1909.

ADAM, Dr. Karl, *The Spirit of Catholicism*. London, 1929.

AMANN, E., *L'Epoque Carolingienne (Histoire de l'Eglise, VI)*. Paris, 1937.

BARUZI, Jean, *Leibniz et l'organisation religieuse de la Terre*. Paris, 1907.

BASCH, Victor, *Les doctrines politiques des philosophes classiques de l'Allemagne*. Paris, 1922.

BAUDRILLART, Cardinal, *L'Eglise Catholique—La Renaissance—Le Protestantisme*. Paris, 1908.

BAZIN, G., *Windthorst, ses Alliés et ses Adversaires*. Paris, 1896.

BELASCO, Philip S., *Authority in Church and State*, with a foreword by G. P. Gooch. London, 1928.

BENDA, Julien, *Esquisse d'une histoire des Français*. Paris, 1932.

BERDYAEV, Nicolas, *The End of Our Time*. Paris, 1930. London, 1933.

—— *Christianity and Class War*. Paris, 1932. London, 1933.

—— *Freedom and the Spirit*. Paris, 1933. London, 1935.

BETTANINI, A. M., *Benedetto XIV e la Repubblica di Venezia*. Milan, 1931.

BEVAN, Edwyn, *Christianity*. London, 1932.

BLONDEL, Maurice, *La Pensée*, I et II. Paris, 1934–5.

—— *L'Etre et les êtres*. Paris, 1936.

—— *L'Action*, I et II. Paris, 1936–7.

BODY, Auguste, *Le Concordat, sa négotiation, ses dix-sept articles, son histoire de 1801–3*. Lyon, 1903.

BOSANQUET, Bernard, *The Philosophical Theory of the State*. London, 1899.

BOURLON, J., *Les assemblées du Clergé et le Jansénisme*. Paris, 1909.

BRIERE, Ives de la, *L'Organisation internationale et la Papauté souveraine*. Paris, 1924.

—— *La Communauté des Puissances*. Paris, 1932.

BUONAIUTI, E., *Gioacchino da Fiore*. Rome, 1931.

—— *Lutero e la Riforma in Germania*. Bologna, 1927.

—— *Dante come profeta*. Modena, 1936.

BURKHARDT, J., *The Civilisation of the Renaissance in Italy*. The Phaedon Press, Vienna, 1937.

BURY, J. B., *History of the Papacy in the XIX Century*. London, 1930.

BUTLER, Dom Cuthbert, *The Vatican Council*. London, 1930.

CABANE, Henri, *Histoire du Clergé de France pendant la Révolution de 1898*. Paris, 1908.

CAPECELATRO, Cardinal Alfonso, *Storia di San Pier Damiano*. Rome, 1887.

CARLYLE, R. W. and A. J., *A History of Medieval Philosophy in the West*. Vol. I–VI. Edinburgh, 1903–36.

CHENON, E., *Histoire des rapports de l'Eglise et de l'Etat*. Paris, 1913.

CHEREL, Albert, *La Pensée de Machiavel en France*. Paris, 1935.

Church and State—Papers read at the Summer School of Catholic Studies, August 1935. London, 1936.

The Churches survey their Task—The Report of the Conference at Oxford, July 1937, on Church, Community and State. London, 1937.

The Church and the XX Century, edited by G. L. H. Harvey, London, 1936.

CONSTANT, G., *The English Schism, Henry VIII (1509–47)*. London, 1934.

—— *The Reformation in England*. Paris, 1930. London, 1934.

COOLEN, G., *Histoire de l'Eglise d'Angleterre*. Paris, 1932.

—— *L'Anglicanisme d'Aujourd'hui*. Paris, 1933.

CROCE, Benedetto, *Storia del Regno di Napoli*. Bari, 1925.

—— *A History of Italy, 1871 to 1915*. Bari, 1928. Oxford, 1929.

—— *History of Europe in the XIX Century*. Bari, 1932. London, 1934.

CURCIO, Carlo, *Dal Rinascimento alla Controriforma*. Rome, 1934.

DEMPF, Alois, *Sacrum Imperium*—Geschichts-und Staatsphilosophie des Mittelalters und der politischen Renaissance. Munich and Berlin, 1924.

DE RUGGIERO, Guido, *The History of European Liberalism*. Bari, 1925. London, 1927.

DE SARLO, Francesco, *L'Uomo nella Vita Sociale*. Bari, 1931.

DOUMERGUE, E., *Jean Calvin (Vol. V. La Pensée Ecclésiastique et la Pensée Politique)*. Lausanne, 1917.

DUCHESNE, L., *Les premiers temps de l'Etat Pontifical*. Paris, 1898.

DUNCAN-JONES, A. S., *The Struggle for Religious Freedom in Germany*. London, 1938.

FAULHABER, Cardinal, *Judaism, Christianity, and Germany*. London, 1934.

FERRARI, Francesco Luigi, *Le Régime Fasciste Italien*. Paris, 1928.

FESSARD, G., *Pax nostra. Examen de conscience international*. Paris, 1936.

FIGGIS, J. Neville, *Studies of Political Thought. From Gerson to Grotius*. Cambridge, 1907.

—— *Churches in the Modern State*. London, 1914.

FILIPPINI, Francesco, *Il Cardinale Egidio Albornoz*. Bologna, 1933.

FLORI, E., *Il tratto De Regimine Principum e le dottrine politiche di S. Tommaso*. Bologna, 1928.

FONTENELLE, R., *Pius XI*. Paris, 1938.

GASQUET, Cardinal Aidan and BISHOP, Edmund, *Edward VI and the Book of Common Prayer*. London, 1928.

GIANNINI, A., *I Concordati Post-Bellici*, Milan, 1929.

GIERKE, Dr. Otto, *Political Theories of the Middle Ages*, (English edition, with an introduction by F. W. Maitland). Cambridge, 1913.

—— *Natural Law and the Theory of Society (1500–1800), with a Lecture on the Ideas of Natural Law and Humanity by* Ernest Troeltsch, (English edition, with an introduction by Ernest Barker). Cambridge, 1934.

GILSON, Etienne, *The Philosophy of St. Thomas Aquinas*. Paris, 1923. ('*Le Thomisme*.') London, 1924.

GILSON, *Moral Values and the Moral Life. The System of St. Thomas Aquinas*. Paris, 1925. *St. Thomas d'Aquinas*. St. Louis and London, 1931.
—— *The Philosophy of St. Bonaventure*. Paris, 1924. London, 1938.
—— *The Spirit of Medieval Philosophy*. London, 1936.
—— *Pour un Ordre Catholique*. Paris, 1934.
—— *Christianisme et Philosophie*. Paris, 1936.
GOOCH, G. P., *Studies in Modern History*. London, 1931.
GUIRAUD, Jean, *Histoire de l'Inquisition au Moyen Age*. Paris, 1938.
HAWKINS, L. M., *Allegiance in Church and State*, with a foreword by G. P. Gooch. London, 1928.
HAZARD, Paul, *La Crise de la Conscience Européenne (1680–1715)*. Paris, 1935.
JACINI, Stefano, *Il Tramonto del Potere Temporale nelle relazioni degli Ambasciatori Austriaci a Roma*. Bari, 1931.
—— *La politica ecclesiastica italiana da Villafranca a Porta Pia*. Bari, 1938.
JANNI, Ettore, Machiavelli. Milan, 1927.
JARRETT, Bede, O. P., *Social Theories of the Middle Ages. Medieval Socialism*. London, 1926.
JARRY, E., *L'Eglise contemporaine*. Paris, 1935.
JEMOLO, A. C., *Stato e Chiesa negli scrittori italiani del sei e settecento*. Turin, 1914.
JORDAN, W. K. H. D., *The Development of Religious Toleration in England (1603–40)*. London, 1936.
JOURNET, C., *La Jurisdiction de l'Eglise sur la Cité*. Paris, 1931.
LAMBRUSCHINI, Card. Luigi, *La mia Nunziatura in Francia, a cura di Pietro Pirri*. Bologna, 1934.
LA PRADELLE, A. de, *Le Conflit Italo-Ethiopien*. Paris, 1936.
LECANUET, R. P., *La Vie de l'Eglise sous Léon XIII. (L'Eglise de France sous la Troisième République)*. Paris, 1930.
LECLERC, Joseph, S. J., *L'Argument des deux glaives dans les controverses politiques du Moyen Age* (Recherches Religieuses, 1931–2, Paris).
LEGENDRE ET CHEVALIER, *Le Catholicisme et la société*. LABERTHONIERE, *L'Eglise et l'Etat à travers l'histoire*. Paris, 1907.
LESLIE, Steward, *A Century of Anglo-Catholicism*. London–Toronto, 1929.
LEVASTI, A., *Sant'Anselmo, Vita e Pensiero*. Bari, 1929.
LUCHAIRE, Julien, *Les Démocraties Italiennes*. Paris, 1920.
MACENTEE, G. Putnam, *The Social Catholic Movement in Great Britain*. New York, 1927.
MANGANO, Dr. Vincenzo, *Il pensiero sociale e politico di Leone XIII*. Milan, 1931.
MARITAIN, Jacques, *Du Régime Temporel et de la Liberté*. Paris, 1933.
—— *True Humanism*. Paris, 1936. London, 1938.
—— *Les Juifs parmi les Nations*. Paris, 1938.
MARTIN, Victor, *Le Gallicanisme politique et le Clergé de France*. Paris, 1929.
MAUROIS, André, *Histoire d'Angleterre*. Paris, 1937.
MENDIZÁBAL, Alfred, *The Martyrdom of Spain, with a Preface by Jacques Maritain*. Paris, 1937. London, 1938.
MESNARD, P., *L'Essor de la Philosophie Politique au XVI Siècle*. Paris, 1937.
MESSINEO, A., *Giustizia ed Espansione Coloniale*. Rome, 1937.

MORNET, Daniel, *Les Origines Intellectuelles de la Révolution Française (1715–87)*. Paris, 1933.
NITTI, Francesco. *La Démocratie*. Paris, 1933.
NORWICH, The Bishop of, *Church and State*. London, 1936.
OLGIATI, Mgr. Francesco, *L'Anima dell'Umanesimo e del Rinascimento*. Milan, 1924.
—— *Il significato storico di Leibniz*. Milan.
—— *Cartesio*. Milan, 1924.
OMODEO, Adolfo, *Cattolicismo e Civiltà Moderna nel Secolo XIX.—J. De Maistre* (Article in *Critica*, Bari, 1936).
—— *Le Missioni di riconquista cattolica nella Francia della Restaurazione* (*Critica*. Bari, 1938).
PAGANOL, André, *L'Empereur Constantin*. Paris, 1932.
PALMIERI, Aurelio, *La Chiesa Russa, le sue odierne condizioni e il suo riformismo dottrinale*. Florence, 1908.
PINCHERLE, A., *Sant'Agostino d'Ippona*. Bari, 1930.
PRZYWARA, Father Erich, S. J., *Polarity, a German Catholic's Interpretation of Religion*. Translated by A. C. Bouquet. London, 1935.
QUONIAM, Th., *Erasme*. Paris, 1935.
RASTOUL, A., *Le Père Ventura*. Paris, 1906.
RICHARD, P., *Concile de Trente*. Paris, 1930–31.
RIVET, Louis, *La Question Romaine et le Traité du Latran*. Paris, 1931.
RIVIERE, Jean, *Le Problème de l'Eglise et de l'Etat au temps de Philippe le Bel*. Louvain-Paris, 1926.
ROTTA, Paolo, *Il Cardinale di Cusa*. Milan.
ROUSSEAU, F., *L'Idée Missionaire aux XVI et XVII Siècles*. Paris, 1930.
RUFFINI, Francesco, *Religious Liberty*, (Translated by J. Parker Heyes. London-New York, 1912).
—— *La Vita religiosa di Alessandro Manzoni*. Bari, 1931.
SALATA, Francesco, *Per la Storia Diplomatica della Questione Romana*—I. *Da Cavour alla Triplice Alleanza, con documenti inediti*. Milan, 1929.
SALVATORELLI, L., *S. Benedetto e l'Italia del suo tempo*. Bari, 1928.
SALVEMINI, Gaetano, *La Rivoluzione Francese (1788–1792)*. Fifth edition, Florence, 1925.
SCHNITZER, R., *Savonarola*. Italian edition Florence, 1931.
SCHNURER, Gustave, *L'Eglise et la Civilisation au Moyen Age*, with a preface by Edouard Jordan. Paris, 1933.
SFORZA, Count Carlo, *Synthèse de l'Europe*. Paris, 1937.
STOUGHTON, John, D. D., *History of Religion in England. Vol. II. The Church of the Commonwealth*. London, 1881.
STROWSKY, F., *Pascal et son Temps*. Paris, 1923.
STURZO, Luigi, *Italy and Fascismo*. London, 1926.
—— *The International Community and the Right of War*. London, 1929.
—— *Essai de Sociologie*. Paris, 1937.
—— *Politics and Morality*. London, 1938.
TOFFANIN, A., *Storia dell'Umanesimo dal XIII al XVI secolo*. Naples, 1933.
TOSTI, Don Luigi, *Storia del Concilio di Costanza*. Rome, 1887.
TREVELYAN, G. M., *History of England*. London, 1934.

TROELTSCH, Ernst, *Protestantism and Progress*. (Translated by W. Montgomery). London–New York, 1912.

—— *The Social Teaching of the Christian Churches*. (Translated by Olive Wyon). London, 1931.

VACANDARD, E., *Etudes de Critique et d'Histoire Religieuse*. Paris, 1910.

VANDERPOL, A., *La doctrine Scolastique du Droit de Guerre*. Paris, 1925.

VIALATOUX, Joseph, *La Cité de Hobbes*. Paris, 1935.

VILLARI, Pasquale, *The Life and Times of Savonarola*. Florence (2nd ed.), 1887–8. London, 1888.

VOLPE, Gioachino, *Movimenti Religiosi e Sette Ereticali nella Società Medievale Italiana*. (*Sec. XI–XIV*). Florence, 1922.

VOSSLER, Karl. *Medieval Culture*. (Translated by W. C. Lawton.) London, 1929.

WARD, Wilfrid, *Last Lectures*. London, 1918.

WOLFF, Théodor, *Through two Decades*. (Translated by E. W. Dickes.) London, 1936.

ZANATTA, Mario, *I Tempi e gli Uomini che prepararono la Rerum Novarum*. Milan, 1931.

INDEX

D

M